Before She

Before Sherlock Holmes

How Magazines and Newspapers Invented the Detective Story

LeRoy Lad Panek

McFarland & Company, Inc., Publishers

Jefferson, North Carolina, and London

Also of interest are the author's following works from McFarland: *Early American Detective Stories: An Anthology*, edited by LeRoy Lad Panek and Mary M. Bendel-Simso (2008); *The Origins of the American Detective Story*, by LeRoy Lad Panek (2006); *Reading Early Hammett: A Critical Study of the Fiction Prior to The Maltese Falcon*, by LeRoy Lad Panek (2004); and *The American Police Novel: A History*, by LeRoy Lad Panek (2003)

LIBRARY OF CONGRESS CATALOGUING-IN-PUBLICATION DATA

Panek, LeRoy.
    Before Sherlock Holmes : how magazines and newspapers invented the detective story / LeRoy Lad Panek.
        p.   cm.
    Includes bibliographical references and index.

    ISBN 978-0-7864-6787-7
    softcover : 50# alkaline paper ∞

    1. Detective and mystery stories, American — History and criticism.   2. American fiction — 19th century — History and cricicism.   3. Periodicals — Publishing — United States — History — 19th century.   4. American periodicals — History — 19th century.   5. Detective and mystery stories, English — History and criticism.   6. English fiction, 19th century — History and criticism.   7. Periodicals — Publishing — Great Britain — History — 20th century.   8. English periodicals — History — 19th century.   9. Detectives in literature.   10. Crime in literature.   I. Title.
PS374.D4P32 2011
813'.087209 — dc23   2011037385

BRITISH LIBRARY CATALOGUING DATA ARE AVAILABLE

Manufactured in the United States of America

McFarland & Company, Inc., Publishers
    Box 611, Jefferson, North Carolina 28640
    www.mcfarlandpub.com

For
Audrey Elizabeth

Contents

Introduction

Occasionally a short list of forgotten writers — Godwin, Bulwer-Lytton, Ainsworth — gets a brief, retrospective nod, but the usual, conventional, traditional formula for the history of the detective story goes: Poe to Dickens to Collins to Gaboriau to Conan Doyle, and then off to the races. This formula, to be sure, gives people some things to talk about. But consider the following:

• In March 1838, William Edwin Burton published a detective story entitled "The Cork Leg," and from September 1838 to May 1839 followed it with nine stories about French detective Vidocq — not from his *Memoirs*. The month after the last Vidocq story, Burton announced that he had hired Edgar Allan Poe as the editor of his magazine.

• When Poe published "The Murders in the Rue Morgue" in 1841, *Graham's Magazine* had 5,000 subscribers, but eight years later, when *Chambers' Edinburgh Journal* began its series of stories collectively entitled Recollections of a Police-Officer, it had 95,000 subscribers — and some of those stories were picked up by *Harper's New Monthly Magazine* and a dozen or so newspapers in the United States.

• In April 1859, the month before Arthur Conan Doyle was born, *Harper's New Monthly Magazine* printed "The Costly Kiss: A New York Detective Experience." The year before installments of *The Moonstone* appeared in *All the Year Round* and *Harper's Weekly*, "Escaped from Justice," "The Pen-Knife Blade," "The Fatal Woman," "A Detective's Story," "Dr. Puffer's Lost Opportunity," "The Counterfeit Bill," "Only a Cent," and the first installment of Charles Dickens' "Hunted Down" (for which the publisher paid him $12,000) appeared in *The New York Ledger*, which had a weekly circulation of 400,000.

• Three years after Wyatt Earp left Dodge City, Kansas, for Tombstone, Arizona, *The Dodge City Times* — beneath a piece of shaped verse entitled

"Fishing"— ran "Circumstantial Evidence," a story copied from the *Cincinnati Enquirer* about a detective and a somnambulist.

   • Two years before Agatha Christie was born and decades before Edgar Wallace's fiasco with his *The Four Just Men* contest, *The Boston Daily Globe* offered $200 to the reader who could correctly predict the ending of its serial *Written in Red* before it appeared in the paper.

   This seems like a lot to miss — and it is.

   It wasn't just Poe, Dickens, Collins, Gaboriau and a few other writers; the nineteenth century was quite literally awash in detective stories. But many of them, like the so-called detective notebooks, have been beyond the reach of even the most dedicated reader/scholar. Charles Martel's collection of short stories *The Diary of an Ex-Detective* (1860), for instance, resides in only six libraries worldwide — or did until Google's initiative to digitize the contents of several of the world's greatest libraries. And even more of those detective stories languished in newspaper morgues and the back rooms of local historical societies in both the United States and Great Britain — before the on-going movement to digitize historic magazines and newspapers.

   For the past several years I have been assembling and musing on a lot of that newly available material in an attempt to renovate my own views on how and where the detective story began and trying to piece together an introductory survey of the development of detective fiction during its formative years. That process has yielded the following chapters, which examine the major developments of the genre before the publication in 1891 of the short stories which came to comprise *The Adventures of Sherlock Holmes*.

   While during the nineteenth century crime literature and detective stories certainly existed in countries other than Great Britain and the United States — with Vidocq's *Memoirs* in the 1830s and Gaboriau's novels in the 1860s as notable examples — the modern detective story mainly evolved from the transatlantic literary exchanges that took place from the 1840s onward between the United States and Great Britain. Thus, just as he would influence Conan Doyle in the 1880s, Poe influenced Wilkie Collins in the 1850s, and then Collins, published in both of Harper's magazines, went on to inspire American writers to take up the sensation novel in the 1870s and 1880s. More importantly, perhaps, was the flourishing literary market in America that motivated publishers in the United States to buy or borrow detective stories printed in British magazines. This began in earnest when stories originally appearing in *Chambers' Edinburgh Journal* in the late 1840s under the series title Recollections of a Police-Officer became the first of the "detective note-books" when they were collected and published as *The Recollections of a Policeman* in New York in 1852. And while American magazines and newspapers continued to publish British imports up to the appearance of the Sherlock Holmes stories, the demand they created in the growing market in the United States motivated both American publishers and writers to make the detective story their own. But it was not simply or even originally the skill, novelty, or ingenuity of writers, or the enterprise of aggressive publishers on both sides of the Atlantic that made the detective story an Anglo-American phenomenon. The law had a lot to do with it.

Inextricably tied to the origin and development of the detective story in the nineteenth century was the fact that Great Britain and the United States shared the same concepts, principles, and practices of law. And throughout the century those concepts, principles, and practices underwent dynamic changes. Capital punishment, access to counsel, definition of legal responsibility, admissibility of testimony, and the nature of evidence; each of these was the subject of intense debate throughout the century — and had a significant, even informing impact on fiction. Thus Bulwer-Lytton, Ainsworth, and Dickens all had much to say about capital punishment, and access to counsel became one of the major themes of detective stories in the first half of the century. Indeed, for a time it even appeared that lawyers rather than detectives would be the heroes of the new kind of fiction. But the most important facet of Anglo-American law affecting detective fiction then and now was the consciousness of the possibility of innocents being wrongly accused, prosecuted, condemned, and executed. At the center of that concern resided the nature and function of both direct and circumstantial evidence — and that, in turn, became the particular subject of a host of nineteenth-century detective stories.

While the concern for the flaws of judicial processes, especially the debated value of circumstantial evidence, reflected a basic concern for real-world issues in both Britain and the United States, the evolving detective story had a problematic relationship with other contemporary issues during its formative years. There were no detective police in Britain (and few real police forces at all in America) before 1842, and the new profession of detective (versus lawyer or police officer) became the subject not only of Charles Dickens' journalistic crusade on behalf of the new detective department but also a shelf of seemingly biographical or autobiographical titles: thus *The Recollections of a Policeman, The Diary of an Ex-Detective; The Detective's Note-Book; The Experiences of a Real Detective; The Autobiography of an English Detective; The Revelations of a Private Detective; The Female Detective; Secret Service: or, Recollections of a City Detective; Strange Stories of a Detective: or Curiosities of Crime;* and *Leaves from the Note-Book of a New York Detective.* While these collections of stories do describe some routines and practices of actual detectives, they were neither biographies nor autobiographies but collections of short fiction jinned up by anonymous writers or publishers themselves to capture readers' interest in the new profession. Further, in the aggregate (and there is a lot to aggregate) nineteenth-century detective fiction certainly reflected some interest in crimes *de jour*— from numerous pieces that turn on threatened bank or business failures caused by absconding officials to the torrent of stories about tracking down counterfeiters. But stories based on real crimes (like the Constance Kent material in *The Moonstone* or the Ripper allusions in the serial *Marked for a Victim,* "Founded on Whitechapel's Tragedies," in Joseph Pulitzer's *Evening World* in the spring of 1889) are decidedly in the minority. Insofar as contemporary detective fiction was concerned, the seven attempts to assassinate Queen Victoria as well as the entire American Civil War never happened. This paradox of a genre centered on crime that avoids events that are profoundly troubling is repeated in the identity of heroes of nineteenth-century detective stories, thus, while there were a number of famous contemporary detectives (the Forrester brothers, Charles Frederick Field, John Townshend, Jonathan Whicher, and Allan Pinkerton), they were rarely made into the heroes of detective stories — except in Pinkerton's stories that he had written to promote his own business.

In addition to being a response, albeit a particular one, to real issues in nineteenth-century Britain and America, the rise of detective stories had literary origins as well. These began to be noted late in the nineteenth century and Dorothy L. Sayers summed them up in *The Omnibus of Crime* in 1929 as being several apocryphal books of the Bible, Herodotus, deMailly, Voltaire, and William Godwin. This list posits two relatively different sorts of ancestor for the detective story: the story about a clever individual solving problems, puzzles, or riddles, and the story grappling with crime, criminals, and concepts of justice. Rather than any direct connection, the relationship between problem and puzzle stories with the rise of detective fiction in the nineteenth century is more spiritual than genealogical. Thus, the major British and American writers of the period who wrote detective stories — Poe, Dickens, and Collins — while not directly connected to the tradition of puzzle writing, manifest a kindred *joi de vivre* in delineating their detective heroes and creating plots to tantalize and entertain their readers. A closer relationship exists between fiction about social justice and the rise of the detective story. Godwin and Holcroft and then the Newgate novels of Ainsworth, Bulwer-Lytton, and Dickens have much to say about class prejudice and the evils of the judicial system, particularly the "bloody code" that made even trivial crimes hanging offenses. They were, however, old school — laden with sentiment and fundamentally committed to a belief in a providential universe in which real criminals look like criminals and in which, ultimately, "murder will out." Reacting against this kind of fiction was on Poe's mind when he turned to write his Dupin stories and Dickens wrote his first real detective (sub) plot in *Bleak House* when for the first time his murderer does not wear the mark of Cain.

While detective stories were a response to social conditions and took part in identifiable literary traditions, they were also one the first branches of literature to feel the effect of mass marketing. In the middle of the nineteenth century, printing technology, increased affluence, increased literacy, and other factors led to an explosion in the kinds and number of media published in Britain and the United States. Every party, trade, special interest, and sect had its own magazine, and every town, village, or hamlet had its own newspaper. By the end of the century the new medium of the nationally distributed family story paper could periodically claim circulation of up to a million copies an issue. And newspapers, often hungry for copy, freely borrowed from one another and a piece of fiction could spread from coast to coast and even to what was then the Kingdom of Hawaii and the so-called Indian Territories within a matter of months. Thus, in the nineteenth century and perhaps up into the beginning of the twentieth century, a lot more people found what literature they read in magazines and in newspapers rather than in books. And they found detective stories in them early and often. Thus, for example, on October 10, 1849, two months after "The Gambler's Revenge — Recollections of a Police Officer" came out in *Chambers'* in Edinburgh, the story appeared under the heading of "Tales and Sketches" on the front page of Wellsboro, Pennsylvania's *Tioga Eagle*— without attribution to *Chambers*. And the extent to which detective stories penetrated the magazine market perhaps can be gauged by noting that "A Romance of a Railway Carriage," a story about a detective nabbing a disguised murderer on the Dover Express, was published in *The Locomotive Engineer's Monthly* printed in Cleveland, Ohio in 1870.

One of the things that all of this means is that over the last decade trying to understand what was going on with detective fiction in the nineteenth century has gone from famine to an overloaded smorgasbord, from those few big names — Poe to Dickens to Collins to Gaboriau — to quite literally thousands of pieces of fiction, and probably many more which have yet to be discovered; my colleague Mary Bendel-Simso and I have already identified over a thousand pieces of short detective fiction published in the United States before 1891 for the online Westminster Detective Library, and we are confident that there is a like number yet to be identified and cataloged in U.S. magazines, newspapers and family story papers that we have not yet examined.

In the following chapters I have tried to begin to rewrite the history of the detective story in the nineteenth century by looking both at the major writers and at the new media that brought detectives to readers in Britain and the United States. It is, however, only a first step. There is a great deal of material yet to be collected and discussed. Thus below I say very little about the detective story serials that began to appear in the 1880s and probably played a significant role in the newspaper circulation wars in the U.S. in the 1890s. I also say almost nothing about the role of detective stories in British newspapers and family story papers, an area likely to yield other insights. And I say nothing at all about the drama, another popular genre that might shed light on the development of the detective hero and the detective story in the nineteenth century.

My thanks to the indefatigable Mary Bendel-Simso, to the librarians at Hoover Library at McDaniel College, and to my wife. As always, any and all of the errors and infelicities in the following are my own.

Chapter One

Life Before Detectives

Edgar Allan Poe usually gets the credit for inventing a new way of telling stories — the way of telling stories which came to be called the detective story — when he wrote "The Murders in the Rue Morgue" for *Graham's Magazine* in 1841. Not much problem about that; everybody pretty much agrees. And Arthur Conan Doyle's repeated admissions that he based his Sherlock Holmes stories on Poe's Dupin tales makes the assertion pretty much gospel for most. But while he may have gotten the credit for creating the detective story, Poe had little or nothing to do with inventing stories about detectives, or, for that matter, about crime. He never thought about his Chevalier Dupin as someone responsible to the law, for upholding it, or for bringing criminals to justice — recall that the criminal in the first story is an orangutan and that nothing happens to Minister D — beyond losing the letter he has stolen. In fact, the crimes in Poe's stories exist principally as examinations of perception and that meant demonstrations of and celebrations of genius. He was, after all, a romantic. But more on Poe later, after a look at the backgrounds of that other kind of detective story, the kind which came about because of changes in attitudes toward law, crime, society, providence, human nature, journalism, and the creation of police and detectives — detectives that had little similarity to Poe's grouchy, condescending, misanthropic genius. And that means going back to the beginning of the eighteenth century and glancing at the ways in which the law changed.

Thoughts on Government and the Law

Back in the days of divine right and absolute monarchy, the whole business of the law as both an abstract principle and practical entity was relatively simple. Law was what the monarch said it was, and kings' edicts had both temporal and spiritual oomph because kings were, after all, God's agents, and in England, of course, they eventually had their own church to make that point abundantly clear. Then, too, power as well as wealth were concentrated in a small ruling class that could pretty much turn their whims into law — with only a few inconveniences (like trial by jury established in Common Law) acting as grossly inadequate protections of individuals' rights. But in England on January 30, 1649, the rationale for absolute monarchy became as dead as Charles I's headless corpse on the scaffold. And what that meant was that in England a great deal of thought and tinkering had to be done in order to accommodate the law — both abstract and practical — to the realities of the new world, a world with no divine right and one which ever so slowly acknowledged, granted, and then even began to protect the rights of the individual.

At the same time that most of them were musing on the complex nature of how we know what we know, what with the king dead and the less-than-liberating experience of Cromwell's dour commonwealth, most of the big brain British thinkers of the Enlightenment also thought a good deal about the origin and nature of government. There was Hobbes' *Leviathan* (1651), and then Locke's *An Essay concerning The True Original, Extent, and End of Civil-Government* (1689), followed at mid-eighteenth century by Hume's *Of the First Principles of Government* and *Of the Origin of Government* (1742), and even chemist Joseph Priestley got into the act with *The First Principles of Government and the Nature of Political, Civil and Religious Liberty* (1768). While short on practical suggestions about what to do about the law in action — especially as it touches on crime and punishment — readers of these treatises would, in time, bring real changes to government on both sides of the Atlantic. For most people during the 1700s in Britain, however, musings about government didn't mean a whole lot: poverty, class prejudice, crime, and a justice system inherited from the middle ages made life, in Hobbes' terms, "poor, nasty, brutish, and short."

Crime and Punishment in the Age of Reason

It wasn't that people weren't aware that there was a problem with crime. Eighteenth-century Parliaments made several notable (albeit futile) attempts to rein crime in — especially crime against the gentry. They did this first by passing laws that made almost everything a hanging offense. In the sixteenth century there were eleven capital crimes in England (murder, rape, piracy, arson, etc.). But by 1723 death was the punishment for 150 offenses, ranging from murder to stealing fish from ponds or damaging parks or forests. There were, of course, no police or prosecutors to bring those who murdered, stole fish from damaged ponds, or damaged parks or forests to justice — those roles were the duties, responsibilities, and obligations of individuals — and parliament encouraged citizens to take those duties seriously by paying them to do so and act as their own police and prosecutors. To that end, an act of 1692 set the precedent for what was to become an extensive system of cash rewards; it promised £40 (along with the malefactor's horse, arms, and cash) for the arrest and conviction of highwaymen. But neither draconian punishments nor paying citizens to rat out their brethren worked very well — indeed they did the opposite.

Shortly after it was instituted, the reward system led to the exposure of such monstrous abuses that the perpetrators became the stuff of criminal legend. First there was the trial of William Chaloner, investigated and prosecuted for counterfeiting coins in 1699 by Isaac Newton, then Warden of the Royal Mint — and amateur detective. As a sideline to Chaloner's admitted coining of £30,000 worth of bogus currency, he dabbled in the impeachment business by luring people into phony conspiracies and then reporting them as conspirators for the rewards. Then followed the career of Jonathan Wild, the "hero" of *A True Discovery of the Conduct of Receivers and Thief-Takers in and about the City of London* (1718). At the same time that Wild assumed the title of "thief-taker general," however, he was the head of organized crime in the capital and used the reward system both to discipline members of his gang of criminals by turning them in and to fatten his purse by impeaching others. Finally there was the Stephen McDaniel scandal of 1754 which, in the words of John Fielding, magistrate at Bow Street, exposed a system which allowed McDaniel "and his hellish crew, to prostitute the useful employment of a thieftaker, to the procuring both public and private rewards, at the shameful and mocking price of innocent blood" (*A plan for preventing robberies within twenty miles of London*, 1755). James Caulfield is more precise about "innocent blood" in *Persons, from the Revolution in 1688 to the End of the Reign of George II* (1819):

> Stephen Macdaniel was one of those detestable villains that no epithet is vile enough to brand their infamy. This fellow, in conjunction with John Berry, James Egan, and James Salmon, followed the profession of swearing away the lives of innocent unsuspecting persons, for the sake of the reward given by government, for the conviction of capital offenders:— the young, friendless, and destitute, were sure to become their prey; and father and motherless lads, of from sixteen to eighteen years of age, were their most favourite game. This profitable merchandise was carried on for a series of years, undiscovered and indeed unsuspected.

Wild's career was to provide material for John Gay's *The Beggar's Opera* (1728) and Henry Fielding's *The Life and Death of Jonathan Wild, the Great* (1743).

In addition to these literary diversions, however, the periodic exposure of gross failures of the reward system — as well as routine lying on the part of those connected with law enforcement — did much to retard the growth and development of professional police and detectives in Britain.

If the reward system flopped badly, capital punishment didn't do a whole lot better in controlling crime. At the same time that Parliament was making more and more acts capital offenses, it also introduced a way around the death penalty — in part because of the increasing chorus of outrage about what came to be known as the "Bloody Code." Beginning in 1718 the British government introduced transportation both as a destination for convicted debtors and as an alternative to hanging felons — until 1776 they sent them to America. With that option lost and the number of convicted felons multiplying, in 1776 the hulks of old warships moored in the Thames served as makeshift prisons. Using the hulks as prisons continued for eighty years, long after the government discovered a new destination for transported criminals when the first shipload of felons set off for New South Wales in 1787.

The Literature of Crime

By the beginning of the eighteenth century criminals provided much of the substance for cheap literature. Ballads, broadsides, pamphlets, magazines (like *Applebee's Magazine,* which had Daniel Defoe on the payroll to cover trials), newspapers, and books featured the lives, exploits, and deaths of criminals. These provided several different points of view toward crime and criminals — some were picaresque, extolling the freedom and excitement of the highwayman's life; some were (more or less) narrative reporting; some were moralistic cautionary tales; and some were a combination of all three. From the late seventeenth century onward, ballads like "Devol's last Farewel: Containing an Account of many frolicksom Intrigues and notorious Robberies which he committed: Concluding with his mournful Lamentation, on the Day of his Death" (1670) combined adventure and *joi de vivre*— or his "frolicksom Intriegues" — with a dollop of censure —"his mournful lamentation." Ballads extolling the romance of crime, especially highway robbery, continued throughout the next century. Thus ballads like "The Female Robber" (1735):

> Ye females of every station,
> Give ear to my frolicksome song;
> The like was ne'er known in the nation,
> 'Twas done by a female so young.
>
> She bought her a horse and a bridle,
> With saddle and pistols also;

Resolving not to remain idle,
But on the highway she would go.

She clothed herself in great splendour,
Her breeches and sword she had on;
Her body appeared mighty slender,
'Twas dressed like a pretty young man.

And thus like a robber so pretty,
She mounted with speed on her mare;
She left all her friends in the city,
And steered her course toward Ware
[*Pedlar's Pack Ballads And Songs*].

There were also ballads about specific, legendary figures such Dick Turpin:

On Hounslow Heath, as I rode o'er,
I spied a lawyer riding before;
"Kind sir," said I, "are you not afraid,
Of Turpin that mischievous blade?"
O rare Turpin, hero,
O rare Turpin, O ["Turpin's Valour" from
Pedlar's Pack of Ballads and Songs].

Most of the ballads and broadsides about criminals were ephemeral, but a whole lot of them were printed, plagiarized and then reprinted over and over. But it wasn't only ballads and broadsides that flooded the market with stories about crime and criminals. There were Tyburn and Newgate Calendars, and the strange, eventful (and voluminous) history of the so-called Newgate Calendars serves as an apt demonstration of the place of criminals and crime in the eighteenth century.

Newgate Calendars

The ordinary, or chaplain, of Newgate prison provided both spiritual consolation to the condemned and, for various reasons (not the least of which was commercial), wrote out a record of their lives, their confessions, and their last words. These were then published as a kind of reverse of Foxe's *Book of Martyrs*, recording the lives of sinners as opposed to those of saints. The earliest of these collections, or "calendars," was compiled by Samuel Smith, Ordinary between 1676 and 1698. Released in huge printings, there were more than 400 of the variously entitled "Newgate" calendars issued before the first decades of the nineteenth century (www.oldbaileyonline.org). Their titles advertised literature with the same allure found in the ballads — news, sensation, morality, adventure, and even a bit of black humor. Here is a sample of titles:

*Hell upon Earth; or the Most Pleasant and Delectable History of Whittington's Col-
lege, Otherwise Called Newgate, Giving an Account of the Humours of those Colle-
gians who are strictly examined at the Old Baily, and take their highest Degrees near
Hyde Park Corner* [1703];

    *A General and True History of the Lives and Adventures of the Most Famous
Highwaymen, Murderers, Street-Robbers etc. To which is added a genuine Account
of the Voyages and Plunders of the Most Noted Pirates, Interspersed with several
remarkable Tryals of the most Notorious Malefactor* [1734];

and

    *The Newgate Calendar or MALEFACTORS' BLOODY REGISTER containing: Gen-
uine and Circumstantial Narrative of the lives and transactions, various exploits and
Dying Speeches of the Most Notorious Criminals of both sexes who suffered Death
Punishment in Gt. Britain and Ireland for High Treason Petty Treason Murder
Piracy Felony Thieving Highway Robberies Forgery Rapes Bigamy Burglaries Riots
and various other horrid crimes and misdemeanours on a plan entirely new, wherein
will be fully displayed the regular progress from virtue to vice interspersed with strik-
ing reflexions on the conduct of those unhappy wretches who have fallen a sacrifice to
the laws of their country [1774–1778].*

All of these collections of criminal biographies had an ostensible moral purpose. Hence *The New and Complete Newgate Calandar, or Villainy Displayed
in all its Branches* (1795?) opens with this bit of verse on the title page:

> How dreadful the Fate of the Wretches who fall,
> A victim of Laws they have broke!
> Of Vice, the Beginning is frequently small,
> But how fatal at length is the Stroke!
> The contents of these Volumes will amply display
> The steps which Offenders have trod;
> Learn hence, then, each Reader, the Laws to obey
> Of your County, your King, and your God.

And the biographies of most criminals that follow this admonition stress failed
morals. Thus, there was Thomas Savage who murdered a fellow servant:

THIS unhappy wretch was born of very honest parents in the parish of St Giles's
in the Fields, and between fourteen and fifteen years of age bound apprentice to
one Mr. Collins, a vintner, at the Ship Tavern at Ratcliff Cross, with whom he
led but a very loose and profligate sort of life for about two years.

    Breaking the Sabbath (by his own confession, he having never once heard a
whole sermon during that time) was the first inlet to all his other vices, especially
whoredom, drunkenness and theft, for he used commonly to pass away the Sab-
baths at a bawdy-house in Ratcliff Highway with one Hannah Blay, a vile common strumpet, who was the cause of his ruin, and brought him to his shameful
end [www.exclassics.com].

And Tom Rowland who

was born at Ware, in Hertfordshire, and by his parents was put an apprentice to a bricklayer; but after he had served his time, being then of a slothful, idle disposition, he kept such company as soon brought him to follow evil courses; and, to support his extravagancy in a most riotous way of living, he stole a horse out of the Duke of Beaufort's stables, at his seat at Badminton, in Gloucestershire; and then, going on the highway, committed several most notorious robberies, for above eighteen years; but he always robbed in women's apparel, which disguise was the means of his reigning so long in his villainy. Whenever he was pursued he then rode astride; but at last, being apprehended in this unlawful habit for robbing a person on Hounslow Heath of a quantity of bone-lace, to the value of twelve hundred pounds sterling...However, whilst he lay under sentence of death he was very refractory, and was so abominably wicked that the very morning on which he died, lying in the Press Yard, for he wanted for no money whilst under confinement, a common woman coming to visit him, he had the unparalleled audaciousness to act carnally with her, and gloried in the sin as he was going to execution, which was at Tyburn, on Friday, the 24th of October, 1699 [www.exclassics.com].

There's a crowd of very nasty people in the pages of *The New and Complete Newgate Calandar*: Tom Astin who "murdered his aunt, wife, and seven children"; George Caddell who "murdered Miss Price, whom he had seduced and promised marriage"; The Rev. Thomas Hunter, M.A., who "murdered out of revenge two children"; and Sawney Bean who, "with his Wife, lived by murder and cannibalism in a cave." Interspersed with these monsters, however, there are narratives which stress the bizarre. There was William Nevison, a highwayman who, "dying of the plague as was thought, reappeared as his own Ghost"; Jonathan Simpson, a highwayman who "was witty with a halter round his Neck and, being reprieved, found that Newgate would not have him"; Jacob Halsey, "the Quaker highwayman, who after being fooled by a 'Spirit' led a life of crime"; and Dick Hughes, "a robber whose thoughtful Wife bought the Rope to hang him" [www.exclassics.com].

In time, some Newgate calendars began to do more than present examples of people drawn into lives of crime. Significantly, some came to include accounts of innocents wrongly accused, tried, and, in some cases, executed: there are 19 such cases in the Knapp and Baldwin edition of 1825. Thus the tales of John, Richard, and Joan Perry, "Mother and Sons, executed in 1661 on the false Statement of the First for the alleged Murder of Mr. William Harrison, who appeared alive two Years later after strange Adventures"; William Shaw, "Executed in 1721 for 'Murdering' his Daughter, who, it was afterwards proved, committed Suicide"; Robert Fuller, "Convicted of shooting Mr. Bailey, June Sessions, 1743, and pardoned because he was wrongly identified"; and Christopher Woodland, "Another Victim of the horrid gang of Thief-takers" [www.exclassics.com].

More than simply including brief biographies which illustrated miscarriages of justice, later issues of Newgate calendars came to include brief editorial comments on the state of law and order in the kingdom. In 1779, for instance, there is this comment on public order in the preface of *The Malefactor's Register*:

> IN an age abandoned to dissipation, and when the ties of religion and morality fail to have their accustomed influence on the mind, the publication of a New Work of this nature makes its appearance with peculiar propriety.
>
> It has not been unusual, of late years, to complain of the sanguinary complexion of our laws; and if there were any reason to expect that the practice of felony would be lessened by the institution of any laws less sanguinary than those now in force, it would be a good argument for the enacting of such laws.
>
> Wise and virtuous legislators can wish nothing more ardently than the general welfare of the community; and those who have from time to time given birth to the laws of England, have indisputably done it with a view to this general welfare. But as the wisest productions of the human mind are liable to error, and as there is visibly an increasing depravity in the manners of the age, it is no wonder that our laws are found, in some instances, inadequate to the purposes for which they were enacted: and, perhaps, if, in a few instances they were made more, and in others less severe than they are at present, the happiest consequences might result to the public.
>
> It is with the utmost deference to the wisdom of their superiors, that the editors of this work offer the following hints for the improvement of the police of this country, and the security of the lives and properties of the subject [1780].

Although in the preface to their 1825 edition of the *Newgate Calendar* Knapp and Baldwin cite one of the powerful voices opposed to capital punishment —

> Mr. Colquhoun observes, "Can it be thought a correct system of jurisprudence, which inflicts the penalty of death for breaking down the mound of a fish-pond, whereby the fish may escape; or cutting down a fruit-tree in a garden or orchard; or stealing a handkerchief or any trifle from a person's pocket, above the value of twelve-pence; while the number of other crimes, of much greater enormity, are only punished with transportation and imprisonment; and while the punishment of murder itself is, and can be, only death, with circumstances of additional ignominy?" [www.newgatecalendar.co.uk]

— the editors nonetheless hold the old line, and argue the social utility of killing people as examples to others. But by 1828, Knapp and Baldwin felt compelled to add an appendix to their *Calendar*— an analysis of crime and punishment in Britain; and after toting up the figures asked, rhetorically, "If we inquire whether, with this increasing severity, crime has been kept under, the answer is very much the reverse."

More on Government and the Law

Coincident with the outpouring of popular literature about crime and criminals swirling around in the middle of the eighteenth century, thinkers in England and its colonies as well as on the continent began to consider the law in new and more practical terms. The first and most far-reaching manifestation of this new phenomenon was in the publication and popularity of William Blackstone's *Commentaries on the Laws of England* (1765–1769). Before Blackstone, British Common Law was an unsystematic jumble of hundreds of years of legislation which he sought to organize, codify, and explain in accessible language. The hugely popular *Commentaries* both provided a new and coherent way of looking at law and laws and also changed the way in which the law was taught and practiced — in both Britain and America. The *Commentaries*, however, was a conservative work meant to systematize and explain the law as it existed rather than question its efficacy or purpose — or to change it. There was, however, a movement afoot to at least question the law — particularly insofar as it related to the rules of evidence and the ways in which evidence was used to find individuals innocent or guilty. This began on the continent with Cesare Bonesana, Marchese di Beccaria's *Dei deliti e delle pene* (*On Crimes and Punishments*) published in 1764. Rather than just looking at laws, Beccaria looked at their defects, finding that

> the cruelty of punishments, and the irregularity of proceedings in criminal cases, so principal a part of the legislation, and so much neglected throughout Europe, has hardly ever been called in question. Efforts, accumulated through many centuries, have never yet been exposed by ascending to general principles; nor has the force of acknowledged truths been ever opposed to the unbounded licentiousness of ill-directed power, which has continually produced so many authorised examples of the most unfeeling barbarity. Surely, the groans of the weak, sacrificed to the cruel ignorance and indolence of the powerful, the barbarous torments lavished, and multiplied with useless severity, for crimes either not proved, or in their nature impossible, the filth and horrors of a prison, increased by the most cruel tormentor of the miserable, uncertainty, ought to have roused the attention of those whose business is to direct the opinions of mankind [http://www.constitution.org/cb/crim_pun00.txt].

And in his examination of the law's defects, in chapter 13 ("Of the Credibility of Witnesses") and chapter 14 ("Of Evidence and The Proofs of a Crime and the Form of Judgment") Beccaria opened up a consideration of the nature and function of evidence that would become the center of interest and controversy for hundreds of years. In Britain practicing justices had been worrying about the same thing: evidence. To that end, in *An Enquiry Into the Causes of the late Increase of Robbers, &c. With Some Proposals for Remedying this Growing Evil* (1751), Justice-turned-novelist Henry Fielding wrote, "There is no

Branch of the Law more bulky, more full of confusion and Contradiction, I had almost said of Absurdity, than the Law of Evidence as it now stands." To remedy this, at the turn of the nineteenth century a number of lawyer/writers took up the subject of evidence. William Godwin added a chapter "Of Evidence" to his *Enquiry Concerning Political Justice and its Influence on Modern Morals and Manners* (1793). Of far greater influence was Evans' translation from the French of Pothier's *A Treatise on the Law of Obligations or Contracts* (1806), which in chapter XVI (Of Public Evidence) contained detailed sections on handwriting and hearsay evidence as well as on the competence of witnesses. Jeremy Bentham contributed to the literature with *A Treatise on Judicial Evidence* (1813), book five of which confronts the issue that would become a nineteenth-century obsession, "Circumstantial Evidence." And discussions of the nature and function of evidence extended to the new United States with John Dunlap's *Notes and references to American Authorities* added to S.M. Phillipps' *On the Law of Evidence* (1816).

A New Approach to Crime

Even while the century was producing more and more thought on the difficulties and details of applying law to hypothetical situations, at Bow Street in London Henry Fielding and then his brother John were taking the first effectual steps toward active application of the law in order to ensure public safety.

In the way of public policy, government in England had traditionally turned problems over to the public to solve. The ancient institution of the Watch was supposed to prevent and report crime, but from Shakespeare's time forward, it was an ineffectual organization. Indeed, in 1728 the Lord Mayor of London cried out against the decrepitude of the Watch:

> The principal encouragements, and opportunity given to street-robbers is that our streets are so poorly watch'd; the Watchmen for the most part, being decrepid, superannuated Wretches, with one foot in the grave, and the t'other ready to follow; so feeble, that a puff of breath can blow 'em down: Poor crazy mortals! much fitter for an Alms-house than a Watch-house. A City watch'd and guarded by such animals, is wretchedly watch'd indeed.
>
> Nay, so little terror do our Watchmen carry with them, that hardy thieves make a mere jest of 'em, and sometimes oblige even the very Watchmen, who should apprehend 'em, to light 'em in their roguery: And what can a poor creature do, in terror of his life, surrounded by a pack of ruffians, and no assistance near.

He also proposed measures for its reinvigoration

Let the Watch be compos'd of stout able bodied men, and of those at least treble the number now subsisting, that is to say, a Watchman to every 40 houses, 20 on one side of the way, and 20 on the other; for it is observable, that a man cannot well see distinctly beyond the extent of 20 houses in a row; if 'tis a single row, and no opposite houses, the charges must be greater, and their safety less. This man should be elected, and paid by the house-keepers themselves, to prevent misapplication and abuse, so much complain'd of, in the distribution of publick money [http://rictornorton.co.uk/grubstreet/proposal.htm].

But no one listened, and English people instead adhered to the tradition that made every one a police officer and a detective. Henry Fielding describes this in *Enquiry Into the Causes of the late Increase of Robbers, &c. With Some Proposals for Remedying this Growing Evil* (1751):

By the Common Law every Person who hath committed a Felony, may be arrested and secured by any private Man present at the said Fact, though he hath no general or particular Authority, i.e. tho' he be no Officer of Justice, nor have any Writ or Warrant for so doing; and such private Man may either deliver the Felon to the Constable, secure him in a Goal, or carry him before a Magistrate. And if he refuses to yield, those who arrest may justify beating him; or, in case of absolute Necessity, killing him.

Nor is this Arrest merely allowed; it is enjoined by Law, and the Omission, without some good Excuse is a Misdemeanor punishable by Amercement or Fine and Imprisonment.

The problem was that in spite of the carrot of duty and the stick of amercement, crime (or the consciousness of crime) was demonstrably on the rise in eighteenth-century England — hence Fielding's use of "Late Increase" in the title cited above. But rather than being simply a novelist, satirist, and pamphleteer, Fielding had the means to do something about crime: he was a magistrate. In 1748 he became the magistrate at Bow Street. Assisted by his blind brother (and successor to the office) John, Fielding took the first step toward establishing a police and detective force in London. Since the act establishing rewards of 1692, policing was altogether a private enterprise, undertaken by independent thief-takers who detected and apprehended criminals and were compensated by reward money paid by the government. As seen above, this system was open to scandalous abuses and ultimately did more harm than good. What the brothers Fielding did was to organize thief-taking and thief-takers: they hired six former parish constables who worked at first for reward money and later for the salary of one guinea a week to detect and apprehend criminals when crimes were reported to the Bow Street magistrate's office. A number of these Bow Street "Runners," in fact, went on to become well-known detectives, including Henry Goddard, John and Daniel Forrester, John Sayer, and John Townshend.

To the original Runners, John Fielding added a horse patrol in 1763. In 1792 Parliament expanded the Bow Street model to seven other precincts and permitted other jurisdictions to request the aid of a Bow Street officer to act as a detective. The problem was that it was all too little — in personnel, in funding, and in organization — to police London, let alone the whole of England. The population of London had grown from 300,000 in 1700 to over 3,000,000 by 1861. While the Bow Street Runners were to become only a stepping-stone to the creation of a real police force in Britain, they did have an impact, albeit a small one, on literature.

That impact was tardy and mixed. A Bow Street Runner is the hero of what may be the first extended work of fiction concerning the life and work of a professional detective, Thomas Gaspey's (?) *Richmond: Scenes from the Life of a Bow-Street Runner* (1827). After 80-odd pages recounting his early, picaresque life, Richmond casts about for employment:

> I could not submit again to imprison myself at the irksome desk of a counting-house; I had neglected my books too much to think of becoming an usher in a school; I could not degrade myself by wearing a badge of servitude in the form of a livery...and nothing occurred to me that I could endure, but the situation of a game-keeper ... Unfortunately, I was no marksman....

A friend persuades him to become a Bow Street Runner: "That was precisely what accorded with the views I had been forming of a life, partly regular and partly adventurous." And he finds his fellow officers "a jovial set of fellows, — free, careless, merry, and full of anecdotes of their different exploits, which exhibited a more varied picture of human life than I had hitherto met with in all my wanderings." The hero-narrator then goes on to recount five of his cases, involving crimes from kidnapping to grave robbing. The narrative ends with acknowledgment of its mixed purpose:

> My purpose will be answered if what I have recorded in these volumes shall serve to beguile an idle hour, or show to those, who are inexperienced, the innumerable snares which beset the path of life, particularly in this overgrown and bustling metropolis.

In the later nineteenth century, the Bow Street Runners did not fare quite so well in print. Runner John Townshend received a great deal of notice for his work as a detective (a sympathetic and intelligent "officer" named Townshend, for instance, plays a significant role in "The Wife's Evidence," in *Leaves from the Diary of a Law Clerk*, 1857) and Townsend the Bow Street Runner plays a noteworthy role in James Payn's novel *The Lost Sir Massingberd* (1864). But other fiction of the period was not kind to the Bow Street boys. There's an officer in "Aunt Janet's Diamonds" (1860) who does nothing effectual after this introduction:

Josiah returned from London after an absence of three hours; a Bow-Street officer was to follow immediately. From my bedroom window I saw a strange, forbidding-looking man, with a slow, heavy step, come up the house-walk from the common.

In *Night and Morning* (1841) Bulwer-Lytton briefly introduced a semi-sinister Runner named Mr. Sharp, whose principal object is serving the wealthy versus justice or humanity. And the narrator in *Autobiography of an English Detective* (1863), although an apprentice in the corps of Runners, takes it upon himself to outsmart them and prove his real mettle as a detective:

> My pride, of which I had a Luciferian share, was aroused. It was a duel — nothing less — between me and the famous Bow-street runners. Should I succeed — should I baffle those trained sleuthhounds — it would prove at all events, that my astute stepfather had rightly divined the peculiar bent of my genius.

And, of course, he does succeed.

Finally, one of the most dominant voices of the age, Charles Dickens, had no use for Bow Street Runners. Thus, in "A Detective Police Party" in *Household Words* (July 7, 1850) we get this:

> We are not by any means devout believers in the old Bow Street Police. To say the truth, we think there was a vast amount of humbug about those worthies. Apart from many of them being men of very indifferent character, and far too much in the habit of consorting with thieves and the like, they never lost a public occasion of jobbing and trading in mystery and making the most of themselves. Continually puffed besides by incompetent magistrates anxious to conceal their own deficiencies, and hand-in-glove with the penny-a-liners of that time, they became a sort of superstition. Although as a Preventive Police they were utterly ineffective, and as a Detective Police were very loose and uncertain in their operations, they remain with some people a superstition to the present day.

And a decade later he included Runners as characters in *Great Expectations*:

> The Constables, and the Bow Street men from London — for, this happened in the days of the extinct red-waistcoated police — were about the house for a week or two, and did pretty much what I have heard and read of like authorities doing in other such cases. They took up several obviously wrong people, and they ran their heads very hard against wrong ideas, and persisted in trying to fit the circumstances to the ideas, instead of trying to extract ideas from the circumstances. Also, they stood about the door of the Jolly Bargemen, with knowing and reserved looks that filled the whole neighbourhood with admiration; and they had a mysterious manner of taking their drink, that was almost as good as taking the culprit. But not quite, for they never did it.

Victorian Reform

In the first half of the nineteenth century, England went about reinventing itself. Slavery was abolished, protestant dissenters and then Catholics could sit in Parliament, men who didn't own property could vote, child labor began to be regulated, and railroads had to be inspected for safety. And along with this there came about new ways of viewing and coping with crime.

The late eighteenth and early nineteenth centuries saw a number of attempts to improve on and expand the kind of policing begun at Bow Street. The most significant of these was in 1797 when John Harriott and Patrick Colquhoun created the Thames River Police, a body financed by the West India Merchants, and the West India Planters Committees, to protect their property on London's river. Colquhoun, in fact, became one of the most prominent voices calling for police reform — his *A Treatise of the Police of the Metropolis* (1800) and *A Treatise on the Functions and Duties of a Constable* (1803) combined calls for police reform with the consideration of both defects of the law, especially profligate capital punishment, and relief of the poor. While tinkering with and expanding the Bow Street model had some effect, crime and what to do about it remained serious problems in England. Thus the Duke of Wellington began his speech in favor of "An Act for Improving the Police in and near the Metropolis" of 1829 by declaring:

> There can be no doubt that no branch connected with the administration of public justice in this country is so defective as the police. This is clearly proved by the great increase of crime in the metropolis. My Lords, it appears from the returns that in the last six years the total number of criminals committed for various offences has increased in the ratio of two-fifths. The commitments in London and Middlesex in 1822 were 2539; in 1825, 2902; in 1828, 3516. This proportion does not arise from the prevalence of any particular crime, but prevails in almost every species of crime perpetrated in the metropolis and its neighbouring districts during the same period. It is perfectly clear to all who have considered the subject, that this rapid increase of crime arises solely from the deficiency of the police [http://www.historyhome.co.uk/peel/laworder/met bill.htm].

That bill, introduced and shepherded by Home Secretary Robert Peel, began by sweeping away the old order:

> And whereas it is expedient to substitute a new and more efficient System of Police in lieu of such Establishments of Nightly Watch and Nightly Police, within the Limits herein after mentioned, and to constitute an Office of Police, which, acting under the immediate Authority of One of His Majesty's Principal Secretaries of State, shall direct and control the whole of such new System of Police within those Limits....

The bill made the policing of the capital the responsibility of one body, made being a police officer a full-time job with a specified salary, made being a police officer subject to employment criteria and training, and more than doubled the number of policemen in London. The other Victorian reform of policing came about because of Daniel Good. On April 3, 1842, Good murdered a young woman in Putney Park and managed to elude capture for a number of days. Police Inspector Nicholas Pearce and Sergeant Stephen Thornton tracked him around the country until they finally found Good in Tonbridge. In response to the publicity related to Good's escape as well as comments in the press connected with the investigation related to the murder of Lord William Russell two years earlier, Home Secretary Sir James Graham authorized the creation of a detective division of the Metropolitan Police in 1842.

Along with these reforms in public policy related to policing, the nineteenth century saw basic changes to the concept of criminals and crime and how to explain and how to treat them. The Prisoner's Counsel Act of 1836 made an effort to level the field by allowing for the first time those charged with crimes to be represented by legal counsel in court. But more important was the whole issue of capital punishment. Although the House of Lords repeatedly rejected the bills passed in the House of Commons to reduce the number of capital crimes, by 1837 Parliament had removed a number of crimes — sacrilege, letter stealing, returning from transportation, forgery, arson, and burglary — from the capital list and by 1861 conviction for only four crimes — Murder, High Treason, Arson in a Royal Dockyard, and Piracy — called for execution. And in 1823 the Judgment of Death Act made the hitherto mandatory death penalty discretionary for all crimes except murder and treason. All of this happened because of intense public debate about the functions of the law, and the efficacy of punishment going back to Blackstone's maxim: "Better that ten guilty persons escape than one innocent person suffer." This and other anti–capital punishment views were vigorously voiced in Parliament and out by Samuel Romilly and others, and using the bad old days of the Bloody Code as a straw man became one of the prominent motifs of notebook crime fiction in the nineteenth century.

The debate about capital punishment opened up other new ways of viewing crime and criminals. Radical changes evolved with respect to the ways to define certain criminals' behavior. There was a movement, reflected in the Newgate novel, which emphasized the role of social conditions in producing criminals. And there was another which began to see mental illness at the root of at least some crime. This began with the Criminal Lunatics Act. Based on the fact that George Hadfield was acting in a delusional state when he tried to assassinate George III in 1800, he was found innocent. This verdict moved

Parliament to immediately pass an act which mandated indefinite detention, but not execution, for "criminal lunatics." For the next half century British courts went on to define and redefine what it meant to be criminally insane. In Rex v. Arnold (1812) the court's instructions to the jury were that an individual was not responsible for his acts if he was "totally deprived of his understanding and memory, and doth not know what he is doing, no more than a brute, or a wild beast." In 1840 the Insane Prisoners Act allowed the transfer of convicted and condemned mentally ill inmates from prisons to asylums. And finally there was the M'Naghten (sometimes McNaughton) case. Daniel M'Naghten was tried in 1843 for the murder of Prime Minister Peel's private secretary. By finding him not guilty, the court (and the country) established a new, and lasting, definition of why people do bad things — they do them because they are "labouring under such a defect of reason from disease of the mind" and cannot, therefore, distinguish right from wrong (law.jrank.org).

Rewriting the Newgate Calendar

When he looked back from 1832, William Godwin recalled that when he finished his *Enquiry concerning Political Justice, and its Influence on General Virtue and Happiness* in 1793, "It was my fortune at that time to be obliged to consider my pen as the sole instrument for supplying my current expenses." And so he spent the next year writing the novel that became *Things as They Are or, The Adventures of Caleb Williams* (1794). In the same reflection, written as a preface for Bentley's Standard Novels edition of *Fleetwood* (two years after Bulwer-Lytton published the first official "Newgate Novel"), Godwin went on to describe his preparation for writing his first novel:

> I turned over the pages of a tremendous compilation entitled "God's Revenge against Murder," where the beam of the eye of Omniscience was represented as perpetually pursuing the guilty, and laying open the most hidden retreats to the light of day. I was extremely conversant with the "Newgate Calendar," and the "Lives of the Pirates." In the mean time no works of fiction came amiss to me, provided they were written with energy. The authors were still employed upon the same mine as myself, however different was the vein they pursued: we were all of us engaged in exploring the entrails of mind and motive, and in tracing the various reencounter and clashes that may occur between man and man in the diversified scene of human life.
>
> I rather amused myself with tracing a certain similitude between the story of Caleb Williams and the tale of Blue Beard, than derived any hints from that admirable specimen of the terrific. Falkland was my Blue Beard, who had perpetrated atrocious crimes, which if discovered, he might expect to have all the world roused to revenge against him. Caleb Williams was the wife, who in spite

of warning, persisted in his attempts to discover the forbidden secret; and, when he had succeeded, struggled as fruitlessly to escape the consequences, as the wife of Blue Beard in washing the key of the ensanguined chamber, who, as often as she cleared the stain of blood from the one side, found it showing itself with frightful distinctness on the other.

He also notes in the same piece that he constructed the novel backwards — that he wrote the conclusion before he wrote the narrative that led up to it — a technique that Poe would make into the standard mode of construction for the detective story. And looking back almost four decades, Godwin suggested that he conceived part of the novel as what would later be called a thriller: "I bent myself to the conception of a series of adventures of flight and pursuit; the fugitive in perpetual apprehension of being overwhelmed with the worst calamities, and the pursuer, by his ingenuity and resources."

All of this sounds promising, especially for constructing a history for the detective story. *Caleb Williams*, however, largely fails to deliver on that promise. It wasn't that Godwin had no interest in the intellectual complexities associated with crime and detection. Indeed he devotes an entire chapter to discussing the nature and fallibility of judicial evidence in his *Enquiry*, a chapter that ends with:

> Before the intention of any man can be ascertained, in a court of justice, from the consideration of the words he has employed, a variety of circumstances must be taken into the account. The witness heard the words which were employed: does he repeat them accurately, or has not his want of memory caused him to substitute, in the room of some of them, words of his own? Before it is possible to decide, upon the confident expectation I may entertain, that these words will be followed with correspondent actions, it is necessary I should know the exact tone with which they were delivered, and gesture with which they were accompanied. It is necessary I should be acquainted with the context, and the occasion that produced them. Their construction will depend upon the quantity of momentary heat or rooted malice with which they were delivered; and words which appear at first sight of tremendous import will sometimes be found, upon accurate investigation, to have had a meaning purely ironical in the mind of the speaker. These considerations, together with the odious nature of punishment in general, and the extreme mischief that may attend our restraining the faculty of speech, in addition to the restraint we conceive ourselves obliged to put on men's actions, will probably be found to afford a sufficient reason why words ought seldom or never to be made a topic of political animadversion.

And *Caleb Williams*, in fact, has crime in it. The first book depicts the repulsive person and actions of Barnabas Tyrell as well as the admirable person and benevolent actions of Mr. Falkland. Tyrell turns up murdered, and his displaced tenants, the Hawkinses, are accused, tried, and executed for the deed — which they did not commit. In book two, Caleb Williams, who has

raised himself up from humble origins to become Falkland's secretary, becomes
obsessed with the idea that his master, regardless of his genius and magna-
nimity, was Tyrell's real killer; and Falkland privately confesses the fact to
Caleb, who has no intention of turning him in — except the confession infects
both master and servant with galloping suspicion of the other's motives. Caleb
tries to leave Falkland's service, but his master, by means of planted evidence,
accuses him of theft and has him locked up to await his trial. Then follows
sections based on legendary highwayman Jack Sheppard's escapes from Newgate, an interlude of living with a band of bandits, and the vicissitudes Caleb
faces being pursued by thuggish robber turned thief-taker Gines. At the end
of hundreds of pages Caleb finally decides that he must, and is able to, publicly
accuse Falkland of Tyrell's murder. Falkland confesses in open court and more
or less spontaneously dies. During the course of the novel Godwin included
several judicial proceedings — the trial of the Hawkinses for the murder of
Tyrell, Caleb's hearing for theft from his master, and Falkland's trial for the
murder of Tyrell. Two of the three involve miscarriages of justice based on
class prejudice and planted, circumstantial evidence. And when Caleb is
accused of theft Godwin includes a short speech on the obligation of Justices
to listen and judge impartially.

But there were different things on Godwin's mind in 1794 when he wrote
Caleb Williams than there were in 1832 when he recalled his motives and purposes for a very different world. In spite of his interest in the nature and fallibility of evidence, in the novel he treats it with casual disregard; thus, he
pretty much dismisses serious treatment of the evidence which convicted the
Hawkinses of Tyrell's murder:

> Whence came the circumstantial evidence against him, the broken knife and the
> blood, I am unable to tell. I suppose by some miraculous accident.

Instead of "a series of adventures of flight and pursuit," what Godwin settled
on when he wrote his novel was a first person narrative in which the hero
largely examines and reexamines the reasons for his persecution as opposed
to one which focused on the action of flight and pursuit. And this results in
what may be considered a whole lot of self-righteous whining. Indeed what
Godwin ended up with in *Caleb Williams* is not a proto detective story but
something much closer to tragedy and social commentary. Thus it is Falkland's
wealth and status that let him almost get away with murder and persecute an
innocent man, and it is virtues which are also vices that motivate the actions
of the principal characters and devastate both of their lives.

Regardless of its label, however, Godwin's novel became very popular
for decades after its publication. And as it was printed and reprinted, the
aura — if not the substance — of the novel changed. It stopped being entitled

Things as They Are or, The Adventures of Caleb Williams and was retitled as *The Adventures of Caleb Williams, or Things as They Are*, and Godwin added notes about his backward construction of the novel and its Newgate elements to the 1832 edition. Those changes made *Caleb Williams* seem as if it belonged to the hot literary fad of the 1830s — the Newgate novel. But it didn't.

While the sententiousness of *Caleb Williams* keeps it out of the Newgate category, Thomas Holcroft's *Memoirs of Bryan Perdue* (1805) exhibits a number of the elements that would make novels about crime and criminals popular three decades later. Holcroft's novel follows the fortunes of Bryan Perdue from his school days through his "adoption" by a wealthy family, his experiences as a book-keeper in the counting house of a London merchant, his ill-fated amours, his association with the fast and fashionable, his arrest for debt followed by his arrest for forgery, his residence at Newgate and trial, his exile in France, ending with his managing a plantation in Jamaica. Unlike Godwin's whining narrator, Holcroft's first person narrator has a lighter tone as well as a large measure of the *picaro* about him. Thus he frequently addresses the reader as he meanders about the history of his life, muses on the treatises he could have and might someday write, includes poems and songs, and stops occasionally to explain canting slang. For each disreputable thing his professional expertise in gambling precipitates — expulsion from school, damaging young men's fortunes and reputations, keeping a mistress, forging his patron's name — Holcroft includes an equal and opposite benevolent action, including saving a child's life, rescuing his patron's daughter (and important papers) from fire, and reconciling another friend's family to his marriage. This bifurcation, moreover, serves Holcroft's larger purpose of illustrating the redeemable quality of one moved by circumstance and lack of guidance into a life of disreputable acts which betray the trust of others.

As in the picaresque novel, *Bryan Perdue* includes a generous helping of social satire. Thus, for the narrator, high life and low life possess similarities, especially in economics:

> I have the occasion to speak much of gamblers, but it cannot escape the acute reader that commerce itself, in the hands of men like Mr. Hazard, is gambling by wholesale.

From the beginning of the novel, however, Holcroft tells readers that his major concern lies with criminal justice:

> Whenever I have undertaken to write a novel, I have proposed to myself a specific moral purpose. This purpose in Anna St. Ives, was to teach fortitude to females: in Hugh Trevor, to induce youth (or their parents) carefully to inquire into the morality of the profession which each might intend for himself; and, in the present work, to induce all humane and thinking men, such as legislators

ought to be and often are, to consider the general and the adventitious value of human life, and the moral tendency of our penal laws.

It is a subject upon which Holcroft expands when Bryan's disordered life lands him in Newgate. He begins with capital punishment:

> The sacrifice of human victims is not the way to remove offence from the earth, but to create it. Never will men walk in safety, till better modes of correcting vice shall be practiced.

And he goes on to envision a better way to treat vice and crime:

> Oh, that criminals might ever more have these advantages! Oh, that the watchful eye of wisdom, and the benignant hand of power, might henceforth and forever be their protectors! Oh, that the guilty might be sent, like patients afflicted with dangerous disease, to hospitable mansions, that might be humanely constructed for their reception, and reform!
> How many men of enterprise and high faculty would then be preserved! What might the mind of Jack Sheppard have achieved, had its powers been directed to their proper end?...How inestimable might have been the labors of Eugene Aram, than man of extraordinary attainments and stupendous faculties! Nay, how doubtful was his guilt! How doubtful! Even the crime for which he suffered! How easily are minds like these destroyed! But by whom shall they be restored?

Bryan Perdue, however, did not cause an immediate rage for novels about crime. The French Revolution came along at the wrong time for that. Holcroft was charged with treason in 1794, but never tried, and popular reaction against republicanism cast a temporary pall on the drive for reform. After the first burst of reform legislation had begun to remake the British criminal justice system in the 1830s, however, other writers would take up the lives of Jack Sheppard and Eugene Aram with the advantage of having at their disposal a new gallery of techniques and motifs afforded them by experiments in the novel at the turn of the nineteenth century.

The Newgate Novel

Those techniques and motifs resulted in the creation of what came to be called the Newgate novel. The sources of the Newgate novel were various. First there was the publication of Knapp and Baldwin's 1824–28 edition of *The Newgate Calendar*. As noted above, not only did this four-volume work transmit the stories of legendary British felons to nineteenth-century readers, it also reflected the reform movement by including editorial comment on the defects of current criminal law. While the incessant publication of traditional Newgate literature displayed a robust interest in how people became criminals, the bad things they did, and the manner of their deaths, the growth of interest in slang dictionaries displayed a fascination with other aspects of the mores and folkways of criminals. Although interest in criminal slang goes back to Robert Greene's *Cony Catching* pamphlets of the sixteenth century, the rise of dictionaries in the eighteenth century inspired a number of writers to turn to cataloging thieves' language from what might properly be called a scholarly perspective. Thus there were works such as *The Scoundrel's Dictionary; or an Explanation of the Cant Words used by Thieves, Housebreakers, Street Robbers, and Pickpockets about Town* (1754) and Humphrey Tristram Potter's *New Dictionary of all the Cant and Flash Languages* (1795), with the most influential, Francis Grose's *Classical Dictionary of the Vulgar Tongue* (1785) in between. Grose gives this context to his dictionary:

> As this expressive language was originally invented, and is still used, like the cipher of the diplomatists, for purposes of secrecy, and as a means of eluding the vigilance of a certain class of persons, called, *flashicé, Traps,* or in common language, Bow-Street-Officers, it is subject of course to continual change, and is perpetually either altering the meaning of old words, or adding new ones, according as the great object, secrecy, renders it prudent to have recourse to such innovations.

And he follows with definitions of such entries as "Sheriff's Picture Frame: the gallows," "To Shoole: To go skulking about," and "Crump: one who helps solicitors to affidavit men, or false witnesses." In addition to setting forth slang terms and definitions, the canting dictionaries frequently included songs — thus the title page of *The Canting Academy* (1674) adds that it also contains "several new catches and songs," and *The Scoundrel's Dictionary* also boasts that the volume contains "a collection of their flash songs."

At the same time that criminal biographies as well as underworld language and lyrics came to the public's attention, at the turn of the nineteenth century readers made popular several new forms of the novel. While fascination with Fielding's combination of satire and the picaresque in *Joseph Andrews* (1742) and *Tom Jones* (1749) remained strong, the new gothic novel hit a peak of popularity with its furniture of gore and its connections with criminals at the turn of the century — with Ann Radcliffe's *The Mysteries of Udolpho* (1794), Lewis' *The Monk* (1796), and Mary Shelly's *Frankenstein* (1818). In 1814 Walter Scott started a rage for historical novels with the publication of *Waverly*. And, of course, Godwin's and Holcroft's novels (labeled "Jacobin novels" by Gary Kelly) participated in the mix of fiction that would beget the Newgate novel.

All of these elements, in varying combinations, came together to form the substance of what came to be called Newgate novels. These included Thomas Gaspey's *History of George Godfrey* (1828), Bulwer-Lytton's *Paul Clifford* (1830) and *Eugene Aram* (1832), Charles Whitehead's (?), *Autobiography of Jack Ketch* (1835), William H. Ainsworth's *Rookwood* (1834) and *Jack Sheppard* (1839), and Henry Downes Miles, *Dick Turpin* (1840). And then, too, there is Dickens' *Oliver Twist* (1838), which transcends the genre, and Thackeray's *Catherine* (1839), which is a satire of the popular form.

Most of these works draw historical material from Newgate literature. Thus they are based on Eugene Aram ("A Self-Educated Man, with remarkable Linguistic Attainments, who was executed at York on 6th of August, 1759, for a Murder discovered Fourteen Years after its Commission"); Dick Turpin ("A famous Highway Robber, who shot dead one of his own Comrades and was executed at York On 7th of April, 1739"); Jack Sheppard ("A Daring Housebreaker, who made Ingenious Escapes from Prison and even tried to foil his Executioner at Tyburn on 16th of November, 1724"); Jonathan Wild "Director of a Corporation of Thieves, and a most famous Receiver. Executed at Tyburn, 24th of May, 1725"); and William Brandon alias Jack Ketch ("Who beheaded King Charles the First") (www.exclassics.com). Elements of the defective criminal justice system of the last century play significant roles in each — from the extended depiction of Jonathan Wild, "thief-taker general" in *Jack Sheppard*, to episodes of accusation and arrest, to descriptions of prison and prison life, and finally to inevitable one-sided, prejudiced trials and cruel public executions. Rather than viewing these processes as right and proper, moreover, Newgate novels emphasize the indifference and cruelty of things as they were. Ainsworth, for instance, takes great pains to describe the gloomy architecture and cruel routines of Newgate prison in *Jack Sheppard*, and in *History of George Godfrey* readers find fifteen pages devoted to a minute, step-by-step description of the preparation of prisoners for the gallows. These elements, moreover, serve as details in the writers' avowed purpose. Thus Bulwer-Lytton describes his double purpose in the preface to the 1840 edition of *Paul Clifford*. The first was serious social comment:

> First to draw attention to two errors in our penal institutions; namely, a vicious prison-discipline, and a sanguinary criminal code, — the habit of corrupting the boy by the very punishment that ought to redeem him, and then hanging the man at the first occasion, as the easiest way of getting rid of our own blunders.

But there was a comic-satiric element as well:

> A second and a lighter object in the novel of "Paul Clifford" (and hence the introduction of a semi-burlesque or travesty in the earlier chapters) was to show that there is nothing essentially different between vulgar vice and fashionable vice, and that the slang of the one circle is but an easy paraphrase of the other.

In most cases, too, Newgate writers spend time in a creating a sympathetic portrayal of the early years of their criminal protagonists — thus Paul Clifford's upbringing by Peggy Lobkins and Ainsworth's drawing of the apprenticeship of Jack Sheppard and Thames Darrell — and generally explain rather than condemn the causes or accidents which led their heroes to become involved with crime — even confessed murderer Eugene Aram. They also demonstrate a lighter side of crime. Both Bulwer-Lytton and Ainsworth, therefore, provide page after page of robbers' lyrics and properly annotated, canting slang. Newgate writers often describe highway robberies as capers rather than as felonies, and they portray thief-takers, magistrates, and judges as blind, indifferent, and cruel instruments of a perverse legal and social system. The writers also include a generous helping of romance material — separated lovers, exotic locales from caves to crypts, demonic villains, and surprise revelations about parentage occur in most Newgate books. And choosing material based on pursuit, capture and escape, furthermore, made thriller plotting an almost inevitable part of the Newgate novel.

Coincident with the appearance of the Newgate novel in Britain, in 1828 the first work by a real detective appeared in France — and very quickly in translations published in England, Germany, and the United States. It was by Eugene François Vidocq. Partly padded out by ghost writers, Vidocq's four-volume *Memoirs* recounts the transformation of the narrator from felon to thief-taker extraordinaire to chief of the Sûreté. Beginning with narratives of his early life as a juvenile delinquent and progressing through prison-break after prison-break, the *Memoirs* then switch to demonstrations of Vidocq's prowess as a thief-taker — prowess which depends upon quick wit, knowledge of criminals, expertise in disguise, as well as the widespread incompetence of the police and police methods of his day. The book met with enthusiasm from British reviewers who placed it firmly in the tradition of Newgate literature. Thus the review of Vidocq's *Memoirs* in *The Westminster Review* (July 1829) speaks of the "Newgate lessons" of the work, especially with reference to the hero as a reformed criminal:

> He is moreover a shrewd and intelligent man, and we recommend all persons who are interested in the reform of criminals and the suppression of crime, to take up these volumes, if they can forgive the author for being very entertaining. Those benevolent individuals who would regulate the world after the best possible methods, may learn that there may be instruction in a pleasant work, in a book of an agreeable style, and written in a light, and sometimes even in a picturesque manner.

Foreign Quarterly Review (January 1829) took the same view of Vidocq's *Memoirs* as one containing lessons for the legislature about crime and criminals and coupled this with unrestrained praise of Vidocq and the work:

> From a pernicious member of one society, he became a most valuable agent of another; in fact, from being a runaway convict he became a police officer, having passed through the chrysalis state of spy. But what an officer! what a spy! and

what a convict! In the last character he was condemned without a crime: as a spy he was a Proteus; as an officer a Hercules...For our parts, we have faith in genius; Vidocq is known to all the world of Paris as the most celebrated thief-taker that ever existed, and where a man really excels in his art, we maintain that he is not likely to trifle with it. Besides, we trust to internal evidence; either Vidocq has known — and seen — and done — what he has, or his invention does not fall short of the fertility of Defoe, and the vigour of Sir Walter Scott. We allow for a little colouring; we allow for a desire to stand well with the world; we allow for these in all confessions; and when all this allowance is made, it would be extremely difficult to point out a work with more legitimate claims to attention. If the incredulous say it is a fiction, take it as such, and it is superior to any work of the kind; if it is a true story, then let us be amused by its strange pictures of a kind of life we suppose none of our readers have experienced, but which it imports every citizen of a free country to understand. Legislators ought to know exactly what it is to which they condemn men; they should learn the operation of circumstances on different dispositions, and they should meditate better plans than are yet in existence for the decrease of crime and the reform of criminals.

Indeed, the inserted narrative about Adele and the pathos of her fall into a life of crime in *Memoirs* is every bit as sentimental as anything in British Newgate literature.

More Newgate Than Newgate

From the time of Vidocq's *Memoirs,* the French audience was very much interested in what was going on with respect to the police and crime — real and imagined. Indeed Eugene Sue's exposé of crime and poverty, *The Mysteries of Paris* (1842), resonated emphatically in both England and the United States. It inspired a number of books that used urban crime and satire to make a new version of the Newgate novel. The most popular of these were George William MacArthur Reynolds' *The Mysteries of London* and George Lippard's *The Quaker City, or The Monks of Monk Hall.*

Published originally as a "penny dreadful" — a form of inexpensive serial literature which appeared in Britain in the 1830s — *The Mysteries of London* (1845) began a rage for a new sub-set of Newgate literature which came to be called Misery and Mysteries literature. A compound of seemingly countless installments (each with an illustration), Reynolds' work is an amalgam of Eugene Sue's *The Mysteries of Paris* and some of the motifs of the novels of Bulwer-Lytton and Dickens. Roughly following the vicissitudes of Richard Markam who is beset by bad luck, con men, and other assorted felons, *The Mysteries of London* contains repeated descriptions of the fetid lives and living conditions of the poor; thus:

when a member of one of these families happens to die, the corpse is kept in the close room where the rest still continue to live and sleep. Poverty frequently compels the unhappy relatives to keep the body for days — aye, and weeks. Rapid decomposition takes place; — animal life generates quickly; and in four-and-twenty hours myriads of loathsome animaculae are seen crawling about. The very undertakers' men fall sick at these disgusting — these revolting spectacles.

It is a world infested with crime and criminals. Some of the crime arises from harsh and inequitable laws — as in the case of this woman arrested for vagrancy:

"Do not think so, sir! My husband was a hard working man — never spent an hour at the publichouse — never deprived his family of a farthing of his wages. He was a pattern to all married men — and his pride was to see his children well-dressed and happy. Alas, sir — we were too happy not to meet with some sad reverse! My husband in an evil hour went out shooting one afternoon, when there was a holiday at the factory where he worked; and he killed a hare upon a nobleman's grounds near Richmond. He was taken up and tried for poaching, and was sentenced to a year's imprisonment with hard labour! This term expires in six weeks; but in the meantime — O God! what have we not suffered!"

But Reynolds also populates the world with hard-core criminal types:

The parlour of the "boozing-ken" now received some additional guests — all belonging to the profession of roguery, though not all following precisely the same line. Thus there were Cracksmen, Magsmen, Area-Sneaks, Public Patterers, Buzgloaks, Dummy-Hunters, Compter-Prigs, Smashers, Flimsy Kiddies, Macers, Coiners, Begging-Letter Imposters, &c.

And, as in Bulwer-Lytton and Ainsworth, these mugs sing — included are texts to "The Thieves' Alphabet," and "The Body Snatcher's Song."

The Mysteries of London describes trials at Old Bailey, Newgate and a debtors' prison, as well as a public hanging, and depicts the police as a group corrupted by the duties they have been assigned to perform:

Reassured by this conviction, though still strangely excited by the appalling scene which he had witnessed, Richard seated himself by the fire, and soon fell into conversation with the policemen. These men could talk of nothing but themselves or their pursuits: they appeared to live in a world of policeism; all their ideas were circumscribed to station-houses, magistrates' offices, prisons, and criminal courts of justice. Their discourse was moreover garnished with the slang terms of thieves; they could not utter a sentence without interpolating a swell-mob phrase or a Newgate jest. They seemed to be so familiar with crime (though not criminal themselves) that they could not devote a moment to the contemplation of virtue: they only conversed about persons who were "in trouble," but never condescended to lavish a thought to those who were out of it.

And, as in Dickens, conscience provides the real punishment for crime:

But chiefly he beheld before him the tall gaunt form of his murdered wife—with one eye smashed and bleeding in her head:—the other glared fearfully upon him.

This phantasmagoria became at length so fearful and so real in appearance, that the murderer turned his back towards the little grating through which the light struggled into the dungeon in two long, narrow, and oblique columns.

But then he imagined that there were goblins behind him; and this idea soon grew as insupportable as the first;—so he rose, and groped his way up and down that narrow vault—a vault which might become his tomb!

The same year as Reynolds' serial appeared, miseries and mysteries made an American debut with *The Quaker City, or The Monks of Monks Hall* published in ten installments beginning in 1844 by Poe's friend George Lippard. It shares some of the Newgate features with Reynolds' work: Lippard included several instances of criminals' songs, a note about the use of underworld argot, and an extended description of a hanging in *The Quaker City*. Indeed the book even contains an allusion to Ainsworth:

> To say that Luke did not relish these excursions, for the adventure's sake alone, would be doing him rank injustice. He found as much pleasure in pursuing the thread of a difficult enterprize, which combined danger, romance, and mystery, as the most indefatigable novel-reader finds in the pages of a book like Rookwood, where the attention is, from first to last, rivetted and enchained by one passage of breathless interest succeeding another, in transitions as rapid and thrilling as the changes of some well-contested battle.

But *The Quaker City, or The Monks of Monk Hall* derives more from the traditions of Juvenalian satire and the gothic of Monk Lewis than from Bulwer-Lytton or Ainsworth. Lippard underlines the work with repeated, wholesale condemnations of Philadelphia society — the following being but a modest version of the scorn the narrator heaps on Philadelphia society:

> Here they come—one and all—the fools, pretending to despise my science, and yet willing to place themselves in my power, while they affect to doubt. Haha—here are their Nativities one and all—That" he continued, turning over a leaf—"is the Horoscope of a clergyman—Holy man of God!—He wanted to know whether he could ruin an innocent girl in his congregation without discovery. And that is the Horoscope of a lawyer, who takes fees from both sides. His desire is to know, whether he can perjure himself in a case now in court without detection. Noble counsellor! This Doctor—" and he turned over another leaf— "told me that he had a delicate case in hand. A pretty girl has been, ruined and so on—the seducer wants to destroy the fruit of his crime and desires the doctor to undertake the job. Doctor wants to know what moment will be auspicious— ha-ha!"

As the novel proceeds this scorn accelerates until there is a vision of the apocalyptic destruction of the City of Brotherly Love. Along with the inserted rants about universal corruption in the Quaker city, Lippard's narrative is in part based on the 1843 trial of Singleton Mercer for murdering his sister's rapist. From the breathless recreation of the rape that occasioned that murder, Lippard continues to depict of a series of crimes committed by nominally respectable citizens — rape, incest, and adultery attended by murder with a case of forgery added for good measure. All of these take place in or end up at the immense mansion called Monk Hall which is more gothic castle with its catacombs, dungeons, trap-doors, and secret corridors than urban residence. And all of the acts of the novel take place in a world in which justice is largely corrupt, the police are ineffectual "burly men," and conscience fails to operate either as a check on or as a punishment for crime.

Anti-Newgate Reaction

While Vidocq's name and work remained before the English-speaking public for the remainder of the century and books called "mysteries and miseries" of assorted cities continued to be published well into the 1880s, the fad for Newgate novels lasted for a little over a decade. Even at the beginning of its proverbial fifteen minutes of fame there was trouble. First it was about the language — thus this piece from *The Monthly Review* (June 1830) on *Paul Clifford*:

> We must, however, quarrel with our author for introducing into a novel destined to meet the eyes of females, a coarse and almost unintelligible jargon of the vilest slang, which he is frequently obliged to interpret by notes, and which we were often unable to comprehend when not so assisted...We admit that there is a degree of raciness and originality in some of the slang of the lower orders; but we no more wish to be gratified with such occasional relishes at the expense of the disgust which environs them, than we would wish to initiate ourselves in the amusements of a deceased nobleman who sought the company of sympathetic coal-heavers.

There were, however, more serious objections voiced to Ainsworth, Bulwer-Lytton, and the rage for Newgate novels than their unrefined language — objections that held that they were degenerate, even dangerous. Thus this piece on *Jack Sheppard* in *The Monthly Review* (December 1839):

> We have already said that there are great moral incongruities and pictorial falsifications in the delineation of character as given by Mr. Ainsworth; and therefore it is not nature nor real life which he attempts to mirror. But independent entirely of this objection, we deny that it is wholesome to tell the whole truth, when the thing that is to be represented must tend to degrade the spectator or listener, and to infect perniciously the taste, which, unless diseased, or untutored,

must revolt at the horrors, and the grossnesses, which the darkest passages in life, and the practices of the vilest, furnish. Unless diseased or uncultured, we say:— why, it is the morbidity and rude condition of the tastes and attainments of the multitude which has brought such works as Jack Sheppard into vogue, and to which tastes and attainments Mr. Ainsworth has so abundantly catered, and so successfully served to confirm and still further to lower....

But the final blow to the Newgate novel came out of the publicity surrounding the arrest and 1840 trial of B.F. Courvoisier for the murder of Lord William Russell — the same crime that, in part, led to the creation of London's first official detective police at Scotland Yard. In his confession Courvoisier maintained that he was moved to murder his master by reading *Jack Sheppard* and seeing a play based on the novel. The press jumped all over this. There was an outcry from journals from *The Examiner* to *The Phrenological Journal*; *The Monthly Magazine* (July 1840) had this to say:

> We should particularly notice that this attempt is concurrent with several of the recent atrocious murders on record. We have already suggested the cause in the Jack Sheppardism of the age. The manner of the murderer's proceeding in the case of Templeton, is copied from Mr. Ainsworth's romance — it was the novelist who told him how to manage the execrable deed with safety and success. Courvoisier has confessed, that it was reading and seeing Jack Sheppard which induced him to the assassination of his noble master. Can such things be — and yet the present state of literature excite no interest? Wherever we turn — to the drama or to the novel — the essay or the poem — all is the same, with a very few honourable exceptions, and for them the public has no ear. The adder is deaf to all but the discord of hell.

And it wasn't just in Britain that Newgate novels in general and Ainsworth in particular took it on the chin. In 1840 *Burton's Gentleman's Magazine and American Monthly Review* (April 1840) printed this review:

> Mr. Ainsworth is a powerful writer; his "Crichton" stands at the head of the long list of English novels — unapproachable and alone; but if this great glory is fairly Mr. Ainsworth's due, and in our humble opinion the fact is incontrovertible, he must also assume the responsibility of giving to the reading world the most corrupt, flat, and vulgar fabrication in the English language. "Jack Sheppard" is a disgrace to the literature of the day.

Significantly, one of the two editors of *Burton's* in 1840 was Edgar Allan Poe.

Why Not Detective Stories?

In 1841 when Poe wrote "The Murders in the Rue Morgue," the Newgate novel was decidedly yesterday's news. Even though it did not contribute to the creation of either the detective story or the story about detectives, nonetheless the genre represented the culmination of a century's worth of thought about crime and criminals. Over that span, the literary portrayal of criminals changed dramatically. Old school Newgate Calendars focused on those who committed crimes and portrayed them as monsters, or picaros, or sometimes even as buffoons. At the turn of the nineteenth century, however, writers began to show criminal heroes as victims of callous social conditions and mounted arguments against perverse laws and an outmoded judicial system. In older literature writers used criminals' lives principally as caveats for the young, and attributed their apprehension, punishment, and their slim hope of redemption directly to Providence. Newgate novels, on the other hand, portrayed their criminal heroes as gaining redemption with the help of their friends and the achieved potential of their hearts. If English law in effect made every person responsible for apprehending criminals, Newgate novels depicted a world in which exemplary individuals took it upon themselves to provide sympathy and support for the less fortunate — even those involved with crime. Thus in *Jack Sheppard* there is Mr. Wood who makes a practice of taking in orphans. Mr. Browlow does the same in *Oliver Twist*; Mr. Saville becomes the protector of Bryan Purdue even after he has been booted out of school for gambling, and Peggy Lobkins raises the abandoned Paul Clifford as best she can. On top of these and other effects of benevolence demonstrated in the books, in one way or another, in the end sentiment redeems the criminal heroes of these novels. Thus Paul Clifford leaves a successful, thriving, and (in an adolescent male way) fulfilling career as the leader of a band of highwaymen because of his love for Lucy, and Jack Sheppard achieves redemption because of his love for his mother. If good people do the work of Providence in the lives of the criminal heroes of Newgate novels, it plays a more forceful role in the fate of criminal villains. In line with their grounding in traditional romance motifs, several Newgate novels made their plots work by opposing their criminal heroes with irredeemable criminal villains. Thus Jonathan Wild and Fagin and Bill Sykes are very, very bad men who cannot be made into anything different. And with them it is not society or its agents but Providence that has its way in the end, underlining the writers' use of traditional themes of evil being self-destructive and "murder will out."

And if one has Providence on one's side, who needs detectives or anything else? While the rise and fall of the Newgate novel corresponded with and in some measure reflected the rise of serious and broad interest in the nature and fallibility of law and justice in contemporary institutions, the form almost entirely neglected one of the other significant topics in the early nineteenth-century debate about the law. Focusing almost entirely on the horrors of Newgate prison and the "bloody code," writers ignored the growing contemporary interest in the nature and role of evidence in determining guilt. Thus one finds Godwin — who expressed weighty concerns about evidence in *Enquiry concerning Political Justice*— cavalierly dismissing it in *Caleb Williams*: "Whence came the circumstantial evidence against him, the broken knife and the blood, I am unable to tell. I suppose by some miraculous accident." This casual approach to proof exists in part because the heroes of Newgate novels are admittedly criminals, so no one has to investigate or prove anything; it was the product in the form of brutal sentencing upon which the writers were focused, rather than the process in the form of proofs of guilt or innocence. That was going to change.

With the exceptions of Vidocq — whose *Memoirs* reviewers made to fit the criteria of the Newgate novel — and the little-known *Richmond: Scenes from the Life of a Bow-Street Runner*, none of the works of the period is about a detective. While de-facto detectives certainly existed in England at least from the time of the Bow Street Runners, it is worth recalling that there was no official detective force in the country until 1842. It took so long because of a widespread pubic distrust of police and especially plainclothes detectives. Part of that distrust dates back to the trial of Stephen McDaniel and the association of thief-takers with systematic perjury — an association that moved Bow Street magistrate John Fielding to distance himself, his late brother, and all honest thief-takers from the methods and work of "McDaniel and his hellish crew" in his pamphlet *A plan for preventing robberies within twenty miles of London* (1755). The repeated exposure of systematic perjury on the part of law enforcement, in fact, cast a shadow over the heart of the contemporary judicial system — the testimony of one person against another — and would in time cause thoughtful writers to begin to think about how people are proved to be innocent or guilty and portray it in fiction. The other and more immediate reason it took so long for detectives to appear in Britain and in British literature was the French. The French police, especially those in plain clothes, were seen as but another one of Napoleon's devilish instruments. Thus this piece in *The Christian Examiner* (September and October 1827):

> It would seem as if despotism, profiting by the experience of ages, had put forth her whole skill and resources in forming the French police, and had forged a weapon, never to be surpassed, for stifling the faintest breathings of disaffection, and chaining every free thought. This system of *espionage*, (we are proud that we have no English word for the infernal machine,) had indeed been used under all tyrannies. But it wanted the craft of Fouche, and the energy of Bonaparte, to disclose all its powers...[Every] man, of the least importance in the community, had the eye of a spy upon him. He was watched at home as well as abroad, in the boudoir and theatre, in the brothel and gaming house; and these last named haunts furnished not a few ministers of the Argus-eyed police. There was an ear open through all France to catch the whispers of discontent; a power of evil,

which aimed to rival, in omnipresence and invisibleness, the benignant agency of the Deity. Of all instruments of tyranny, this is the most detestable; for it chills the freedom and warmth of social intercourse; locks up the heart; infects and darkens men's minds with mutual jealousies and fears; and reduces to system a wary dissimulation, subversive of force and manliness of character.

Additionally, Newgate novels did not participate in the public debate about the necessity and utility of having detective police in part because of the association of writers like Holcroft with French radicalism. The movement to purify the public through what they read in deference to the sensibilities of the new queen also contributed to the decline of fiction about crime and criminals in the late 1830s. And as historical works which focused on depicting the cruel workings of the last century's justice system defined, the reform movement took away a lot of their subject matter.

And then, too, at the beginning of the nineteenth century a movement began which saw crime and criminals not as a social problem amenable for discussion and depiction in literature but as a medical one. This originated in Germany with Franz Joseph Gall, and his new science phrenology. His works, including *The physiognomical system of Drs. Gall and Spurzheim : founded on an anatomical and physiological examination of the nervous system in general and the brain in particular : and indicating the dispositions and manifestations of the mind* (1815), held that human moral nature was innate and located in a particular area of the brain which, in turn, was reflected in the shape of an individual's skull. Phreonology, moreover, was just one of the indicators of the new approach to crime and criminals as a scientific and medical issue — the most definitive of which was the series of judicial decision relative to the insanity defense. Neither writers nor readers in the mid-nineteenth century had the wherewithal to deal with human actions as irrational and inexplicable.

All of this helps to explain why there were no detective stories — and less than a handful of pieces about detectives — in Anglo-American literature before the 1840s. Instead of developing from novels centered on the lives of criminals, fiction about detectives arose from stories appearing in the burgeoning world of magazines and newspapers in Britain and the United States. In these stories writers developed a hero whose personal and social virtues were less problematic than those of the criminal as well as themes which ranged from the exploration of the current interest in the nature and use of evidence to the reassurance of an increasingly affluent society about the safety and security of their persons and possessions.

Chapter Two

Edgar Allan Poe

After three and a half centuries of making do, in the nineteenth century a lot of clever people began fiddling around with printing presses. In 1814 *The Times* of London speeded up the printing process with Koenig and Bauer's new steam-powered presses, and by the mid–1840s Richard Hoe's "lightning" rotary press could crank out 8,000 impressions an hour — an impressive figure when one considers that the circulation of most contemporary magazines was under 5,000 copies per issue (George Rex Graham, for example, bought out *The Casket* in 1839 mostly for its list of 3,500 subscribers). Like *The Casket's*, most magazines' circulation may have been modest, but during the first half of the nineteenth century an awful lot of them were printed in Britain and the United States. Between 1800 and 1850, for instance, one estimate puts the number of American magazines that saw daylight — however briefly — at 3,333 (www.comp-index.com). Seemingly, toward the middle of the nineteenth century every organization, every region, every political party and every special interest in America had its own magazine. And while few of them could pay writers much, each one of these magazines needed copy. And thereby hangs more than one tale.

The Philadelphia Story

William Edwin Burton was a particular and significant case in point. In 1834 Burton left England and came to the United States where he quickly established himself as a popular comic actor. Taking advantage of his celebrity, as well as an inherited bent for authorship and publishing, in 1837 Burton launched a new magazine in Philadelphia. As the potpourri of images on the cover summoning up patriotism, outdoor sport, the theater, the library, the ballroom, and the battlefield suggest, *The Gentleman's Magazine* (soon to become *Burton's Gentleman's Magazine*) was a miscellany of prose and verse

on divergent subjects. Although it was avowedly American, from the start its contents displayed a definite Gallic tilt (Paris, for instance, is mentioned in twelve places in the first year's issues). In the first year Burton himself contributed two signed pieces to his journal: the lyrics for the song "The Dark-Haired Spanish Maid," and "The Excommunicated, a Tale."

In March of 1838 Burton contributed another tale to his magazine, "The Cork Leg," a story that is, if not the first detective story, a narrative which surely influenced Poe's detective tales. "The Cork Leg" begins with an epigraph that insists that the following narrative is original and not a translation from the French. Then the narrator launches into a description of the idyllic life of a group of friends who live in the French countryside. Among them is Jacques Cloporte, who lost his leg in battle and has acquired an artificial limb made of cork. On a visit to Paris Cloporte engages in a duel in which he severely wounds his opponent and then departs for his friend's chateau. He is pursued to the country estate by M. De Turgot, "an agent of the Paris police," who believes that a murder has been committed and wants an arrest in order to achieve a promotion, but who knows only that the suspect is a man with a cork leg. Forewarned of the police agent's impending arrival — as well as his limited knowledge — Cloporte's two friends pretend that they, too, have artificial limbs and instruct all of the servants to limp as well. Not to be flummoxed, Turgot devises the means to solve the problem of identity: he drops a hot coal as if by accident on one of the pretender's legs, jabs the other in the leg when he is asleep, and sets fire to his bed curtains to observe his hosts' gaits in an emergency. After he has identified his man, however, the friends chase him from the chateau and he returns to Paris only to discover that the supposed victim of the duel has recovered from his wound and there is no case after all. What readers found in "The Cork Leg" was a puzzle story based on a policeman using ingenuity to solve the problem of who has the cork leg, and a comedy displaying the tables turned and authority humbled.

Six months later, in the fall of 1838, Burton moved from writing about made-up police agents to stories about Eugene Francois Vidocq, the most famous detective of the day. Vidocq tales had appeared in Philadelphia as early as 1830 when the short "Vidocq and the Sexton" appeared in the *Philadelphia Album and Ladies Literary Gazette* (February 20, 1830) bearing the heading that it had been "Translated for the New York American." In 1834 Cary and Hart published Vidocq's *Memoirs (Memoirs of Vidocq, principal agent of the French police until 1827)* along with endpapers advertising their New Books *Lives and Exploits of the English Highway* and *Celebrated Trails and Cases of Criminal Jurisprudence.* As both a follow-up to Burton's own police story, "The Cork Leg," and to capture the trailing popularity and publicity of the publication of *Memoirs,* starting in September 1838 and ending in May 1839,

Burton ran nine stories about Vidocq not contained in the Cary and Hart volume. They appeared under the heading "Unpublished passages in the Life of Vidocq the French Minister of Police." These included "Marie Laurent" (September 1838); "Doctor D'Arsac" (October 1838); "The Seducer" (November 1838); "The Bill of Exchange" (December 1838); "The Strange Discovery" (January 1839); "The Gambler's Death" (February 1839); "Pierre Louvois" (March 1839); Jean Monette" (April 1839); and "The Conscript's Revenge" (May 1839). Most are signed at the conclusion with the initials J.M.B.— who may have been more author than translator.

Half of Burton's Vidocq tales concern murder, two turn on attempted murder and burglary, one has forgery as its basis, and one centers on the evils of gambling. Sentiment serves as the basis for all of them. Thus seduction and revenge provide the basis for three ("The Seducer," "Jean Monette," and "The Conscript's Revenge"); marriage above one's station causes the crime in "Doctor D'Arsac"; the burglars in "Marie Laurent" and "Jean Monette" both practice upon innocent women to accomplish their dirty work; guilt and suicide propel both "The Gambler's Death" and "The Bill of Exchange"; and one of them, "Pierre Louvois," concerns the execution of an man wrongly convicted by circumstantial evidence. Vidocq the detective himself does little or nothing in most of the stories beyond, one is to assume, providing the voice of the narrator — they are, after all, supposed to be passages from his life. Indeed he does not appear as an actor in more than half of them ("Pierre Louvois," "The Conscript's Revenge," "The Gambler's Death," and "The Bill of Exchange"), and in several ("Marie Laurent," "Doctor D'Arsac," "The Strange Discovery," and "Jean Monette") his involvement in the denouement is the result of accident rather than his efforts — in "The Strange Discovery," for example, Julie, the falsely accused maid, identifies the men who robbed and murdered her mistress herself, and then goes to Vidocq who arrests them.

In June 1839, the month after Burton ran the last of the Vidocq pieces, *Burton's Gentleman's Magazine* ran a notice that the editor had "made arrangements with Edgar A. Poe, Esq., late Editor of the *Southern Literary Messenger,* to devote his abilities and experience to a portion of the Editorial duties of the *Gentleman's Magazine.*" But the arrangement didn't last long. In May of 1840 Burton fired Poe when he got news of his attempt to start a new magazine. Four months later George Rex Graham bought *Burton's Gentleman's Magazine* and subsumed it into his new journal, *Graham's Lady's and Gentleman's Magazine: Embracing Every Department of Literature Embellished with Engravings, Fashions, and Music, Arranged for the Piano-Forte, Harp, and Guitar.* On February 20, 1841, Graham announced in *The Saturday Evening Post,* which he owned, that beginning with the April issue Poe would become an editor of *Graham's Magazine.*

The Founding Documents

The April 1841 issue of *Graham's* contained poetry, a section on "Sports and Pastimes," book reviews, the music and words for "Oh, Gentle Love," and nine pieces of prose fiction. The books reviewed included Bulwer-Lytton's *Night and Morning* and R.M. Walsh's translation of *Sketches of Conspicuous Living Characters of France*. Bulwer-Lytton's book got faint praise: "In regard to 'Night and Morning' we cannot agree with that critical opinion which considers it the best novel of its author. It is only not his worst." Ignored in the review, however, the novel contains both the sinister Mr. Sharp, a Bow Street Runner, and a French detective based on Vidocq:

> At these words the small companion of the stranger slowly sauntered to the spot, while at the sound of his name and the tread of his step the throng gave way to the right and left. For M. Favart was one of the most renowned chiefs of the great Paris police,— a man worthy to be the contemporary of the illustrious Vidocq.

As for *Sketches*, not only does the book contain a chapter on André-Marie-Jean-Jacques Dupin, an eminent French jurist, it also briefly mentions cryptography in the chapter on Pierre A. Berryer. Poe only briefly cited Dupin in his review, but with cryptography it was another matter — it provided the opening, given his pieces on codes in *Alexander's Weekly Messenger* in 1839, to issue another challenge to readers to send in encoded passages to stump the editor:

> The difficulty of deciphering may well be supposed much greater had the key been in a foreign tongue; yet any one who will take the trouble may address us a note, in the same manner as here proposed, and the key-phrase may be either in French, Italian, Spanish, German, Latin, or Greek, (or in any of the dialects of those languages), and we pledge ourselves for the solution of the riddle. The experiment may afford our readers some amusement — let them try it.

The April 1841 number of *Graham's* also contains the original version of Poe's "The Murders in the Rue Morgue." It occupies 14 double-column pages (from 166 to 179) and develops in six parts: (1) an introductory essay on analysis that begins with a paradox: "It cannot be doubted that the mental features discoursed of as the analytical are, in themselves, but little susceptible of analysis"; (2) the introduction of the narrator and detective: "I was astonished, too, at the vast extent of his reading — and above all I felt my soul enkindled within me by the wild fervor, and what I could only term the vivid freshness, of his imagination ... I felt that the society of such a man would be to me a treasure beyond price"; (3) the detective's deduction demonstration, showing how he knows what the narrator is thinking: "All at once Dupin broke forth with these words:—'He is a very little fellow, that's true, and would do better for the *Théâtre des Variétés*'"; (4) the details of the murder of two women as described in the press: "we were looking over an evening edition of the 'Le Tribunal,' when the following paragraphs arrested our attention. 'EXTRAORDINARY MURDERS'"; (5) a visit to and inspection of the scene of the crime; and (6) Dupin's analysis of evidence and surprise solution. In later editions Poe added the epigraph from Thomas Browne's *Urn Burial* and deleted the original first paragraph.

On May 1 Rex Graham published Poe's review of *Barnaby Rudge* in the *Saturday Evening Post* in which he predicted the ending of Dickens' serial novel before the publication of its last installment. In that piece Poe also discussed the significance of the reader's relationship to the text. Thus

> We may as well here observe that the reader should note carefully the ravings of Barnaby, which are not put into his mouth at random, as might be supposed, but are intended to convey indistinct glimmerings of the events to be evolved, and in this evident design of Mr. Dickens' his ideality is strongly evinced. It would be difficult to impress upon the mind of a merely general reader how vast a degree of interest may be given to the story by such means; for in truth that interest, great as it may be made, will not be, strictly speaking, of a popular cast.
> ...
> Now these incoherences are regarded by Mr. Chester simply as such, and no attention is paid them; but they have reference, *indistinctly*, to the counsellings together of Rudge and Geoffrey Haredale, upon the topic of the bloody deeds committed; which counsellings have been watched by the idiot. In the same manner almost every word spoken by him will be found to have an under current of meaning, by paying strict attention to which the enjoyment of the imaginative reader will be infinitely heightened.

Two months later Poe returned to the subject of cryptography which he had been exploring in *Alexander's Messenger* in the previous years and he included "A Few Words on Secret Writing" in *Graham's Magazine*. By the spring of 1842, however, Poe tired of his connection with the Philadelphia publisher, and on May 25 wrote to Thomas that

> my reason for resigning was disgust with the namby-pamby character of the Magazine — a character which it was impossible to eradicate — I allude to the contemptible pictures, fashion plates, music and love tales. The salary, moreover, did not pay me for the labor which I was forced to bestow. With Graham, who is really a very gentlemanly, although exceedingly weak man, I had no misunderstanding.

A year after he had left *Graham's* Poe began to shop around a new story, "a sequel to 'The Murders in the Rue Morgue.'" First, in June he offered it to George Roberts, editor of the *Boston Notion*:

MY DEAR SIR,— It is just possible that you may have seen a tale of mine entitled "The Murders in the Rue Morgue," and published originally, in "Graham's Magazine" for April, 1841. Its *theme* was the exercise of ingenuity in the detection of a murderer. I have just completed a similar article, which I shall entitle "The Mystery of Marie Roget — a Sequel to the Murders in the Rue Morgue." The story is based upon the assassination of Mary Cecilia Rogers, which created so vast an excitement, some months ago, in New York. I have, however, handled my design in a manner altogether *novel* in literature. I have imagined a series of nearly exact *coincidences* occurring in Paris. A young grisette, one Marie Roget, has been murdered under precisely similar circumstances with Mary Rogers. Thus, under pretence of showing how Dupin (the hero of "The Rue Morgue") unravelled the mystery of Marie's assassination, I, in reality, enter into a very long and rigorous analysis of the New York tragedy. No point is omitted. I examine, each by each, the opinions and arguments of the press upon the subject, and show that this subject has been, hitherto, *unappreciated*. In fact I believe not only that I have demonstrated the fallacy of the general idea — that the girl was the victim of a gang of ruffians — but have *indicated the assassin* in a manner which will give renewed impetus to investigation. My main object, nevertheless, as you will readily understand, is an analysis of the true principles which should direct inquiry in similar cases. From the nature of the subject, I feel convinced that the article will excite attention, and it has occurred to me that you would be willing to purchase it for the forthcoming Mammoth Notion. It will make 25 pages of Graham's Magazine, and, at the usual price, would be worth to me $100. For reasons, however, which I need not specify, I am desirous of having this tale printed in Boston, and, if you like it, I will say $50. Will you please write me upon this point ? — by return mail, if possible.

The same day he sent virtually the same letter offering the piece to Joseph Evans Snodgrass of the *Baltimore Saturday Visiter*. Neither Snodgrass nor Rogers took the bait. Finally in the fall of 1842 *Snowden's Ladies' Companion* picked up "The Mystery of Marie Roget," and published the first two installments in November and December. On November 18, however, *The New York Tribune* published an account of the real facts of Mary Rogers' death:

On Sunday the 25th of July, 1841, Mary Rogers came to her [Mrs. Loss's] house in company with a young physician, who undertook to procure for the unfortunate girl a premature delivery. While in the hands of the physician she died.

This was not the solution Poe had imagined, and it meant a rewrite was in order. He needed until February 1843 to alter the last installment of the tale in order to make it at least not contradict the known facts of the Mary Rogers case. Each installment of "Marie Roget" carries the header that it is "A Sequel to 'Murders in the Rue Morgue," and taken together the three installments total over 20,000 words. In the first installment the Prefect of Police visits Dupin, asks for his help with the unsolved murder of Marie Roget, recites the known facts (though which Dupin sleeps), and offers a generous reward for his help. The narrator then trots out and procures "at the Prefecture, a full report of all the evidence elicited, and, at the various newspaper offices, a copy of every paper in which, from first to last, had been published any decisive information in regard to this sad affair." Readers are given a rather grisly autopsy report, one that (erroneously) rules out sex crimes: "The medical testimony spoke confidently of the virtuous character of the deceased." Dupin comments on several newspaper accounts, and the first installment ends with a brief discussion of the effects of water on dead bodies. The second installment continues the discussion with 1,173 words on bodies in water, extended rumination on the victim's state of mind and the testimony of witnesses, and ends by dismissing the idea that Marie was the victim of a gang. The last installment centers on the idea of one criminal and suggests that finding his boat will be the key to the whole case: "This boat shall guide us, with a rapidity which will surprise even ourselves, to him who employed it in the midnight of the fatal Sabbath. Corroboration will rise upon corroboration, and the murderer will be traced." At that juncture an inserted paragraph cuts off the investigation of the crime and states "We feel it advisable only to state, in brief, that the result desired was brought to pass; and that the Prefect fulfilled punctually, although with reluctance, the terms of his compact with the Chevalier." The final paragraph states that there is no correspondence between the cases of Marie Roget and Mary Rogers and rescinds the concept of parallel worlds briefly brought up in the first installment.

Sometime late in 1842 or early 1843, although Poe was no longer associated with his publications, Rex Graham paid him $50 for "The Gold Bug." When Poe heard about Philadelphia's *The Dollar Newspaper's* story contest, however, he swapped the promise of some reviews for the return of the story and entered it in the contest. "The Gold Bug," of course, won the prize of $100 and appeared in two parts: June 21 and 28, 1843. The first installment proceeds through the depiction of (1) the narrator's visit to Sullivan's Island, the introduction of the reclusive William Legrand, and his peculiar behavior centered on a beetle and a scrap of paper; (2) Jupiter's (Legrand's servant) visit to the narrator in Charleston, his description of his master's strange behavior, and the delivery of an invitation from Legrand; and (3) the meeting of Legrand with the narrator and Jupiter who are conducted on a mysterious expedition to the mainland and after several sightings and measurements they discover a vast hidden treasure. The first installment ends with: "When, at length, we had concluded our examination, and the intense excitement of the time had, in some measure, subsided, Legrand, who saw that I was dying with impatience, for a solution of this most extraordinary riddle, entered into a full detail of all the circumstances connected with it." One week later Part II was added to a reprint of the first week's adventure. In 5,514 words Legrand reveals that the scrap of paper noted at the beginning of the tale was in reality a cipher written in disappearing ink indicating the location of Captain Kidd's treasure. He then explains how to make disappearing ink readable and how to decipher a document written in code — followed by the application of the document's instructions in finding the treasure.

In the fall of 1844 Poe published a number of pieces in *Godey's Lady's Book*; the third of them was "'Thou Art the Man,'" a 5,837-word tale about the investigation of a murder in which the narrator plays "the Oedipus to the Rattleborough enigma" and exposes the murderer by means of a macabre surprise. It begins with the anonymous narrator setting the scene in the country town of Rattleborough and very quickly introducing Mr. Barnabas Shuttleworthy, one of the richest men in town, and "Old Charley Goodfellow," a bonhomous newcomer with no visible means of support. Off on a business trip, Shuttleworthy disappears and his riderless horse returns to town "all bloody from a pistol shot that had gone clean through and through the poor animal's chest." A search is made for Shuttleworthy which results only in finding evidence which seems to suggest that he has been murdered and seems to incriminate his nephew, Mr. Pennifeather. Old Charley finds what townspeople believe to be the conclusive evidence of Pennifeather's guilt in the form of a rifle ball which he maintains he found in Shuttleworthy's horse's body. Pennifeather is tried, convicted and sentenced to death. Before the execution a large box from a vintner is delivered to Old Charley's house, ostensibly from the late Mr. Shuttleworthy. Goodfellow invites in the neighborhood to share in his bounty, but when the box is pried open Shuttleworthy's corpse pops out of it and appears to utter the title phrase, "thou art the man," whereupon Old Charley confesses and dies. At the close the narrator describes his detective work (which turns on the bullet that was not in the horse's body) and the engineering of the surprise at Old Charley's wine tasting.

Late in 1844 Philadelphia publisher Carey and Hart brought out *The Gift; a Christmas, New Year, and Birthday Present 1845*. The volume contained 15 pieces of verse including poems by Longfellow and Emerson, and 12 short stories, including Poe's last detective story, "The Purloined Letter," running from page 41 to page 59. The plot is the simplest of the detective tales. The Prefect of Police comes to Dupin, tells him that Minister D — has stolen an important letter but for reasons of delicacy cannot be prosecuted, and recounts the extent of the minute searches of Minister D —'s property and person which have failed to find the letter. Dupin tells him to go back and look again. After a second exhaustive search the frustrated Prefect returns, whereupon Dupin hands him the letter and explains to the narrator how and where he found it.

Searching for the Source

In the four years from 1841 to 1845 Poe brought together diverse elements and used them to create detective stories. One of those elements was the current state of affairs in Philadelphia. First, there was the issue of the police — never mind detectives, there weren't even any police in Philadelphia in 1841, and that absence was very much a matter of public concern. Indeed, at his death in 1831 Stephen Girard, one of the richest men in America, left a portion of his estate for the purpose of establishing a police force in Philadelphia, a bequest prominently in the news in the early 1840s because of the attenuated legal maneuverings of his disappointed heirs. At the same time that concerned citizens were thinking about police, Philadelphians witnessed the sensational trial of James Wood for the murder of his daughter; Poe wrote about the trial and elaborated on the rationale of the insanity verdict in *Alexander's Weekly Messenger* in April 1840. By the time he wrote the detective tales, in fact, he had begun to think in detail about the nature and fallibility of evidence, long a topic of intense interest in legal circles in America and Britain. Thus in "Marie Roget" Poe has Dupin raise the topic of judicial evidence in general terms:

> I would here observe that very much of what is rejected as evidence by a court, is the best of evidence to the intellect. For the court, guiding itself by the general principles of evidence — the recognized and *booked* principles — is averse from swerving at particular instances. And this steadfast adherence to principle, with rigorous disregard of the conflicting exception, is a sure mode of attaining the *maximum* of attainable truth, in any long sequence of time. The practice, *in mass*, is therefore philosophical; but it is not the less certain that it engenders frequently vast individual error.

And by the time of "Thou Art the Man" he used both the concept and the term that had stirred controversy in legal circles from the beginning of the century and which would provide more than a century's worth of material for both jurists and writers — "circumstantial evidence";

> when the chain of circumstantial evidence ... was considered so unbroken and so thoroughly conclusive, that the jury, without leaving their seats, returned an immediate verdict of "*Guilty of murder in the first degree.*"

Coincident with these influences, Cary and Hart (who were to publish "The Purloined Letter" in *The Gift*) published Vidocq's *Memoirs* in 1834; four years later, William Edwin Burton began to print his series of nine Vidocq pieces in *Burton's Gentleman's Magazine,* ending the month before his announcement of Poe's appointment as editor of the magazine; and Bulwer-Lytton included a character based on Vidocq in *Night and Morning* which

Poe reviewed in 1841. The Vidocq business, of course, both demonstrated the utility of police and detectives to the reading public and later gave Poe a straw man to introduce in "The Murders in the Rue Morgue." On top of the Vidocq background, Poe's profession as reviewer and reporter demonstrated the author's analytical bent that would be displayed and discussed in the detective tales. In the case of his review of *Barnaby Rudge* in the *Saturday Evening Post* (May 1, 1841), Poe extrapolated Dickens' serial's conclusion before the publication of the last installment by noticing clues already in the text, and in "Maelzel's Chess Player" (*Southern Literary Messenger*, April 1836), Poe the reporter put before his readers all of the steps he went through in his analysis of the so-called chess-playing automaton and presented his conclusion about its secret.

There was, moreover, a literary precedent for detective stories for Poe to follow: Burton's 1838 story "The Cork Leg" from *Burton's Gentleman's Magazine*. To begin with, in that tale Poe found a crime story that was not about crime. Thus "The Cork Leg" focuses on the suspects' humorous and clever ruse, the investigator's acumen and originality, and the comedy of authority overthrown; notably, "The Cork Leg" also does not convey the slightest interest in the moral aspect of crime. The story, therefore, demonstrated a way to write about crime and at the same time avoid the contemporary backlash against the characters and themes of the Newgate novel. That backlash was as pronounced in the United States as it was in Britain and was very much present in journals with which Poe was associated. Criticism of Bulwer-Lytton's Newgate books extends from 1838 to 1842 in *The Southern Literary Messenger*. For example:

> We have neither leisure nor space to expose severally the dangerous tendency of the publications of this author. Falkland has long since been outlawed; Eugene Aram and Pelham have been condemned for their false philosophy, their bad moral, and their strained and unnatural sentiment. Devereux and Paul Clifford were written upon a false theory, and with all the graces of inimitable style have long since been censured as clever extravagances [*Southern Literary Messenger* July 1838];

and

> "Paul Clifford I did read, and there I stopped. His earlier novels, some of them, I greatly admired. But I condemn every attempt to invest crime with interest; and when I saw a robber converted into a hero, I saw that the author's mind would no longer be a well of pure and sparkling waters. I have never read another of his books" [*Southern Literary Messenger* April 1842].

And the same view is expressed toward Ainsworth in *Burton's Gentleman's Magazine* when Poe was one of its editors:

[Ainsworth] must also assume the responsibility of giving to the reading world the most corrupt, flat, and vulgar fabrication in the English language. "Jack Sheppard" is a disgrace to the literature of the day [*Burton's Gentleman's Magazine and American Monthly Review* April 1840].

One of the remarked-about virtues of "The Murders in the Rue Morgue" was that it was a crime story that was not about crime. Thus a reviewer in *Blackwood's* in November 1847 specifically connected Poe's tale with the response to Bulwer-Lytton, Ainsworth and the Newgate novel by observing that in it, "unlike most stories of this description, our sympathies are not called upon, either in the fate of the person assassinated, or in behalf of some individual falsely accused of the crime; the interest is sustained solely by the nature of the evidence, and the inferences to be adduced from it." Given these sentiments, therefore, it was not simply coincidence that the one Dupin tale most closely and seriously connected to actual crime, "The Mystery of Marie Roget," was both the least successful one of the series and the story Poe had the hardest time selling to publishers.

Reason v. Ingenuity v. Games

What the 1847 *Blackwood's* reviewer liked, then, was the choice of intellect and the departure from sentiment found in "The Murders in the Rue Morgue." And Poe's detective tales certainly do both. They prominently include discussions and demonstrations of evidence (judicial and otherwise), reason and analysis. Thus, with the exception of "Thou Art the Man," each of the stories presents mini-lectures on analysis and evidence, as well as examples of its application in the main action of the narrative. Poe, in fact, underlined this facet of the stories by applying the term "ratiocination" ("The action or process of reasoning, esp. deductively or by using syllogisms" [OED]) to them — as in his letter to James Russell Lowell: "'The Purloined Letter,' forthcoming in the 'Gift,' is, perhaps, the best of my tales of ratiocination" (July 2, 1844). It is not entirely clear, however, whether Poe applied either the term or concept before writing "The Mystery of Marie Roget"— the first of the stories in which the term "ratiocination" appears. And it wasn't always just reason that he stressed as the principal feature of the detective stories. Sometimes in his correspondence Poe replaced the terms "reason" and "analysis" with "ingenuity" (i.e. skill or cleverness) in describing the core of the detective tales. He used the term as his selling point when he shopped "Marie Roget" to both Snodgrass and Rogers in 1842: "Its theme was the exercise of ingenuity in detecting a murderer." Four years later, moreover, in a letter to Philip Pendleton Cooke in which he again used the term ratiocination, Poe edged the emphasis even a bit further away from reason:

These tales of ratiocination owe most of their popularity to being something in a new key. I do not mean to say they are not ingenious — but people think they are more ingenious than they are — on account of their method and *air* of method.... Where is the ingenuity of unravelling a web which you yourself (the author) have woven for the express purpose of unravelling? [August 9, 1846].

Whether centered on reason, ingenuity, or both, what Poe found in "The Cork Leg" — in addition to the move away from the Newgate variety of crime fiction to depicting crime from a point of view less offensive to Victorian taste — was a story built around puzzles and the solution to those puzzles. And Poe surely liked puzzles. In the winter before he composed "The Murders in the Rue Morgue" he had demonstrated his continuing fascination with them in his multiple pieces about riddles, enigmas, conundrums, puzzles, and ciphers published in *Alexander's Weekly Messenger* (e.g. "Enigmatical and Conundrum-ical" [December 18, 1839]; "Enigmatical" [January 15, 1840]; "Our Late Puzzles" [February 12, 1840]; "Our Puzzles — Again!" [February 19, 1840]; "Our Puzzles Once More" [February 26, 1840]; etc.) and then continuing on the same subject in *Graham's* in the early 1840s (e.g. "A Few Words on Secret Writing" [July 1841]). While many of these articles involve ciphers or "secret" codes, the term "cipher" does not appear in their titles as often as do the terms "puzzle," "enigma," and "conundrum" — thus the term "puzzle" appears in the title of Poe's pieces run in *Alexander's Messenger* on February 12, 19, and 26, and March 4, 11, and 25, 1840; "enigma" appears in the title of pieces run December 18, 1839 and January 15, 1840; and "conundrum" appears in the title of pieces run December 18, 1839, and May 6, 1840. Enigmas and conundrums were, in fact, kinds of puzzles. Indeed, they not only had defined purposes, they also had loosely prescribed formal qualities. Through the 1840s, an enigma was "a short composition in prose or verse, in which something is described by intentionally obscure metaphors, in order to afford an exercise for the ingenuity of the reader or hearer on guessing what is meant" (OED). Conforming to this definition, Griswold entitled Poe's 1848 hidden acrostic sonnet written for Sarah Anna Lewis, "An Enigma." A conundrum, on the other hand, was "a riddle in the form of a question the answer to which involves a pun or play on words" (OED). Both of these forms of the puzzle, then, center on purposeful deception or trickery practiced by the author upon the readers followed by an unexpected conclusion to the question or problem posed. Enigmas and conundrums, moreover, both contain implicit challenges from the writer to the reader, and in Poe's pieces about enigmas, riddles, puzzles, and codes in both *Alexander's Messenger* and *Graham's Magazine* he explicitly challenged readers to submit ciphers, printed those submissions, and then presented the solutions — along with the method used to arrive at them.

When he came to compose the detective stories Poe carried over some of the terms and methods from the cryptography essays to describe their context. Thus in "The Murders in the Rue Morgue" readers find the terms "mystery," "enigma," "conundrum," "hieroglyphic," and "riddle" used to describe the central issues in the story; in "The Gold Bug" Poe used "hieroglyphic," "enigma," "riddle," "mystery," and "cryptograph"; in "The Purloined Letter" the terms "mystery" and "puzzle" come in; for "Thou Art the Man" Poe used only "enigma"; and "Marie Roget" contains only "mystery" to describe the enterprise in which the characters (and the readers) are engaged.

Following the pattern of the riddle-puzzle-enigma-conundrum form, Poe lays a framework of a perplexing question followed by an unexpected, ingenious answer under each of the stories: who killed the L'Espanaye women? who murdered Marie Roget? How did Legrand discover the treasure? where did Minister D — hide the letter? and who murdered Barnabas Shuttleworthy? But in spite of the implied challenge to readers in the detective tales, for a variety of reasons Poe withheld as long as possible the answers to the questions he posed in them. In "The Murders in the Rue Morgue," "The Purloined Letter" and "Thou Art the Man" he keeps the answer from readers in order to surprise them. In "The Gold Bug" rather than following Legrand's reasoning step by step, he kept the explanation of the process under wraps until the second installment of the story. And in "The Mystery of Marie Roget," of course, Poe had no answer to supply his readers. In all of the detective tales, moreover, the emphasis rests both on the surprise solution and on the hero's genius reflected in doing what he does.

While the puzzle element exists in each of them, there is an underlying atmosphere of amusement in most of Poe's detective tales. Going back to his "Enigmatical and Conundrum-ical" essay in *Alexander's Weekly Messenger*, Poe elevated conundrums over enigmas because they evoked more laughter:

> Modern taste, however, at least modern newspaper taste, affects rather the conundrum than the enigma proper. A good enigma, we have said, is a good thing, but a good conundrum *may be* a better. Consequently, we see our brethren of the press trying their hands at *cons* in all directions, and as soon as they perpetrate a decent one (after a severe effort) they set up a cackle forthwith, and the banding goes the round of the papers in a kind of ovation.

And he concluded his proposed challenge about ciphers in *Graham's* with the promise "The experiment may afford our readers some amusement..." Poe extended this notion of puzzle solving as amusement to "The Murders in the Rue Morgue" and in fact sharpened it when he edited the story; in the revised version Poe eliminated the pseudo-scientific musings on phrenology of his original first paragraph and moved to the top the paragraph about play and games, a paragraph which twice mentions the player's joy:

We know of them, among other things, that they are always to their possessor, when inordinately possessed, a source of the liveliest enjoyment.

and

He derives pleasure from even the most trivial occupations bringing his talents into play.

Indeed, after Poe's failed crime-solving experiment of "The Mystery of Marie Roget," the tone of the detective tales becomes successively lighter. "The Gold Bug" not only has no crime in it and focuses on the analytical process of cipher solving but it also adds the racist comedy of Jupiter as diversion. The coy narration and the jack-in-the-box surprise of "Thou Art the Man" echo the levity of some of Poe's early *Southern Literary Messenger* pieces. Finally in "The Purloined Letter" instead of being invited to try to do the brain-work connected with solving the puzzle, readers have a ringside seat at a contest between two mental heavyweights with no distraction of color commentary about analysis, no artificial problems posed to lead them astray, and with the added buffoonery of the Prefect.

All of this was only one aspect of the enjoyment gained from literary fooling around — an occupation very much to Poe's liking. From early on Poe was fond of playing with readers' — even the reading public's — expectations. This occurs as early as "The Unparalleled Adventure of One Hans Pfaall" in the *Southern Literary Messenger* (1835) in which Poe presents a narrative of Pfaall's supposed balloon trip to the moon and then concludes by adding five pieces of evidence (which the narrator dismisses) that prove the story a hoax. This facetious use of evidence, argument, and analysis, in turn, corresponds to a distinct vein of authorial fooling around in Poe's miscellaneous undertakings in the early forties, from "Raising the Wind; or, Diddling Considered as One of the Exact Sciences" (October 14, 1843) with its tongue-in-cheek catalog of clever cons, to his own revisiting of the idea of "Hans Pfaall" with the diddle presented to the public in "The Balloon Hoax" (April 13, 1844). He, moreover, extended this spirit to his detective stories. Poe fools around with his readers in "The Murders in the Rue Morgue" in a number of ways, most notably by tantalizing them with the illusion that they can solve a puzzle which they cannot and then demonstrating that the hero can. And his hero's name, C. Auguste Dupin, seems to underline this same motive. Throughout all three Dupin stories the narrator remains unnamed, but the detective's name appears in two different forms: in "The Murders in the Rue Morgue" he is "Monsieur C. Auguste Dupin" and then, as if to clarify that the C. in the hero's name is not an abbreviation for the title chevalier, in "Marie Roget" he is "Chevalier C. Auguste Dupin." Given Poe's predilection for puns (or conundrums), the bias of American pronunciation which usually places the emphasis on the first syllable of two syllable names, and the tendency of casual speech, especially casual Southern speech, to drop the final "g" from the "ing" ending of gerunds and progressive continuous verbs, it is at least possible that Poe inserted a hidden sentence in his hero's name: see (c) majestic (august) duping (dupin).

The Detective Story

To the puzzle and the play Poe added the technical elements which made his stories the pattern for future detective stories. First, as noted in *Blackwood's*, he focuses almost exclusively on the detective rather than the criminal or the victim, and justice is really never a very serious consideration. Indeed Poe gives only a nod (and very little sympathy) to the accused innocents in both "The Murders in the Rue Morgue" and "Thou Art the Man." The latter, moreover, is the only one of the detective stories in which Poe shows even the slightest interest in the criminal and personally brings home his confession — and here it is as much connected with displaying the narrator's cleverness and surprising the reader as it is with justice. But other narrative elements that Poe used for the first time are just as important for the future of the detective story. First there is the disjointed chronology — the detective stories do not proceed from beginning to middle to end: "Rue Morgue," "Marie Roget," and "Purloined Letter" start in the middle, recreate the beginning and move swiftly to the end; "The Gold Bug" and "Thou Art the Man" begin at the beginning but move the middle until after the conclusion of the action has been reached. Thus in "The Murders in the Rue Morgue" Poe starts his narrative after the women have been killed. Readers don't know what happened and Dupin recreates the beginning for them before the tale can end. In "The Gold Bug" Legrand and company find and dig up the treasure at the end of the first installment and in the second he recounts how he knew where Captain Kidd's treasure was buried. Directed toward the same end of obscuring facts from readers, in the Dupin stories Poe created his unnamed, naïve, semi-dense narrator who has to be told the significance of what he sees. To these he added several varieties of legerdemain, especially in "The Murders in the Rue Morgue." First, Poe provides readers with testimony from witnesses who are native-speakers of a variety of languages, thereby suggesting that discerning the real language of the killer is only a matter of comparison and elimination. But he does not include a witness fluent in ape. In another place in the same story Poe simply omits mentioning significant facts until the conclusion of the narrative — thus Dupin knows that a sailor is involved because he finds a sailor's ribbon at the crime scene — but the narrator doesn't mention this (or know about it) until near the end of the story. Indeed in his detective stories Poe mirrors the structure of the joke — a narrative with deviously inserted clues designed to be overlooked followed by a surprise revelation which highlights and reinterprets the overlooked or misinterpreted clues. "The Murders in the Rue Morgue," "The Purloined Letter," and "Thou Art the Man," therefore, principally work because they end with an unexpected surprise. "The Mystery of Marie Roget" doesn't.

Accompanying these narrative techniques is a long list of items which would provide material for generation upon generation of detective story writers. There is the locked room that is not locked, the contest between investigators, the contest between the amateur and the professional, the contest between detective and mastermind, the newspaper advertisement, the so-called "arm-chair" detective in which the detective solves the crime without leaving his rooms, the enigmatic clue, the red herring, forensic evidence (like the discussion of bodies in water in "The Mystery of Marie Roget" or the rifle ball in "Thou Art the Man"), and the deduction demonstration showing how smart the detective is before the real beginning of the story. But Poe's creation of the genius detective hero is just as important as all of his other technical innovations.

Poe's Detective

Dupin appears first in "The Murders in the Rue Morgue," but before proceeding to the story about the deaths of the L'Espanaye women Poe conducts readers through a discussion about games and analysis: it takes him 1,148 words to gets to the introduction of the narrator and his friend Dupin. After the prefatory material, the narrator introduces Dupin by telling readers (1) that he is a ruined aristocrat, (2) that he is a recluse, (3) that he is a scholar, (4) that he only goes out at night, (5) that he has an astonishing ability to read others' thoughts ("that most men, in respect to himself, wore windows in their bosoms"), (6) that he undergoes physiological changes when engaged in the latter, and (7) that he and the narrator live in "a time-eaten and grotesque mansion, long deserted through superstitions into which we did not inquire, and tottering to its fall in a retired and desolate portion of the Faubourg St. Germain." On a simple level, there is a suggestion of elements from *The Tempest* in the situation of Dupin; like Prospero in Shakespeare's play he is the exiled prince who lives in isolation with books and then joins the corrupt world and exercises his powers to solve problems. But, practically, Poe took more than a bit of both Dupin and Legrand from his own story "The Fall of the House of Usher" (published three years earlier). Roderick

Usher, the ruined aristocrat, stands behind the new heroes, and both the remote, eerie, deserted settings of Dupin's mansion and Legrand's hut on Sullivan Island draw from the setting in the earlier story. Additionally, the narrators comment on the abrupt changes in the heroes' moods in "The Fall of the House of Usher," "The Murders in the Rue Morgue," and "The Gold Bug." In "Rue Morgue," in fact, the narrator describes the same kind of variation in the quality of the hero's voice as that used to describe Roderick Usher's voice; thus, Dupin's is "usually a rich tenor, rose into a treble which would have sounded petulantly but for the deliberateness and entire distinctness of the enunciation," and Usher's "varied rapidly from a tremulous indecision (when the animal spirits seemed utterly in abeyance) to that species of energetic concision — that abrupt, weighty, unhurried, and hollow-sounding enunciation." On top of the influence of Roderick Usher, Vidocq the man and the myth contributed a bit of background about the Paris police to the stories, but more importantly they gave Poe the idea of the contest between the effective investigator and the inept bureaucrat, as well as the straw man he created to have his hero play off of. Thus while Vidocq's *Memoirs* as well as the stories Burton ran in *The Gentleman's Magazine* concentrate on the superficial, practical mechanics of thief-taking, in "The Murders in the Rue Morgue" Poe saddled him with faulty analytical technique:

> Vidocq, for example, was a good guesser, and a persevering man. But, without educated thought, he erred continually by the very intensity of his investigations. He impaired his vision by holding the object too close. He might see, perhaps, one or two points with unusual clearness, but in so doing he, necessarily, lost sight of the matter as a whole. Thus there is such a thing as being too profound.

Thus instead of serving as the model for his detective hero, Poe transformed Vidocq into an example of wrong-headed approaches to problems and echoed this in the bumbling Prefect of Police in his tales.

In addition to these origins, taken on face value, Poe based most of Dupin's acumen on playing cards — an occupation with which he was perhaps too familiar. Thus before he introduces the narrator and Dupin, Poe tells the readers of "The Murders in the Rue Morgue" that "the narrative which follows will appear to the reader somewhat in the light of a commentary upon the propositions just advanced."

The most apparent of those "propositions just advanced" in the introduction is the description of the qualities possessed by a successful card player:

> Our player confines himself not at all; nor, because the game is the object, does he reject deductions from things external to the game. He examines the countenance of his partner, comparing it carefully with that of each of his opponents. He considers the mode of assorting the cards in each hand; often counting trump by trump, and honor by honor, through the glances bestowed by their

holders upon each. He notes every variation of face as the play progresses, gathering a fund of thought from the differences in the expression of certainty, of surprise, of triumph, or chagrin. From the manner of gathering up a trick he judges whether the person taking it can make another in the suit. He recognizes what is played through feint, by the air with which it is thrown upon the table. A casual or inadvertent word; the accidental dropping or turning of a card, with the accompanying anxiety or carelessness in regard to its concealment; the counting of the tricks, with the order of their arrangement; embarrassment, hesitation, eagerness or trepidation — all afford, to his apparently intuitive perception, indications of the true state of affairs. The first two or three rounds having been played, he is in full possession of the contents of each hand, and thenceforward puts down his cards with as absolute a precision of purpose as if the rest of the party had turned outward the faces of their own.

After this introduction, when readers arrive at the narrator's description of Dupin they learn that he has an astonishing ability to read others' thoughts ("that most men, in respect to himself, wore windows in their bosoms"). And the first incident in "The Murders in the Rue Morgue" is the narrator's 1,044-word recreation of the observations and conclusions Dupin uses to "read the narrator's mind": observations and conclusions parallel to those of the successful card player. Indeed the term "calculus of possibilities" used in the stories, Poe found in Edmond Hoyle's *Hoyle's Games Improved* where it refers to counting cards and therefore knowing what has been and what has not been played.

In addition to giving Dupin the attributes of a successful card player (one of which is keeping one's cards close to one's vest), Poe portrayed both Dupin and Legrand as aloof, grouchy and misanthropic — characteristics made necessary in part by the kinds of plots he designed for their stories. In the Dupin stories and "The Gold Bug," relying entirely on the narrators' obtuseness and lack of curiosity in order to make the surprise endings work ran the danger of forfeiting some of the readers' sympathy and potentially risked alienating them by their identification with a less-than-intelligent-and-observant narrator. And so Poe made the genius hero, the one with the answers: an aloof, reticent, arrogant, and thin-skinned individual upon whom one had to wait. Thus Legrand is moody and over-sensitive; in "The Gold Bug" he tells the narrator at the end of part one that he has not confided in him earlier because the narrator had expressed concern for his mental health early in the narrative: "Why, to be frank, I felt somewhat annoyed by your evident suspicions touching my sanity, and so resolved to punish you quietly, in my own way, by a little bit of sober mystification." And Dupin is downright arrogant: in "The Purloined Letter"; for instance, he sends the Prefect and his men off to ransack Minister D—'s apartments a second time without advising them how and where to look, and then taunts the Prefect with his anecdote about taking advice in spite of the fact that the Prefect has come to him to ask for advice. The only justifications Poe gives for what amounts to rude, arrogant, and uncivil self-absorption on the part of Dupin and Legrand is that they have lost their birthrights, thus

> this young gentleman was of an excellent — indeed of an illustrious family, but, by a variety of untoward events, had been reduced to such poverty that the energy of his character succumbed beneath it, and he ceased to bestir himself in the world, or to care for the retrieval of his fortunes ["Murders in the Rue Morgue"].

When he came to write "Thou Art the Man" Poe provided readers with a new perspective for the character of the detective hero. In that story the hero is also the narrator and he takes readers into this confidence to a far greater extent than one finds in the other detective tales. Thus the tale begins with the narrator's direct address to his readers; "I will expound to you — as I alone can — the secret of the enginery that effected the Rattleborough miracle." Unlike the Dupin stories, moreover, the narrator of "Thou Art the Man" gives his readers real clues — the rifle ball found in the horse versus the pistol ball "that had gone clean through and through the poor animal's chest." What Poe emphasizes here is the stupidity of the townspeople in the story and plays off the name of the town and portrays its citizens as "rattle-brains" (empty-headed, noisy people).

Readers and reviewers knew that in Poe's detective tales they found things that were new and different. And so did Poe — that's why he made them into a series, and gave the series a name, "tales of ratiocination." One of those new things he did was to center the stories on the use and abuse of evidence in arriving at a solution to a simulated problem. This was something new. As we have seen, while Jacobin and the Newgate novels dealt with crime, they both concentrated on sentiment versus evidence and proof. Thus, while aware of the contemporary controversies surrounding the discussion of judicial evidence, Godwin chose to ignore it and focused on the corrosive effects of tragedy on his heroes. In the case of Newgate fiction, writers acknowledged that their heroes committed crimes, and therefore there was no need to detail or discuss the evidence needed to prove that they had done so. While Poe touched on human traits in the detective tales they are incidental, and in fact he obscures most of the sentimental potential implicit in his characters and situations. Thus the heroes' ruined fortunes and misanthropy along with the fact that Dupin and Legrand both have devoted friends are personal details, but Poe used these facts only as background and does nothing to exploit their implications for his characters. Additionally, in "The Purloined Letter" Poe not only never brings the antagonist, Minister D —, on stage, he postpones mention of Dupin's personal history with him ("D —, at Vienna once, did me an evil turn") until the last paragraph of the story and there depicts Dupin's triumph over his adversary as a practical joke. And with wrongly accused innocents, Poe refuses to play the sentiment game. He introduces Pennifeather in "Thou Art the Man" more from his desire to emphasize the surprise ending than to elicit sympathy for him as a person; few readers can even recall the name or even the existence of Adolphe Le Bon, the wrongly accused innocent in "The Murders in the Rue Morgue." Neither of these accused innocents appears in person in the stories. Thus while Poe does include a small allotment of human details in his depiction of his characters, the principal object of the detective tales is to portray the hero as an analyst — in effect as an aloof intellect solving problems. Given that premise, his challenge was how to prevent his stories from becoming simply boring presentations of points of argument. And so he inserted truncated bits of character material to enliven the analytical cores of the stories. In this respect Poe was fortunate in that his medium was the short story — a form in which elimination of some or many elements of characterization can pass without notice.

Poe, however, sought to portray more than the quiet satisfaction of solving a difficult problem or to elicit merely the silent approbation of seeing one solved. He chose to make both the problems and the solutions in the detective tales complicated and also sensational, bizarre, outré. Not only are there perplexing situations — a locked room, a thoroughly ransacked apartment, a multitude of damning evidence, a secret code — but Poe adds gothic touches — the woman stuffed up a chimney, details of the effects of water on corpses, the death's head nailed to a tree branch — and then neutralizes them by joining them to the intellectual problem of the story. He makes the problems unsolvable to the people in the world of the story (i.e. the narrator and the police) as well as to his readers, but he does so in order to magnify the surprise endings of the detective tales and to evoke wonder and awe from observers inside and outside of the world of fiction.

On both sides of the Atlantic Poe's detective tales met with a lively reception. In France a translation of "The Murders in the Rue Morgue" appeared as "Un meurtre sans exemple dans les Fastes de la Justice" in *La Quotidienne* from June 11 to 13, 1846, and a second version, "Une Sanglante Enigme," came out in *La Commerce* four months later and led to a much publicized trial for plagiarism. In 1849 another translation of "The Murders in the Rue Morgue" ("L'Assassinat de la Rue Morgue") appeared in another French newspaper, *La Démocratie Pacifique.* While all of this hoopla as well as Baudelaire's translations in 1855 hold significance for the history of the detective story as it grew in France, of more immediate importance was that on November 30, 1844, in the second column of page 343 of *Chambers' Edinburgh Journal*: a brief laudatory notice about *The Gift, a Christmas, New Year, and Birthday Present 1845* appeared followed by an abridged reprint of "The Purloined Letter."

Chapter Three

Notebooks

As in the United States, in the first half of the nineteenth century Britain experienced an explosion of magazine publication — bringing readers titles like *Blackwood's, The Westminster Review, Punch, The Athenaeum, Ainsworth's Magazine*, and, of course, Dickens' diverse periodical ventures. One of this flurry of new journals was *Chambers' Edinburgh Journal. Chambers'* was the work of brothers William and Robert Chambers who in 1832 founded the magazine that would become one of the most popular, and most poached, periodicals of its day, achieving an international circulation of 90,000 by 1845. By the 1840s the range of *Chambers'* contents included sections entitled Familiar Sketches and Moral Essays, Poetry, Tales, Biographical Sketches, Miscellaneous Articles of Instruction and Entertainment, and Anecdotes and Paragraphs; sections on Popular Science and Notices of Books were added in the 1850s. The content reflected the Chambers brothers' dedication to science, rationality, and reform, as well as travel and the semi-exotic — most numbers, for instance, contained either fact or fiction about the world outside of Britain. As a hot topic in the 1840s, *Chambers'* also began to run stories about crime and then stories about detectives.

Beginning in the early 1840s *Chambers'* displayed occasional interest in legal issues and in the police both at home and abroad. The magazine's pieces on circumstantial evidence span the decade from "Remarkable Cases of Circumstantial Evidence: Bradford the Innkeeper" (February 22, 1840) and "Circumstantial Evidence: Thomas Geddely's Case" (April 4, 1840) to "Circumstance" (January 9, 1847) and "Anecdote of Circumstantial Evidence" (October 6, 1849). Likewise, pieces on the police stretch from an article on the French police, "The Police Agent" by Armand Duratin (July 4, 1841), to "Thief-taking and Thief-making" (July 17, 1847). On November 30, 1844, as noted above, after a brief laudatory notice about *The Gift, a Christmas, New Year, and Birthday Present 1845, Chambers' Journal* published an abridged version of Poe's "The Purloined Letter." Finally, on October 6, 1849, *Chambers'* ran an editorial entitled "Murder-Mania." Earlier in the year, on January 13, 1849, *Chambers'* transferred its interest in crime from fact to fiction; "The March Assizes" began an eleven-part run of stories by an unnamed author published under the heading "Experiences of a Barrister" which ended with "The Refugee" on June 1, 1850. Perhaps more importantly, on July 28, 1849, the publication of "The Gambler's Revenge" began a series of 11 stories in *Chambers'* by an unnamed author, entitled "Recollections of a Police-Officer" which ended on April 24, 1852, with "The Monomaniac."

Experiences of a Barrister

The stories run under the head "Experiences of a Barrister" represent the fictional reminiscences of an anonymous, conscientious, compassionate barrister devoted to his wife and daughters and dedicated to justice and the law — in that order. All of the stories which he narrates in the first person are set either at the close of the eighteenth century or at the beginning of the nineteenth, and many of them take place outside of London. Many of them also revolve around the injustice and iniquity of British law before the passage of reform legislation in the first half of the nineteenth century. The most prominent target is capital punishment and the bloody code. Indeed, "March Assizes" and "Esther Mason" recount the execution of innocents, and several of the rest of the stories depict the narrator or Providence uncovering the means to save innocents from execution. To make the connection with historical trends apparent, in "Esther Mason" the narrator drops the name of one of the most zealous opponents of Britain's death penalty, Sir Samuel Romilly ("The amiable and enlightened Sir Samuel Romilly not only attached his name, but aided us zealously by his advice and influence"). And in both "March Assizes" and "Esther Mason" the narrator comments to the readers on the hypocrisy of capital punishment:

> This man [the judge] possessed great forensic acquirements, and was of spotless private character; but, like the majority of lawyers of that day — when it was no extraordinary thing to hang twenty men in a morning at Newgate — he was a staunch stickler for the gallows as the only effectual reformer and safeguard of the social state ["March Assizes"].

> The offence with which she was charged had supplied the scaffold with numberless victims; and tradesmen were more than ever clamorous for the stern execution of a law which, spite of experience, they still regarded as the only safeguard of their property ["Esther Mason"].

Indeed, both "March Assizes" and "Esther Mason" tie vengeance to unjust capital punishment. In the former the innocence of the victim and the culpability of the judge are both exposed in open court whereupon the jurist falls dead on the bench. In "Esther Mason" vengeance is visited upon the entire nation; thus after his wife is hanged

> war soon afterwards broke out with the United States of America, and Mr. Friend discovered that one of the most active and daring officers in the Republican navy was Henry Mason, who had entered the American service in the maiden name of his wife; and that the large sums he had remitted from time to time for the use of Willy, were the produce of his successful depredations on British commerce.

In addition to centering on the evils of capital punishment, several stories in "Experiences of a Barrister" focus on the unfairness of the British legal system before the passage of the Prisoners' Counsel Act (1836) which for the first time permitted accused persons to be represented by counsel in court. The narrator mentions the restraint on counsel in "March Assizes," and he decries his inability to speak for the accused in court in "Esther Mason." In "Circumstantial Evidence" the accused makes a public protest about his lack of counsel:

> I hold in my hand a very acute and eloquent address prepared for me by one of the able and zealous gentlemen who appears to-day as my counsel, and which, but for the iniquitous law which prohibits the advocate of a presumed felon, but possibly quite innocent person, from addressing the jury, upon whose verdict his client's fate depends, would no doubt have formed the subject-matter of an appeal to you not to yield credence to the apparently irrefragable testimony arrayed against me.

Although these stories in the series provide problems of the law beyond the capacity of one individual to repair or redress, others show individual actors solving problems and giving succor to potential victims of unjust suspicion and accusation. These stories ("Contested Marriage," "Mother and Son," "The Writ of Habeas Corpus," "The Marriage Settlement," "The Second Marriage," "Circumstantial Evidence," and "The Refugee") involve crimes from murder to forgery, from false imprisonment to perjury and touch not only the lives of the victims but also those of falsely accused innocents. In one way or another all of the crime and persecution arise from the transfer of wealth — through marriage, inheritance, or both. Significantly, they also involve crimes which the discovery of true witnesses and exposure of false testimony will solve. Some of this occurs in the cross-examination of witnesses at the culmination of trials, but some of it happens because of the work of an individual who can lay claim to being called a detective.

In "The Contested Marriage," the third story in the Experiences of a Barrister series, the narrator receives a letter introducing a client as well as advice about how to handle her problem:

My advice is, to look out for a sharp, clever, persevering attorney, and set him upon a hunt for evidence. If he succeed, I undertake to pay him a thousand pounds over and above his legal costs. He'll nose it out for that, I should think!

That man is Samuel Ferret who appears in this story, "The Writ of Habeas Corpus," and "The Marriage Settlement." Musing on Ferret in the first story, the narrator describes him this way:

> Ferret was just the man for such a commission. Indefatigable, resolute, sharpwitted, and of a ceaseless, remorseless activity, a secret or a fact had need be very profoundly hidden for him not to reach and fish it up. I have heard solemn doubts expressed by attorneys opposed to him as to whether he ever really and truly slept at all — that is, a genuine Christian sleep, as distinguished from a merely canine one, with one eye always half open ["The Contested Marriage"].

In "The Contested Marriage" Ferret both discerns the meaning of the enigmatic "Z.Z." written in a parish register and tracks down the "bombshell" witness, Rev. Zachariah Zimmerman. In "The Writ of Habeas Corpus" it is Ferret and not the narrator who devises the chicanery that frees a young woman from oppressive and greedy relatives. And in "The Marriage Settlement" Ferret's wide knowledge of people helps to set the trap which the narrator allows him to spring at the conclusion of the story.

Recollections of a Police-Officer

Five months after beginning the publication of the Barrister stories, *Chambers'* introduced a new set of ten continuing stories which would be interleaved with lawyer stories for the next three years. This time they were about a police officer, and, as such, claim a particular place in the history of detective fiction.

Like the narrator of the Barrister stories, the narrator-hero of the Police-Officer stories is married and occasionally lovingly refers to his wife and daughters in the narratives. Unlike the unnamed barrister, however, the middle-class hero-narrator of the Police-Officer stories has fallen upon hard times because of an addiction to gambling. He has a name — Waters — and as the stories proceed readers gain some personal insight into both his circumstances and his character. He has, for instance, personal motives in several of the stories: in "Mary Kingsford" he saves a childhood friend of his daughter's and in "The Gambler's Revenge" he apprehends the confidence man who lured him into gambling and cheated him of his fortune. Two of the stories, "Legal Metamorphosis" and "The Revenge," offer continuing action with the villains from the first story returning from transportation and plotting to murder the hero for foiling their plot. And most notably from the character perspective, in "The Pursuit" Waters acknowledges his own fallibility by telling the story of being outwitted by an absconding embezzler. Often the stories begin outside of London and include an allusion to an off-stage crime and solution and then return to the metropolis for narration of a second central crime and solution — hinting, thereby, at the incessant work of the police. Like the Barrister tales, the setting of the Police-Officer stories goes back almost two decades — several stories mention dates in the 1830s. Here historical issues arise: although they were published after the creation of the official detective police in Britain, the Police-Officer stories take place in the transitional period before the creation of legitimate detectives in 1842 and after the dissolution of the Bow Street Runners in 1829. While in two of the stories, "Mary Kingsford" and "Guilty or Not Guilty," the narrator uses the term "detective officer," Waters, the hero, is in fact portrayed as a regular police officer who is especially chosen by the commissioner to work in plain clothes. Indeed one of the minor themes of the stories is the social status of police officers. Thus in the first paragraph of the first story, "The Gambler's Revenge," readers learn that being a policeman is for the narrator a last resort:

> A little more than a year after the period when adverse circumstances — chiefly the result of my own reckless follies — compelled me to enter the ranks of the metropolitan police, as the sole means left me of procuring food and raiment, the attention of one of the principal chiefs of the force was attracted towards me by the ingenuity and boldness which I was supposed to have manifested in hitting upon and unraveling the clue which ultimately led to the detection and punishment of the perpetrators of an artistically-contrived fraud upon an eminent tradesman of the West End of London.

And "The Widow" includes a snapshot of how "respectable" people view the police:

> "I dare say you have, Waters," he replied, reassuming his insolent, swaggering air. "I practice at the Old Bailey; and I have several times seen you there, not, as now, in the masquerade of a gentleman, but with a number on your collar."

Nonetheless, the stories reveal that Waters chooses to become a dedicated police officer and in the third story he even describes police work as his vocation and points to it as "...one which can scarcely be dispensed with, it seems, in this busy, scheming life of ours" [X.Y.Z.].

The Police-Officer stories manifest some concern about larger issues of the law: indeed "The Twins" begins with a police officer's lament (one that would echo across centuries) on the inefficiency of the judicial process:

> THE records of police courts afford but imperfect evidence of the business really effected by the officers attached to them. The machinery of English criminal law is, in practice, so subservient to the caprice of individual prosecutors, that

instances are constantly occurring in which flagrant violations of natural justice are, from various motives, corrupt and otherwise, withdrawn not only from the cognizance of judicial authority, but from the reprobation of public opinion. Compromises are usually effected between the apprehension of the inculpated parties and the public examination before a magistrate. The object of prosecution has been perhaps obtained by the preliminary step of arrest, or a criminal understanding has been arrived at in the interval; and it is then found utterly hopeless to proceed, however manifest may have appeared the guilt of the prisoner.

This, however, differs in both degree and kind from the continued concerns about the law expressed in the Barrister pieces. The principal focus of the stories that comprise *Recollections*, moreover, lies more in individually and collectively protecting the public than it does with sticking points of the law.

A few of the stories in the series display the same interest as those in the Barrister collection in righting wrongs associated with the transfer of wealth — especially "The Widow" and "The Twins." A number of the Police-Officer stories, however, deal with what is in effect organized crime. Thus in "The Gambler's Revenge" the hero's mission involves a "'gang of blacklegs, swindlers, and forgers,' concluded the commissioner, summing up his instructions. 'It will be your object to discover their private haunts, and secure legal evidence of their nefarious practices.'" There are receivers of stolen goods in "Guilty or Not Guilty," "X.Y.Z.," and "Flint Jackson." Professional criminals appear in a number of the stories. There are the "three buckishly-attired, boldfaced looking fellows — one of whom I thought I recognized, spite of his fine dress" in "Guilty or Not Guilty." In "Legal Metamorphosis" the narrator talks of the "dangerous game I was risking with powerful and desperate men," and to prove the point in the next story the villains return from transportation and attempt to murder the hero. As if to off-set the narratives about dangerous, habitual criminals, two of the Police-Officer tales show the hero taking the initiative to protect the powerless from the potential ravages of predators. Thus in "The Widow" the narrator on his own takes on the protection of a woman he has seen threatened with persecution and in "Mary Kingsford" he undertakes the same kind of paternal protection of a family friend.

The Ball Starts to Roll

Five months after publishing the last story in the Barrister series, with the publication of "Life Policy" on October 19, 1850, *Chambers'* began a new series of stories labeled at first "Confessions of an Attorney" and then with "Every Man His Own Lawyer" (run on June 7, 1851), the generic title changed to "Reminiscences of an Attorney." The eight stories in the series involve cases handled by the law firm of Flint and Sharp. Contrary to their names, however, the partners are humane and compassionate — in addition to being knowledgeable about the minutiae of the law. Indeed, because they come in contact with problems before they have become absolutely critical, Sharp, the narrator, has a closer association with clients than does the hero of the Barrister stories. As with the Barrister series, the stories sometimes touch on the inhuman laws of the last century:

> The criminal business of the office was, during the first three or four years of our partnership, entirely superintended by Mr. Flint; he being more *au fait*, from early practice, than myself in the art and mystery of prosecuting and defending felons, and I was thus happily relieved of duties which, in the days when George III was king, were frequently very oppressive and revolting. The criminal practitioner dwelt in an atmosphere tainted alike with cruelty and crime, and pulsating alternately with merciless decrees of death, and the shrieks and wailings of sentenced guilt. And not always guilt! There exist many records of proofs, incontestable, but obtained too late, of innocence having been legally strangled on the gallows in other cases than that of Eliza Fenning. How could it be otherwise with a criminal code crowded in every line with penalties of death, nothing but — death? Juster, wiser times have dawned upon us, in which truer notions prevail of what man owes to man, even when sitting in judgment on transgressors; and this we owe, let us not forget, to the exertions of a band of men who, undeterred by the sneers of the reputedly wise and *practical* men of the world, and the taunts of 'influential' newspapers, persisted in teaching that the rights of property could be more firmly cemented than by the shedding of blood — law, justice, personal security more effectually vindicated than by the gallows ["Jane Eccles"].

One of the series, "Jane Eccles," centers on the bloody code and the Attorney stories do occasionally tip in some of the big names in English law — Romilly, Bentham, and Fortescue. The Attorney series, however, has a different kind of lawyerly emphasis than the Barrister stories. That distinction, in fact, is between the roles of the barrister, one trained in the law who practices before courts, and the attorney, one trained in the law who often prepares cases before they come to trial. "Every Man his Own Lawyer" in the series emphasizes the absolute necessity of lay people seeking and following legal counsel about any sort of problem or contract. Therefore the Attorney stories don't show issues argued in court but show resolution achieved through finding things like wills, marriage certificates, and witnesses to set things right.

On March 27, 1850, while *Chambers'* was in the middle of publishing both the Barrister and Policeman stories, Charles Dickens reentered the magazine business. In the first year of publishing his new journal, *Household Words*, Dickens followed *Chambers'* lead and ran a number of lawyer stories — "The

Young Advocate," "The Gentleman Beggar: An Attorney's Story," and "The Law at a Low Price"; "The One Black Spot" followed in 1851. In the first year several think-pieces on prisons appeared as well as several on crime — "Innocence and Crime" (July 27, 1850), and "Two Chapters on Bank Note Forgeries" (September 7 and 21, 1850). And then, as did *Chambers',* Dickens switched to the police. While his treatment of lawyers and the law in *Household Words* reflected the same outrage found in his novels, Dickens began to present the new police and detectives in a very different light in his magazine than that reflected in his fiction of the time. This new view appeared first in a three-part piece which began with "The Modern Science of Thief Taking" (July 13, 1850) and continued with two stories both entitled "A Detective Police Party" (July 27 and August 10, 1850). These were followed by the semi-attached "The Spy Police" (September 21, 1850) which tags itself to the foregoing three articles in its opening paragraph.

The bosses at Scotland Yard could not have wished for better puff-pieces. "A Detective Police Party," for instance, begins with the assertion that the new detective police force "is so well chosen and trained, proceeds so systematically and quietly, does its business in such a workmanlike manner, and is always so calmly and steadily engaged in the service of the public, that the public really do not know enough of it, to know a tithe of its usefulness." Unlike the thief-takers and Bow Street Runners in his early novels, for whom Dickens had no use, the new detectives are exceptionally intelligent middle-class men:

> They are, one and all, respectable-looking men; of perfectly good deportment and unusual intelligence; with nothing lounging or slinking in their manners; with an air of keen observation and quick perception when addressed; and generally presenting in their faces, traces more or less marked of habitually leading lives of strong mental excitement ["Party"].

In "Modern Science" readers learn that knowledge and experience endow the detectives with special abilities:

> Sometimes they are called upon to investigate robberies so executed, that no human ingenuity appears, to ordinary observers, capable of finding the thief. The robber has left no trail; not a trace. Every clue seems cut off; but the experience of a Detective guides him into tracks invisible to other eyes.

That experience means that the detective possesses a thorough knowledge of the Swell Mob and other denizens of the underworld. But in addition to expertise, the first run of articles on detectives in *Household Words* stresses their humility — indeed the first two narratives in "A Detective Police Party" describe clever and dogged detective work which ends in disappointment. The last piece in the series, "The Spy Police" begins with a comparison of the lot of the British citizen with those unfortunates who dwell on the other side of the Channel:

> WE have already given some insight into the workings of the Detective Police system of London, and have found that it is solely employed in bringing crime to justice. We have no political police, no police over opinion. The most rabid demagogue can *say* in this free country what he chooses, provided it does not tend to incite others to *do* what is annoying to the lieges. He speaks not under the terror of an organised spy system. He dreads not to discuss the affairs of the nation at a tavern, lest the waiter should be a policeman in disguise; he can converse familiarly with his guests at his own table without suspecting that the interior of his own liveries consists of a spy; when travelling, he has not the slightest fear of perpetual imprisonment for declaring himself freely on the conduct of the powers that be, because he knows that even if his fellow passenger be a Sergeant Myth or an Inspector Wield, no harm will come to him.
>
> It is not so across the Channel. There, while the criminal police is very defective, the police of politics is all powerful... Austria, in some of the German states, and in Italy, political *espionage* is carried to a point of refined ingenuity of which no Englishman can form an idea ["Spy Police"].

And then "The Spy Police" goes on to narrate a story about the abuse of police power on the Continent.

On September 14, in the issue before "The Spy Police," Dickens published "Three Detective Anecdotes" which amplified the story-telling inclinations of "A Detective Police Party." The piece recounts three disparate episodes of police work, two narrated by Inspector "Wield" and one by Sergeant "Dornton." The three short anecdotes demonstrate the perspicacity of the members of the detective police and continue the effort of public reassurance found in the first series of police articles in *Household Words*—thus the first anecdote shows Inspector "Wield" following up on circumstantial evidence and discovering its misleading nature. Perhaps more importantly, Dickens works at developing a distinct voice for "Wield" who narrates the first two anecdotes — a voice which combines slang with modest deference to his listener. In 1851 Dickens found a new way to promote the police — the eyewitness account of daily activities. "The Metropolitan Protectives" (April 26, 1851) was the first piece to take this new approach to *Household Words'* program of promoting the police:

> Now, to the end that the prophets [of doom] and their disciples may rest quietly in their beds, we have benevolently abandoned our own bed for some three nights or so, in order to report the results of personal inquiry into the condition and system of the Protective Police of the Metropolis:— the Detective Police has been already described in the first volume of "Household Words." If, after our details of the patience, promptitude, order, vigilance, zeal and judgment, which watch over the peace of the huge Babylon when she sleeps, the fears of the most

apprehensive be not dispelled, we shall have quitted our pillow, and plied our pen in vain! But we have no such distrust ["Protectives"].

In June of 1851 Dickens applied the same technique as used in "Metropolitan Protectives" to Scotland Yard's star detective with "On Duty With Inspector Field" (June 14, 1851). The earlier story recounts one night spent at the Bow Street, Covent Garden police station and goes from inspection of officers and what would become known as reading the crimes, to a barrage of complaints brought to the station that range from destitution, juvenile delinquency, robbery, lost dogs, and drunkenness, to dealing with prisoners in the "holding tank," to the slack, dead time of 5:00 A.M. While in "Metropolitan Protectives" the emphasis principally rests on petty crime caused by poverty, "On Duty With Inspector Field" raises both the stature of the officer and the crimes. While "Metropolitan Protectives" principally describes the pathos of the victims of a broken social system, "On Duty" takes readers into a frightening urban wilderness. A night's duty takes the narrator into streets as hellish as any Dickens ever portrayed:

> How many people may there be in London, who, if we had brought them deviously and blindfold, to this street, fifty paces from the Station House, and within call of Saint Giles's church, would know it for a not remote part of the city in which their lives are passed? How many, who amidst this compound of sickening smells, these heaps of filth, these tumbling houses, with all their vile contents, animate and inanimate, slimily overflowing into the black road, would believe that they breathe *this* air? How much Red Tape may there be, that could look round on the faces which now hem us in — for our appearance here has caused a rush from all points to a common centre — the lowering foreheads, the sallow cheeks, the brutal eyes, the matted hair, the infected, vermin-haunted heaps of rags — and say "I have thought of this" ["On Duty"].

And its inhabitants are hellish as well. At Rats' Castle the narrator describes a gang in its headquarters as being "strong enough to murder us all, and willing enough to do it." The only force that prevents that murder is the heroic Inspector Charles Frederick Field. Gone is the deferential and informative Inspector "Wield" of the "Detective Police Party" and "Three Detective Anecdotes." Inspector Field on the job is a comprehensive national treasure:

> Inspector Field is, to-night, the guardian genius of the British Museum. He is bringing his shrewd eye to bear on every corner of its solitary galleries, before he reports "all right." Suspicious of the Elgin marbles, and not to be done by cat-faced Egyptian giants, with their hands upon their knees, Inspector Field, sagacious, vigilant, lamp in hand, throwing monstrous shadows on the walls and ceilings, passes through the spacious rooms. If a mummy trembled in an atom of its dusty covering, Inspector Field would say, "Come out of that, Tom Green. I know you!" If the smallest "Gonoph" about town were crouching at the bottom

of a classic bath, Inspector Field would nose him with a finer scent than the ogre's, when adventurous Jack lay trembling in his kitchen copper ["On Duty"].

Between the two daily life police stories, *Household World* ran "Disappearances"—by Elizabeth Gaskell—on June 7, 1851. It begins with a reference to and perspective on all of the previous police pieces in the journal:

> I am not in the habit of seeing the "Household Words" regularly; but a friend, who lately sent me some of the back numbers, recommended me to read "all the papers relating to the Detective and Protective Police," which I accordingly did—not as the generality of readers have done, as they appeared week by week, or with pauses between, but consecutively, as a popular history of the Metropolitan Police; and, as I suppose it may also be considered, a history of the Police force in every large town in England.

From there the narrator marvels at the efficiency of the new detective police and muses that

> there could be no more romances written on the same kind of plot as Caleb Williams; the principal interest of which, to the superficial reader, consists in the alternation of hope and fear, that the hero may, or may not, escape his pursuer. It is long since I have read the story, and I forget the name of the offended and injured gentleman, whose privacy Caleb has invaded; but I know that his pursuit of Caleb—his detection of the various hiding places of the latter—his following up of slight clues—all, in fact, depended upon his own energy, sagacity, and perseverance. The interest was caused by the struggle of man against man; and the uncertainty as to which would ultimately be successful in his object; the unrelenting pursuer, or the ingenious Caleb, who seeks by every device to conceal himself. Now, in 1851, the offended master would set the Detective Police to work; there would be no doubt as to their success; the only question would be as to the time that would elapse before the hiding-place could be detected, and that could not be a question long. It is no longer a struggle between man and man, but between a vast organised machinery, and a weak, solitary individual; we have no hopes, no fears—only certainty.

After this panegyric the narrator recounts a number of historical cases of individuals disappearing—punctuated in each case with a reference to the new efficiency of the Detective Police: "I will answer for it, the Detective Police would have ascertained every fact relating to it in a week." At the end of the piece, however, all of these reassurances, seem disingenuous when the narrator closes with "Once more, let me say, I am thankful I live in the days of the Detective Police; if I am murdered, or commit bigamy, at any rate my friends will have the comfort of knowing all about it."

Taken together, the stories about lawyers and police officers published in *Chambers'* and *Household Words* became the founding documents of what would very quickly and very soon become a thriving industry—printing and reprinting stories about crime and detectives.

Detective Books

On May 1, 1842, from Niagara Falls Dickens wrote to this friend Henry Austin:

> Is it not a horrible thing that scoundrel book-sellers should grow rich here [in the United States] from publishing books, the authors of which do not reap one farthing from their issue by scores of thousands; and that every vile blackguard, and detestable newspaper, so filthy and bestial that no honest man would admit one into his house for a scullery door-mat, should be able to publish these same writings, side by side, cheek by jowl, with the coarsest and most obscene companions?

Dickens, and others, had good cause to complain. It didn't take long for stories to cross the ocean, and in the 1850s American publishers caught the police bug from British periodicals. On October 10, 1849, for instance, two months after "Recollections of a Police-Officer — The Gambler's Revenge" came out in *Chambers'*, Wellsboro, Pennsylvania's *Tioga Eagle* printed it; the next month *The Milwaukee Sentinel and Gazette* printed the second story in the "Recollections of a Police-Officer" series, "Guilty or Not Guilty," which had come out in August in Edinburgh. In January 1851 *Harper's New Monthly Magazine* printed "Recollections of a Police-Officer — The Robber's Revenge" originally published by *Chambers'* on November 9, 1850, and, to add insult, in a footnote referred readers to "New Monthly Magazine for November." But perhaps the most energetic of the new American privateers in the 1850s were the book publishers; and of that lot, perhaps Cornish and Lamport were the earliest freebooters.

In 1852 Cornish and Lamport, of 8 Park Place in New York, issued several significant pieces of literary pilfering. First there were the lawyer books: *The Experiences of a Barrister* "by Warren Warner of the Inner Temple," and *Confessions of an Attorney to Which are Added Several Papers on English Law and Lawyers by Charles Dickens*, "by Gustavus Sharpe." And more importantly there was *The Recollections of a Policeman*, "by Thomas Waters, An Inspector of the London Detective Corps." All three books are collections of anonymous pieces originally run in British magazines. The contents of *Experiences of a Barrister* came from *Chambers'* Barrister series published from January 1849 to June 1850, *Chambers'* Reminiscences of an Attorney series run from November 1850 to September 1851, and three pieces purloined from *Household Words*—"The Gentleman Beggar," "A Fashionable Forger," and "The Young Advocate." The last story in *Experiences of a Barrister*, "Murder in the Time of the Crusades," in fact exhibits almost jaw-dropping plagiarism — Cornish and Lamport found the original in Peter Burke's *The Romance of the Forum* (London: Colburn, 1852), dropped the story into *Experiences of a Barrister* in

1852 and then published it in a pirated version of Burke's original work in 1853. The same kind of pilferage characterizes *Confessions of an Attorney*— to which the name Samuel Warren was attached in the Cornish and Lamport 1853 combined edition of *The Experiences of a Barrister, and Confessions of an Attorney*— with its contents drawn from *Chambers'* and *Household Words*.

With the policeman book, *The Recollections of a Policeman*, the publishers are almost candid about the source of the stories; the Preface to that book begins:

> Some of the tales included in this volume have already appeared in some of our American Magazines, and they proved exceedingly popular. It is believed they deserve a more permanent form — that this collection will gratify those familiar with their merits, and interest and instruct those whose interest is now for the first time directed to them.

In its American book form *The Recollections of a Policeman* caught on relatively quickly. After New York it was issued in Boston by Wentworth and also by Thayer and Eldridge in 1856, and in the same year it jumped back across the Atlantic and was published in London as *Recollections of a Detective-Police Officer*. The Cornish and Lamport version contained nine of the eleven Recollections stories published in *Chambers'* from 1849 to 1851 (it does not contain "The Monomaniac" published in 1852 or "The Partner" published in 1853) along with three of Dickens' pieces ("Sketches of the London Detective Force from Household Words"): "The Modern Science of Thief Taking," "A Detective Police Party," and "Three Detective Anecdotes."

The author's identification on the title page of *Recollections of a Policeman* as "Thomas Waters, An Inspector of the London Detective Corps," has not been taken seriously. While there are no authorial attributions in the original publications in *Chambers',* the name of William Russell has been attached to what would become the small library with Waters' name on the covers published in England and the United States. Thus *Leaves from the Diary of a Law Clerk* (1857), *A Skeleton in Every House* (1860), *Recollections of a Sheriff's Officer* (1860), *The Heir-at-Law and other Tales* (1861), *Experiences of a French Detective Officer* (1861), *The Recollections of a Policeman* (1861), *Undiscovered Crimes* (1862), *Experiences of a Real Detective* (1862), *Autobiography of an English Detective* (1863), *Strange Stories of a Detective* (1863), *Diary of a Detective Police Officer* (1864), *and Leaves from the Journal of a Custom-House Officer* (1868) all bear the name Waters. And in many cases their contents are as phony as their nominal author. *Leaves from the Diary of a Law Clerk*, for instance, simply republishes a miscellany of pieces, many originally in *Chambers'* or *Eliza Cook's Journal*, reprinted in *Experiences of a Barrister* and *Confessions of an Attorney* or the joint volume *The Experiences of a Barrister, and Confessions of an Attorney* published by Cornish and Lamport in 1853. Indeed, the title *Recollections of a Policeman* became a loose container into which several American publishers deposited a continuing miscellany of stories vaguely related to the law and the police. To the 13 stories of the 1852 *Recollections*, in 1861, under the same title, Thayer and Eldridge of Boston added eight pieces, most of which were taken from *Confessions of an Attorney*, and in 1864 Dick and Fitzgerald of New York under the title of *The Diary of a Detective Police Officer* published the original ten Recollections stories from *Chambers'*, added "The Monomaniac," the last in the *Chambers'* series, and nine pieces ("Mark Stretton," "The Dramatic Author," "The Two Widows," etc.) from other sources. While some of the Waters books published in Britain and not reprinted in the United States seem to have been assembled with less cavalier plagiarism, additional research in contemporary British periodicals might yield magazine sources for many or all of the stories.

A New Set of Stories

In 1860 while the first batch of Waters collections bounced from continent to continent, from publisher to publisher, and from reader to reader, Ward and Lock in London moved into the detective story business with two titles by Charles Martel that alleged to be a detective's reminiscences: *The Diary of an Ex-Detective* and *The Detective's Note-Book*. Neither a detective or Charlemagne's grandpa, however, "Charles Martel" was the pseudonym of bookseller Thomas Delf (1810–1865).

The Diary of an Ex-Detective contains 15 stories plus an appendix. It begins with a dedication to John and Daniel Forrester, celebrated Bow Street Runners who set up as private inquiry agents. Indeed, "Inspector John F—" narrates all the stories in the collection, taking attentive readers back to the dedication. In some ways the stories possess a degree of atmospheric verisimilitude lacking in other early collections of stories about detectives. Several of the stories make note of the policeman's lot of standing about in foul weather, and "The Murdered Judge" notes that patches of boredom partly characterize life at the station house reminiscent of "The Metropolitan Protectives":

> It was my turn on the night-watch. About six in the morning of the 3rd of April, 18 —, I was sitting in the station-house at — warming my toes by the expiring embers of what had been a pretty good fire; for it was a late spring, and the nights were damp and chilly. We had had a very quiet night of it — no charges of any consequence except a drunken tailor or so, and two or three quarrelling "unfortunates." I felt rather drowsy, and was not sorry that the hour for going home to my bed had arrived.

While little comes out in the collection about the personal life of Inspector F — or the chronology of the stories, one, at least, briefly touches on the personal lives of his subordinates. Thus this mixture of professional and personal details:

> A bill, of which the above is a copy, was placed in my hands one morning as I entered the Street station. Turning to two or three of my staff who were warming their backs at the fire, I addressed them:—
> "This can't be a very difficult case, boys. Suppose we go in for it?"
> "With all my heart," replied Pike, who had a scent like a bloodhound.
> "Things are very slack just now, and the hundred pounds will come in very handy, for my wife presented me with twins yesterday..."
> "Wish you joy, Pike. Take the matter up by yourself, and if you find you want any help, let me know" ["The Murdered Judge"].

While *The Diary of an Ex-Detective* contains several different kinds of crime story—"The Lost Portfolio," for example, is a spy story, "The Innkeeper's Dog" describes a foiled murder attempt, "The Burglar's Hat" centers on finding the meaning of an apparently obvious piece of circumstantial evidence, and a number of stories depend on the detective working in disguise—the dominant emphasis in the collection is moral. "Moneybags and Son," "The Beggar's Ring," and "The Pawned Jewels" deal with illicit relationships, out-of-wedlock pregnancies, and prostitution; "The Gamester" demonstrates the evils of gambling, and "Robbing the Mail" shows tobacco to be the cause of ruin: at the end of the story that murderer confesses:

> I trace all my errors, all my follies, and even my crimes to the use of tobacco. I smoked tobacco contrary to the express injunctions of my father. Smoking led me to drinking and bad company. I became idle, dissipated, and lost my character. In this extremity I resorted to crime—the awful crime for which I am now about to suffer.

Vice preoccupies many of Inspector F—'s cases: in some of them, as in "The Gambler," he is a mute observer of others' misery, in some, as in "Robbing the Mail," he posts Newgate Calendar-style confessions for the readers, and in some, as in "The Beggar's Ring" and "Moneybags and Son" he takes it upon himself to try to protect innocents from the aggression of the vicious. There is, however, one strikingly modern element in *The Diary of an Ex-Detective*. "Cheating the Gallows" centers on the use of scientific expertise and uses blood tests as evidence:

> Of course I examined the prisoner's apartments and office. Upon turning up the carpet of the latter I observed several large stains on the boards, which looked as if they might have been *blood*. The boards had, however, been washed, and in some places scraped. I immediately obtained the assistance of a chemist, who, by dint of much ingenuity and care, satisfactorily ascertained that the stains were of blood—of human blood. I must confess that my admiration of the chemist's art is very great. How often it leads to the detection of crime! By his wonderful skill

he can not only tell, from a drop of dried blood you may give him, what animal it belonged to, but also whether it was shed while the animal was living or dead. Then again, in cases of poisoning, how sure are the means by which the detection of the minutest particle of the deadly drug is arrived at! Many's the wretch that has had to swing through the evidence of the analytical chemist.

In 1860, of course, none of this was true — it was not until the early 1900s with the Precipitin and Reichart tests that this kind of proof was possible. But it attains such importance in *The Diary of an Ex-Detective* that the author provides readers with both the statement in the story and an appendix: "Note to Cheating the Gallows. On the Means of Detecting Sports of Blood," which drops the names of a variety of Teutonic scientists to reinforce the validity of using "blood" as evidence:

> But the tests given by the above and other chemists, although on the whole very satisfactory, are still far inferior in precision, clearness, and facility of execution, to that indicated by Dr. Brücke, of Vienna, and which is based on the formation of the crystals of *hemine* of Teichmann, of Göttingen.

The other Charles Martel book, *The Detective's Note-Book*, contains fourteen stories. The collection begins with a dedication, this time to the celebrated Inspector Charles Frederick Field, and commences with a series of random reminiscences by John "Jack" Bolter, a supposed former detective as told to a listener interested in hearing about crime, the police, and detectives. Thus the first story contains Bolter's account of how he became a policeman:

> You want to know how I became a policeman. Well, sir, I'll tell you. 'Twas partly luck, partly choice. I think I was born for the thing; cut out for it; one of Nature's policemen — it came quite natural. Why, sir, I was a policeman long before the new police was thought of. When a boy, I was mighty 'cute at finding out things. If I saw anything going on wrong, didn't I follow it up and ferret it out! Many's the nice little game I have spoiled by poking my nose in where I had no business; but I couldn't abear to see anything wrong about ["The Marked Money"].

Unlike the inconsistent attempts to establish an intimate relationship between the speaker and the readers in *The Diary of an Ex-Detective*, subsequent stories in *The Detective's Note-Book* have almost folksy inserted addresses to the readers about police history and police practices. Take this passage featuring Bolter on criminals:

> I expect you've no idea how scientifically burglars do their work sometimes. It's a regular trade; I don't know but you might call it one of the arts and sciences. Folks generally think a burglar is a rough-looking villain, with a horrid face and bushy eyebrows, who breaks into any house or shop where he thinks there's anything worth taking, and kills everybody that makes any resistance. Just let me show you a burglar (turning to the Rogues' Gallery), one of the best of them.

There, that fellow, number 203. You wouldn't think *he* was a rascal; he looks
more like a Methodist parson, doesn't he? Now that fellow had as nice a kit of
tools as you'd care to see. His "skeletons," with movable wards, were made with a
polish on 'em. Give him a chance, and he'd open any lock in town ["The Button"].

The narrator also translates the fusion of police and underworld argot for his
readers:

Well, there seemed a poor show for making much in this case, and our plan
seemed to be to watch round for the next attempt, and meanwhile to "turn up"
(search) some of the "fences" (receivers of stolen goods), to see if we could find
any of the property; though it's only by chance that you ever make anything that
way, the "fences" are too "fly" (smart) ["The Button"].

Several of the stories in *The Detective's Note-Book* center on the detective's
discovery of evidence. "The Button," for instance, recounts the discovery of
a lost button at a crime scene and the detectives' search for the coat from
which it was loosened; and "The Forger's Cipher" includes a description of
how to decipher secret codes as patient and clear as Poe's. The Bolter stories
include "The Absconding Debtor" which ends in a chase scene on ice skates.
And unlike most earlier detective fiction, several of the stories include violence:

Luckily for me that I tiptoed behind him. I was just in time to see him reach out
his hand for a revolver that lay on the shelf, when I brought my "billy" down
whack on his arm, just above the elbow, and broke it. What with his pain and
the surprise, and his anger at having his pretty little plan spoiled, his face *wasn't*
particularly amiable when he turned round on me. I asked him afterward if he
intended to shoot me ["The Forger's Cipher"].

Nonetheless, like *The Diary*, a number of the stories center on pathos and
sentiment: "The Libertine's Victim" recounts Bolter's attempts to save the
virtue of a young woman, "The Ex-Policeman's Story" and "The Doctor's
Story" reveal the havoc wrought by fallen women, and "The Closest Shave
of My Life" dwells on the pathos of a prisoner watching his family's home
from his prison cell. In "The Libertine's Victim" the narrator voices the traditional answer for why bad things happen:

"Perhaps, Mr. Moreton, all may yet turn out for the best; and Providence has
designed that I should not discover you, in order to further its own beneficent
ends for her good and your happiness."

After five stories ("The Marked Money," "The Button," "The Forger's Cipher,"
"How Sergeant Bolter's Prisoner Escaped," and "The Absconding Debtor"),
The Detective's Note-Book begins to fall apart. Several of the later stories lack
detective elements—"The Closest Shave of My life," for instance. In "The

Wrong Burglar" Bolter retells a story told him by a barrister. And the last four stories in the collection do not come from a detective's notebook — "Hanged by the Neck" is a first-person narration by a monomaniacal thrill seeker and "The Doctor's Story," of course, is told by a hard-working physician. And small wonder that the collection falls apart: it is one more example of the epidemic of transatlantic plagiarism that characterizes so-called notebook fiction in the 1850s and 1860s. While there is some attempt to anglicize place names and other details, the opening stories appeared first in *Harper's Weekly Magazine* in 1857–8.

Fresh Waters?

In the early 1860s English publishers added new subjects to the Waters oeuvre including stories of true crime (in *A Skeleton in Every House* and *Undiscovered Crimes*), stories to exploit the British curiosity and distaste for the French police system (*Experiences of a French Detective Officer*), and stories about detectives somewhat less anachronistic than those published in the *Recollections of a Police Officer*. In 1862 Ward and Lock's publication of *The Experiences of a Real Detective* announced that it was "edited" by "Waters." A replacement for the oft-reprinted 1852 collection, *Real Detective* contained eleven tales held together (by implication only) by several sentences in the first story which attribute their origin as a detective's notebook:

> I do not know that I should have yielded to the suggestion, had I not a few months since made acquaintance with a gentleman who writes for the best of the London periodicals. He warmly urged me to pitch together the incidents retained in my memory with the memoranda thickly scribbled in my note-book, promising on his part to see the product carefully through the press. I agreed to do so and this series of tales is the result. Tales, certainly, but tales of truth. It is I who have furnished the pen which jots down these recollections; my literary friend having done nothing more than point and nib it ["The Robbery at Osborne's Hotel"].

While several of the stories in *The Experiences of a Real Detective* mention dates in the 1830s, including Queen Victoria's coronation, none of the stories makes any stylistic indication of creating the illusion of having come from or having been based upon an actual detective's notebook — or notebook of any sort for that matter. The narrator is identified on the title page, and several places in the text, as Inspector F —, the name of the narrator in Charles Martel's *The Diary of an Ex-Detective* — a fact which gives one pause regarding the ultimate sources of these stories. While the stories hardly present a coherent picture of the narrator (in "The Robbery at Osborne's Hotel" he mentions a

wife and in "Bigamy and Child Stealing" he is "without encumbrances"), several references to the creation of the new police and to police routines occur
in the text. Thus:

> Several months previous to the organization, in 1829, by Sir Robert, then Mr.
> Peel, Secretary for the Home Department I had made myself conspicuous to a
> certain degree in neighborhood of Covent-garden as an amateur, supplementary
> sort of constable, and in several instances wherein the Charleys were completely
> nonplussed, succeeded in bringing criminals to justice. This seemed to be my
> natural vocation; and when the new police force was in process of definitive for-
> mation, I received a communication from Colonel Rowan, proposing to appoint
> me inspector, if such a post were worth my acceptance ["Osborne's Hotel"].

and

> I was first made acquainted with the leading facts, of the case by printed slips,
> always forwarded without delay, when any startling or extraordinary crime has
> been committed, to every police station, for the information and guidance of the
> officers ["Caught at Last"].

and

> There is a sick fund in the Force, to which from the first I had been a subscriber,
> and much surprise was expressed that I did not throw myself upon the Fund.
> Well, I could not do so. The 19th clause stipulates that no officer can receive
> assistance from that particular fund, except for sickness occasioned by hurts
> received whilst on actual duty ["Mrs. Waldegrave's Will"].

Many of the stories also include a brief citation of details intended to
show the hectic business of the police detective's professional life before the
main narrative begins. Several touch on points of law — in "Rueben Gill,
Mormon Saint," for example, a murderer is acquitted because of a technical
error. And there is also one story linked with the nineteenth century's protracted debate about circumstantial evidence — as opposed to the emphasis
on protests about capital punishment found in earlier police and lawyer stories.
Indeed the story entitled "Circumstantial Evidence" has an address on the
subject of evidence directed to readers:

> This shows that I do not concur in the common cry which brands circumstantial
> evidence as wholly unreliable; on the contrary, I believe that a chain of circum-
> stantial evidence in which there shall be no material break, that might be filled
> up, if all the circumstances were known, in a manner that would establish the
> accused's innocence, by giving a new turn, a different colour to other parts of
> that chain — to be the most reliable testimony upon which human judgment can
> be based — since a circumstance cannot be perjured, or bear corrupt testimony
> ["Circumstantial Evidence"].

Nonetheless, as in the Recollections stories from *Chambers',* part of the
purpose of the *Real Detective* stories is to demonstrate both the acumen and

the kindliness of the detective narrator. Correspondingly, the majority of the stories involve the detective's uncovering facts which clear a wrongly accused innocent. In this respect several of the pieces resemble the stories in the Confessions of an Attorney series in that the detective narrator is assigned to assist a lawyer as he prepares an accused person's defense. (See "Bigamy and Child Stealing" and "Circumstantial Evidence.") Several of the stories involve murder (see "The Tragedy in Judd Street," "Isaac Gortz, the Charcoal Burner," and "Circumstantial Evidence"). The collection, however, introduces robbery as the central crime in many of the stories (see "The Robbery at Osborne's Hotel," "The Gold Dust Robbery in Barbican," "Caught at Last," "Mr. James Bunce," and "The Two Musicians"), and several of these feature the theft of jewelry and absconded embezzlers. The detective work in the stories almost inevitably depends on people as opposed to things — chasing absconded embezzlers or unmasking assumed or hidden identities rather than finding and interpreting material evidence — in spite of the narrator's discussion of circumstantial evidence cited above. Indeed the overall context of police work and justice is vaguely evangelical. A number of the stories pinpoint vice as the cause of crime, depict criminals as unable to hide their guilt from the detective ("A dagger suddenly aimed at Mr. Hedlam's breast could not have caused him to leap back in wilder alarm, have blanched his face more instantaneously, than did these words of mine" ("Isaac Gortz"), and assume a Providential universe — thus "A strange blunder of a world this, my masters, were there not a compensation hereafter" ("Circumstantial Evidence").

The year after "Waters'" *The Experiences of a Real Detective* appeared in London, John Maxwell and Company of Fleet Street published *The Autobiography of an English Detective* (1863) also by "Waters" in two volumes; each volume containing eight stories. Both *The Experiences* and *The Autobiography* are fundamentally miscellanies, but while *The Experiences* makes only a perfunctory attempt at coherence, alluding only once to the source as the narrator's notebook, *The Autobiography* makes a more consistent attempt at coherence both in developing the individuality of the narrator and in carrying out the pretense that the individual stories are indeed from a detective's notebook. On the individuality side, readers of the *Autobiography* can attach a name (or at least an assumed name) to the narrator — Henry Clarke. A number of the stories connect the detective element in the narrative with facts and events (albeit with cavalier chronology) in Clarke's life. The first story, "Detective in the Bud," for example, describes the facts and events which led the narrator to become an apprentice Bow Street Runner, facts which the narrator continues to develop in "Coiners and Forgers," the second story. In "Mr. Charles Frodsham" one of Clarke's old flames plays a significant role, and a number of the other stories spring from or involve in a tangential way Clarke's old friends. Besides these, *The Autobiography* tries to develop a distinctive voice for the narrator. Thus readers witness his silent response when addressed in an over-familiar manner: "I did not much like his 'Clarking' me in such bumptious, patronizing fashion, but I let that quietly pass" ("The Murder of Anthony Louvel, 1794"); and Clarke sometimes breaks out in bursts of aphorisms:

> And now to follow up the promising start I had made. That was the pressing question. Handle the unhatched egg gently, warm it into life with watchful care. Certainly; but how — how to set about the process? Lie low, completely out of sight, and sing small, or, better still, not sing at all for a time ["Coiners and Forgers"].

In an effort to sketch the legitimacy and background of the stories in *The Autobiography,* "Detective in the Bud," the first story in the first volume, describes the source and purpose of the narratives, saying:

> a few months since superannuated upon a fairly-liberal pension — it has occurred to me that I might improve my income, and at the same time amuse, if not instruct, that portion of the public who prefer facts, to fiction however airily tricked out, by transcribing from the tablet of memory the most striking of the scenes which gleam through the dimming mists of those four-and-forty years.

But there's more than memory — throughout both volumes the narrator reminds readers about the stories' origin — the detective's notebook covering 44 years in law enforcement. In "Sir William and Lady Devereaux," for example, they learn the particulars of the narrator's notebook:

> I very early acquired a habit of transcribing in durable ink, before I retired to rest, such pencil memoranda as I had jotted down during the day of singular incidents which I had myself observed or been told of. Standing alone, these were with out apparent significance, but might thereafter prove to be invaluable links in a tangled chain of circumstance. The date, locality, the names of informants or witnesses were strictly recorded. In ninety-nine cases of a hundred I simply had my trouble for my pains; but the hundredth, as in the case I am about to relate, abundantly compensated the lost labour.

Buttressing this reassurance of the accuracy of the narratives, *The Autobiography* includes snippets of police history — thus, "Colonel Rowan, Chief Commissioner of Metropolitan Police, into which body the Bow-street Runners had been absorbed" ("Sir William and Lady Devereaux"), and "There is the tragedy of Lord William Russell — supposed to be murdered in his bed by Courvoisier" ("The Murder of Anthony Louvel"). While many of the stories in *The Autobiography* center on the same kinds of plots found in the earlier Waters collections — bigamy, wills and legacies, and problems of identity — a number of them show new directions in the detective story's subject matter.

First, while stories about absconding felons weren't new, stories like "Detective in the Bud," "My First Trip Across the Atlantic," and "Richard Watson" add international chases mostly absent in earlier works. And *The Autobiography* includes one story, "Lost Under Dartmor," which includes a seasoning of violence to the Waters oeuvre:

> Meanwhile, I held a half-cocked double-barreled pistol in each of my hands. Long practice had enabled me to shoot almost as truly with the left as the right; and any attempt to harm her would, swift as lightning....

Finally, and most significantly, *The Autobiography* follows the lead of *The Diary of an Ex-Detective* and includes a story which turns on scientific evidence. Thus "Murder Under the Microscope" in the second volume describes the detective's acquaintance with and use of science to prove an accused man innocent:

> Once when I attended a lecture by a celebrated man, he had stated that every animal had in its blood globules differing in size from those of any other kind. This knowledge had been arrived at by very slow steps. There was no doubt, however, of its scientific accuracy, or that with the aid of a powerful microscope a professional man of skill and experience could decide, without chance of committing a mistake, from the slightest stain whether the blood, if blood, had flowed in the veins of a human being or other animal.

The Detective Book Club

In 1860 Ward and Lock published the two "Charles Martel" books about detectives (*The Diary of an Ex-Detective* and *The Detective's Note-Book*), and in 1862 they went back to the old standby "Waters" for *The Experiences of a Real Detective*. The next year they added another name (or pseudonym) to their list of detective story writers, Andrew Forrester Jun. whose name was attached to *The Revelations of a Private Detective* (1863), *The Female Detective* (1864), and *Secret Service: or, Recollections of a City Detective* (1864). *The Revelations of a Private Detective* contains a preface and 13 stories — many of them very short — *The Female Detective* contains an introduction and eight stories, and *Secret Service* contains 17 stories. Just as Martel's introduction of blood evidence provides some compensation for reading the rest of the pieces in *The Diary of an Ex-Detective,* the Forrester collections mix several remarkable stories with a medley of largely pedestrian fiction.

The stories in *The Revelations of a Private Detective* reflect what was probably the principal occupation of private detectives in mid-nineteenth century England: they did lawyers' leg work. Thus most of the stories revolve around problems involving estates, trusts, contracts, insurance claims, marriage settlements, and even a divorce settlement (see "Emily H —: A Sad Story"). The narrator detective's occupation in most of the stories turns on uncovering fraud of one sort or another for the lawyer who has hired him. These pieces, however, hardly reflect well on lawyers, the courts, or justice. "The Fraudulent Trustee" gives readers a mini-version of Dickens' Jarndyce vs. Jarndyce, and in the contents of *The Revelations of a Private Detective* readers encounter lawyers named Goosequill, Keene, Sharp, Timewell, Slingem, Tortuous Dodge, Serjeant Birdlime, Serjeant Heavy, Loosetongue, Mr. Commissioner Jaw, Sleeky, Yellowboy, Starch, Barking, Closet Worm, Quick, Stickit, Gawker, Popular Silk, Q.C., and Messrs. Smoothy and Grinder. Rather consistently the tales end with some variety of perversion of justice:

> When a motion was made in the Court of Queen's Bench to make the rule absolute for a new trial, neither Mr. Serjeant Birdlime nor any other man, in silk-gown or stuff held a brief for the plaintiff. The company escaped the extortion of damages and costs; but public justice was defrauded of its title to submit Miss Wilkinson and a nameless paramour to penal servitude for a few years ["A Railway 'Plant' Blighted"].

> Were not the conspirators prosecuted? asks my reader. Oh no! The Unimpeachable Assurance Company saved their £3,000; and were content ["Miss Fitzgerald's Life Policy"].

There is, however, no perversion of justice in the last piece in the collection, "Arrested on Suspicion." But it is not simply that; "Arrested on Suspicion" is completely different from everything in the collection. It has an amateur detective narrator hero as opposed to the jaded private investigator who narrates the rest of the stories. And it is quite consciously and energetically based on Edgar Allan Poe. To begin with, the narrator is an admirer — in fact a defender of Poe even in the days of Griswold's calumnies:

> I may as well say, at once, that this statement never could have been made had I not been, as I remain, an admirer of Edgar Allan Poe; and if ever I have time, I hope to show that his acts were the result, not so much of a bad, as a diseased mind. For one thing, I believe his eyes were affected with an inequality of sight, which, in itself was enough to over balance a very excitable brain.

And during his investigation to free his sister from suspicion of picking pockets he bases his deductions on principles he learned from Poe:

> Of course I do not wish to hide from the reader that I was trying to copy Edgar Poe's style of reasoning in this matter; for confessedly I am making this statement to show how a writer of fiction can aid the officers of the law.

First this involves a search for a hidden letter:

> I remembered that in the case of a search for a letter by the French police, recounted by Poe, that while the officers were hunting for the missive, even in

the very legs and backs of the chairs, that it was stuck in a card rack, openly, with a dozen others; and though this knowledge was the basis upon which I built up my argument....

Once the narrator finds the letter (in a rather obvious place), he discovers that it is written in code and as he decodes it he explains the process to his readers, thereby combining "The Gold Bug" with "The Purloined Letter."

The stories in *The Female Detective* show, if anything, an even stronger influence of Poe. In "The Unknown Weapon," for example, the narrator gives him both praise and credit:

> The great enigma-novelist, Edgar Poe, illustrates this style of concealment where he makes the holder of a letter place it in a cardrack over the mantelpiece, when he knows his house will be ransacked, and every inch of it gone over to find the document.

In addition to using "The Purloined Letter" trick, in *The Female Detective* Forrester followed Poe's example of having a fictional detective work on crimes unsolved in the real world. Thus "The Unravelled Mystery" puts forth a possible solution to the Bridge case, an actual case involving a carpetbag containing dismembered human remains found on an abutment of Waterloo Bridge on October 9, 1847; and "A Child Found Dead: Murder Or No Murder" reexamines the facts brought forth in connection with the Road Murder (June 30, 1860), the case in the background of *The Moonstone*. Indeed, the conclusion of "A Child Found Dead" reflects the same kind of temporizing Poe found necessary when the real facts of the death of Mary Rogers became known:

> At this point the MS. breaks off. Should I obtain its sequel, I will, if I find it advisable to do so, publish the paper immediately. I never learnt my informant doctor's address.

As in the earlier collection, the stories in *The Female Detective* pay particular attention to scientific evidence; there is a mini-lecture on ballistics in "The Judgement of Conscience," a "microscopic chemist" analyzes material in "The Unknown Weapon," and a bit of misbegotten anatomy comes into "The Unravelled Mystery":

> While the hips of foreigners are wider than those of Englishmen, foreign shoulders are not so broad as English; hence it results that while foreigners, by reason of the contrast, look generally wider at the hips than shoulders, Englishmen for the greater part, look wider at the shoulders than the hips.

The use of scientific evidence, moreover, is part of the overall intention of the collection to explain to the readers how detectives work. In every one of the stories the narrator includes asides describing how detectives do their jobs. For example:

Accustomed to weigh facts, and trace out clear meanings, something after the manner of lawyers, a habit common to all detectives, before I began in a loose, half-curious way to question Flemps upon the history he had betrayed to me, I had made out a tolerable case against the lady ["Tenant for Life"].

Now, I need not tell the reader that detectives are as much excited by one of these rich government rewards as — as a ladies' school by the appearance of a new and an elegant master ["Judgement of Conscience"].

To be sure the most significant of these asides concern the principal breakthrough of the collection — the use of a female detective hero. Added to the skills possessed by all detectives, the narrator takes pains to demonstrate the unique advantages of women as detectives. Thus, for example:

It is the peculiar advantage of women detectives, and one which in many cases gives them an immeasurable value beyond that of their male friends, that they can get into houses outside which the ordinary man detective could barely stand without being suspected ["Tenant for Life"].

But without going into particulars, the reader will comprehend that the woman detective has far greater opportunities than a man of intimate watching, and of keeping her eyes upon matters near which a man could not conveniently play eavesdropper ["Tenant for Life"].

It was not much above a whisper, but the breeze set my way, and my ears are uncommonly fine and sharp; indeed, I believe it is admitted that we women detectives are enabled to educate our five senses to a higher pitch than our male competitors ["Tenant for Life"].

Under my corkscrew-like qualities as a detective he had no more chance than a tender young cork with a corkscrew proper. I believe that to the end of the chapter he never comprehended that I was a detective. His mind could not grasp the idea of a police officer in petticoats ["Unknown Weapon"].

Quite as important as portraying a female detective hero, in "The Unknown Weapon" Forrester introduces narrative techniques that would become standard in the fully developed genre. First comes the summary enumeration of facts discovered by the investigation:

And now as I have set out a dozen inferences which rest upon very good evidence, before I go to the history of the work of the following days, I must recapitulate these inferences — if I may use so pompous a word.
  They are as follow:
1. That the key found on the body opened a receptacle containing treasure.
2. That the mask found on the body was of foreign manufacture.
3. That the handkerchief found on the body had very recently belonged to a young lady named Frederica, and to whom the deceased was probably deeply attached.
4. That the circumstances surrounding the deceased showed that he had been engaged in no poaching expedition, nor in any housebreaking attempt,

notwithstanding the presence of the mask, because no house-breaking implements were found upon him...

Allied with this, but more important, is the narrator's use of lists of focusing questions. Thus:

1. Why did the father refuse to offer a reward?
2. Why did the deceased have one of the household keys with him at the time of his death, and how came he to have it at all?
3. What did the box mean? ["The Unknown Weapon"].

Both kinds of lists establish a relationship in which the writer invites readers to try to solve the enigmas presented by the plot and highlighted by the narrator at the same time the narrator works to solve them.

Back in the U.S.

At mid-century William Brisbane Dick and Lawrence R. Fitzgerald teamed up in New York City and formed Dick and Fitzgerald, publishers. Their list leaned heavily on books about games and song books. In 1863 they published *Strange Stories of a Detective; or Curiosities of Crime* by "A Retired Member of the Detective Police." It is another of the dizzying cases of plagiarism in an age of plagiarism. Its contents were lifted from *Harper's Weekly*, *The Detective's Note-Book*, and *The Diary of an Ex-Detective*. The Introduction was fudged up to make the assemblage seem uniformly American instead of British. Thus, for example, when the English narrator of *The Detective's Note-Book* wrote,

> I continued in this until the new police was established by Sir Robert Peel, and I must not omit to pay my tribute of admiration to the genius of that enlightened statesman, who was far in advance of his time. Well, I joined the force, and you have no idea what a difference there was between the new system and the old, or rather, between system and no system. There was a good deal of animosity against us for a long while, and all sorts of opprobrious epithets were bestowed upon us. We were "Bobbies," "Bluebottles," "Peelers," and "Jenny Darbies" *(gens d'armes)*. I am rather quick-tempered, I must confess, and it required a wonderful deal of resolution to forbear pitching into some of the saucy vagabonds who used to taunt and try to aggravate those very useful public servants, the policemen. People took it into their heads that we were "spies," and that foreign tyranny was being introduced under our blue uniforms. It took some time for the public to become reconciled to us; but they settled down to right notions at last, and I think the excellent discipline and general good conduct of the men have fairly entitled them to the favour they now enjoy from all good citizens [*The Detective's Note-Book*].

The publishers of *Strange Stories* altered it to make their book seem American:

> I continued in this until the new police was established. Well, I joined the force,
> and you have no idea what a difference there was between the new system and
> the old. Or rather, between system and no system. There was a good deal of ani-
> mosity against us for a long while, and all sorts of opprobrious epithets were
> bestowed upon us. They called us Mayor's Pups, and dear knows what. I am
> rather quick-tempered, I must confess, and it required a wonderful deal of reso-
> lution to forbear pitching into some of the saucy vagabonds who used to taunt
> and try to aggravate those very useful public servants, the policemen. People
> took it into their heads that we were "spies," and that foreign tyranny was being
> introduced under our blue uniforms. It took some time for the public to become
> reconciled to us; but they settled down to right notions at last, and I think the
> excellent discipline and general good conduct of the men have fairly entitled
> them to the favor they now enjoy from all good citizens [*Strange Stories*].

Shortly after releasing *Strange Stories* Dick and Fitzgerald published
"Waters'" *The Experiences of a French Detective*, and took the stories from the
decade-old *Recollections of a Policeman* (1852), padded them out with nine
stories lifted from other sources (including "The Stolen Letter" by Wilkie
Collins run in *Harpers* in 1855), and published them both as *The Diary of a
Detective Police Officer* (1864) and as *The Autobiography of a London Detective*
(1864). They also added the category of "Our Celebrated Series of Detective
Tales and Adventures" to the advertisements on the end papers of their other
publications. Included in that thin list of patched together pilferings was
another of Dick and Fitzgerald's forays into publishing detective fiction —
Leaves from the Note-Book of a New York Detective (1865). The title page and
introduction allege that the volume contains accounts of the cases of detective
James Brampton as edited by Dr. John B. Williams — hardly.

Given Dick and Fitzgerald's presumptive business plan, one might suspect the truthfulness of the assertions of the front matter of *Leaves from the
Note-Book of a New York Detective*. And indeed they are certified baloney.
First of all, not all of the stories in the book are about the said Brampton or
even about detectives; while some do recount passages from the life and work
of the detective, some don't — indeed after the 22nd story in the collection,
a note informs readers:

> The stories which follow and conclude this series are not details of my own
> experience, nor are they strictly of a detective character. They are adventures of
> personal friends of mine, and I am certain that they are for the most part strictly
> true. In two or three of them perhaps, the relators may have allowed imagination
> to supply the place of facts. I have thought them sufficiently interesting to
> deserve a place in this collection — J. B.

But it's not just the last seven stories that aren't leaves from a detective's
notebook; there are stories included in the collection subtitled "A Leaf from

a Lawyer's Note-Book" and "A Leaf from a Physician's Note-Book." Subtracting all of this filler, *Leaves from the Note-Book of a New York Detective* contains an introduction and 15 stories (one of which, "The Knotted Handkerchief," is a second third-person introduction to the hero) about James Brampton. More importantly, those stories had nothing to do with Dr. John B. Williams — Dick and Fitzgerald swiped the Brampton stories from *Ballou's Dollar Monthly Magazine* where they appeared from 1862 to 1863, where the author of many of them is listed as "A New York Detective," and where Ballou printed the label of "Original" before the titles.

The Late Entrants

While the heyday of the collections of detective stories passed off as the work and words of actual detectives lasted for only a little more than a decade, the same kind of miscellany continued to occasionally appear until the 1890s. Among the most popular of these books were those "written" by George S. McWaters and James M'Goven. George McWaters actually was a New York City policeman from 1858 until 1870. Widely advertised, McWaters' *Knots Untied: or, Ways and By-Ways of the Hidden Life of American Detectives* (1871) contains 32 short stories only a few of which reflect McWaters' own experiences. The second McWaters' book, *Detectives of Europe and America, or a Life in the Secret Service* (1877), reprints most of the stories in the *Knots Untied* and adds a handful of new ones (e.g. "Experience of John Spindler, the London Detective"; "A Gang of Bold Robbers in France"; and "Experiences of Mr. Breitenfeld, the Austrian Detective"). In Britain a series of collections of occasionally connected stories — *Brought to Bay* (1878), *Hunted Down, or Recollections of a City Detective* (1879), and *Traced and Tracked, or Memoirs of a City Detective* (1884) — recount cases of the putative author, James M'Govan, and his friend on the Edinburgh police force, M'Sweeny. They were not, however, the work of policeman M'Govan but of writer William Cranford Honeyman. Meriting brief mention, however, are the works of a real Edinburgh policeman, James McLevy: *Curiosities of Crime in Edinburgh During the Last Thirty Years* (1861), and *The Sliding Scale of Life, or Thirty Years' Observations of Falling Men and Women in Edinburgh* (1861?).

The First (Extended) Decade

From 1852 to 1864 a number of collections of stories about what can be called detection appeared on both sides of the Atlantic. Uniformly their titles advertised them as actual experiences of real detectives or lawyers. In the main, however, they are not original works — indeed, patient research might show that even more of the stories in the collections whose originals have not yet been identified were, in fact, taken from contemporary magazines, as stories from *Chambers'* were appropriated to fill the first two "notebooks," *The Experiences of a Barrister* and *The Recollections of a Policeman*. Added to the fact that these books mostly did not contain original fiction, they also were not the memoirs, or notebooks, or diaries they were advertised to be, and they were not written by former detectives or lawyers. They were written or assembled by book people about whom we know next to nothing because of the ubiquity of pseudonyms. And in the main they were carelessly made collections often with miscellaneous stories pasted in without concern for coherence but only to bulk up the size of the volume. They were also the creations of publishers and not writers, publishers whose principal concern was capitalizing on public interest in the new phenomena of the detective police and changes in the Anglo-American judicial system. Regardless of their negligible literary value, however, these books represent the first body of Anglo-American fiction concerned with telling stories centered on detection and crime after Poe's pioneering tales.

The first collections of detective stories appeared two decades after Victorian reform legislation began to be passed in Britain. From all of the easy pickings for piracy presented in contemporary British magazines, the publishers of the first book of short detective fiction, Cornish and Lamport, no doubt chose the stories from *Chambers'* for the contents of their *Recollections of a Policeman* because they had something in them that sold — a new profession as well as a new way of presenting crime. Crime fiction of the last generation was partly conceived to influence public opinion on legal reform — foremost, the abolition of the bloody code. In the first half of the century, however, the number of capital crimes in Britain had been winnowed down from the hundreds to the teens; and instead of the bloody code, concern about the law began to shift to the nature and function of evidence. Both professional and popular discussions of the law on both sides of the Atlantic in the first half of the nineteenth century are littered with discussions about direct versus "circumstantial evidence" — about the testimony of people, the historical foundation of Anglo-American law, versus the testimony of things as interpreted by experts. Indeed, the first monuments to this new movement were published in the mid–1840s: Alfred Swaine Taylor's *Manual of Medical Jurisprudence* (1844), and *Medical Jurisprudence* (1845). Thus the new stories acknowledged the bad old days of the bloody code during which the whole concept of justice came into question but went on to focus more on the contemporary concern about how to make justice work better — a subject few would argue against. And that meant writing about evidence, especially about physical or circumstantial evidence. Thus readers find a number of short stories entitled "Circumstantial Evidence" among the fiction of the first decade of magazine/book detective fiction, and in them, and in many others, the discovery of proper evidence (whether absent or incorrect witnesses' testimony or material or scientific evidence) became the central concern in many of the new stories about detectives.

Newgate literature of the last generation focused readers on the criminal hero and the pathos of a life wasted because of an inequitable and harsh society and a justice system indifferent and hostile to human potential and redemption. Removing promiscuous capital punishment from the judicial system opened up the prospect or even the reality that equitable justice could be achieved — but sometimes with more than a little help. Thus the focus of crime fiction shifted from the criminal and his adventures and tribulations highlighted in Newgate fiction to the work of the lawyer and then the detective who defended the powerless and whose gifts, knowledge, and actions prevented fatal mistakes and made justice work as it should. But the evolution of this new hero involved first a gradual move away from the courtroom and the lawyer hero and then a conscious effort to counteract more than a century of prejudice which saw the thief-taker as brutal and corrupt as well to combat the British public's fears about police in France who were seen as threats to both personal and political freedom. One of the ways in which the first generation of detective story writers sought to counteract some of the accumulated bias against those connected with law enforcement was by making their heroes solid middle-class individuals, often with homes, wives, and children. In the humanizing department, many of the works of the period include stories in which the detective works hard but fails — see especially Dickens in the early *Household Words* pieces. Furthermore the collections often include stories in which the detective has a personal relationship with those involved in the case — thus "Mary Kingsford" and "The Widow" in Recollections of a Police-Officer. Although the majority of the cases concern protecting the sanctity of property, and thus people with property, the crimes the heroes of these early stories solve and people they serve are not exclusively the gentry — even in the opening spate of lawyer stories. Thus, for instance, "The Beggar's Ring" in *The Detective's Note-Book* concerns a destitute woman and her illegitimate child; "Farmer Williams and his Bride" in *Revelations of a Private Detective* involves a naïve countryman duped by a confidence scheme; and "Judgement of Conscience" in *The Female Detective* focuses on the trials of an impoverished shoemaker. Even though one can find brief mentions of police routines and police hierarchy in these early stories, it is markedly infrequent; in the majority of stories the heroes' actions often seem more those of independent agents operating out of their own homes than public servants in an agency with the kind of paramilitary organization envisioned by Charles Rowan and Richard Mayne when they designed the Metropolitan Police in 1828. Then, too, the first generation of stories about detectives often take pains to describe how detectives do their jobs — a feature which becomes more marked in the 1860s and can be especially seen in *The Female Detective*. Further, the memoir form and the ubiquitous first-person narration also work toward establishing a trusting and intimate relationship with the readers. But perhaps the most important ingredient in these stories which qualifies the detective for the status of popular hero is that one of the most popular plots in all of the collections is that showing the detective saving a wrongly accused innocent from persecution.

Chapter Four

Charles Dickens

In discussing the history of Anglo-American detective fiction, one has several Dickenses to deal with. First there is Dickens the journalist who wrote about (and in some measure served as publicist for) the new official detective division of the Metropolitan Police. Then there is Dickens the editor/publisher who told, second hand, the stories related by real detectives, and printed pieces about detectives written by others. There is Dickens the literary lion whose name American publishers attached to collections of detective stories in order to boost their sales. We have already seen the impact made by these facets of Dickens' work. But there is also Dickens the novelist who introduced criminals, police, detectives, and the solution to mysteries as increasingly important parts of his serial, triple-decker novels.

Old-School Crime Writing

Dickens had more than a causal connection with the last generation's literature about crime. The years when he was making himself into a writer were those marked by the passage of some of the most important Victorian reform legislation — particularly those bills associated with reforming the police and the judicial system. They were also the years when Bulwer-Lytton took up the Newgate novel — *Paul Clifford* came out in 1830 and *Eugene Aram* in 1832, the year before Dickens' first publication. That Dickens named one of his sons Edward Bulwer Lytton Dickens is but one sign of his admiration for Lytton. His other direct connection with Newgate literature was that Dickens was immediately succeeded as editor of *Bentley's Miscellany* by William Harrison Ainsworth whose *Rookwood* appeared in 1834 and whose *Jack Sheppard* (1840) was published during the first year of Ainsworth's editorship. It is not, therefore, wholly a surprise that Dickens left the picaresque good humor of his earliest works and took up Newgate themes in *Oliver Twist* in 1838.

Oliver Twist, of course, is about crimes — crimes of society focused on Oliver's treatment as a ward of the state, crimes against persons seen in Fagan's corruption of children for his own ends, crimes against property perpetrated by Fagin and company, and finally a crime against life in Bill Sikes' murder of Nancy. On one hand these concerns reflect new, or at least Newgate, attitudes about understanding the ways in which individuals become criminals as well as society's complicity in creating criminals. Unlike earlier crime fiction, however, *Oliver Twist* pays some attention to the use of evidence. Just as there is no need to prove that Jack Sheppard or Dick Turpin or Paul Clifford or any of the other Newgate heroes committed crimes, there is no need in *Oliver Twist* to argue that Fagin or Bill Sikes are criminals — or even to ask why they are criminals. But from the beginning of the novel Dickens establishes in his readers a need to discover the truth of Oliver's birth and parentage. And the discovery of that truth involves evidence — thus Monks' efforts to find and destroy physical evidence and Mr. Brownlow and lawyer Grimwig's search for and discovery of legal proof of Oliver's birth and Monks' perfidy. While the search for and defense of evidence would become one of the staples of the detective story, in *Oliver Twist* it is more one of the bag of tricks of the romance writer — recall that Dickens also named one of his sons Henry Fielding Dickens. What underlines this point is the book's emphasis on the role of Providence as opposed to human agents in making justice prevail. Indeed *Oliver Twist* rests on attitudes about crime, detection, and punishment which would not have been out of place in the twelfth century.

Human agents aren't entirely responsible for detecting or destroying crime in *Oliver Twist*. Although there may be people obliquely associated with exposing and punishing crime in the novel, they simply assist justice meted out by Providence or stand by as witnesses to the self-destructiveness of evil. The case of Bill Sikes is instructive. Readers see Bill murder Nancy and then flee the scene of the crime. As he flees he is pursued, not by the hue and cry but by the embodied knowledge of his crime:

> Every object before him, substance or shadow, still or moving, took the semblance of some fearful thing; but these fears were nothing compared to the sense that haunted him of that morning's ghastly figure following at his heels. He could trace its shadow in the gloom, supply the smallest item of the outline, and note how stiff and solemn it seemed to stalk along. He could hear its garments rustling in the leaves; and every breath of wind came laden with that last low cry. If he stopped it did the same. If he ran, it followed — not running too: that would have been a relief; but like a corpse endowed with the mere machinery of life, and borne on one slow melancholy wind that never rose or fell.

As if this were not obvious enough, the narrator here tells readers: "Let no man talk of murderers escaping justice, and hint that Providence must sleep. There were twenty score of violent deaths in one long minute of that agony of fear." And at the end of the novel it is not pursuers who find Sikes or the courts that visit justice upon him but his own dog that leads pursuers to him and finally the vision of Nancy's eyes which causes him to slip and literally place the rope around his own neck. Indeed Dickens also applies this sense of Providential justice to Mr. Brownlow's exposure of Monks. Thus:

> "Every word!" cried the old gentleman, "every word that has passed between you and this detested villain, is known to me. Shadows on the wall have caught your whispers, and brought them to my ear; the sight of the persecuted child has turned vice itself, and given it the courage and almost the attributes of virtue. Murder has been done, to which you were morally if not really a party."

But then again in 1838 Dickens had just thought about using serious crime as a plot element and had little knowledge (or even faith) in the New Police. There were also in Dickens' world no such things as detectives, and nobody had written a detective story. In a few years that would change.

The First Murder Mystery

Things began to change by the time Dickens published the first of the installments of *Barnaby Rudge* in his weekly magazine *Master Humphrey's Clock* in April 1840. But the nature and magnitude of that change depended on one's point of view — and a couple of those points of view are important to the history of detective fiction.

First of all, *Barnaby Rudge* has a better claim on being labeled Newgate fiction than a lot of other contemporary novels — after all Dickens, does portray the historical liberation of the prisoners and burning of Newgate Prison during the Gordon riots of 1780 in the novel. And up front he tagged *Barnaby Rudge* with one of the principal features of Newgate fiction — the demonstration of the monstrous inhumanity of capital punishment. In his 1841 Preface to the novel, Dickens mentions the actual trial and execution of Mary Jones as validation for the novel's portrayal of capital punishment and by the 1849 Preface he enlarged the reference by adding a historical citation to underline the pathos of that event:

> That the case of Mary Jones may speak the more emphatically for itself, I subjoin it, as related by SIR WILLIAM MEREDITH in a speech in Parliament, "on Frequent Executions," made in 1777.
>
> "Under this act," the Shop-lifting Act, "one Mary Jones was executed, whose case I shall just mention; it was at the time when press warrants were issued, on the alarm about Falkland Islands. The woman's husband was pressed, their goods seized for some debts of his, and she, with two small children, turned into the

streets a-begging. It is a circumstance not to be forgotten, that she was very young (under nineteen), and most remarkably handsome. She went to a linen-draper's shop, took some coarse linen off the counter, and slipped it under her cloak; the shopman saw her, and she laid it down: for this she was hanged. Her defence was (I have the trial in my pocket), 'that she had lived in credit, and wanted for nothing, till a press-gang came and stole her husband from her; but since then, she had no bed to lie on; nothing to give her children to eat; and they were almost naked; and perhaps she might have done something wrong, for she hardly knew what she did.' The parish officers testified the truth of this story; but it seems, there had been a good deal of shop-lifting about Ludgate; an example was thought necessary; and this woman was hanged for the comfort and satisfaction of shopkeepers in Ludgate Street. When brought to receive sentence, she behaved in such a frantic manner, as proved her mind to he in a distracted and desponding state; and the child was sucking at her breast when she set out for Tyburn."

And he put lots of material about the bloody code in the novel itself. There is not only the hangman's passing allusion to Mary Jones in his conversation with Gashford about capital crimes, but also there is the fact of the execution of Hugh's mother:

She had been tempted by want — as so many people are — into the easy crime of passing forged notes. She was young and handsome; and the traders who employ men, women, and children in this traffic, looked upon her as one who was well adapted for their business, and who would probably go on without suspicion for a long time. But they were mistaken; for she was stopped in the commission of her very first offence, and died for it.

But the most important comment on capital punishment comes in Dickens' protracted description of Dennis, Hugh, and Barnaby awaiting execution. In addition to the material on the bloody code, in *Barnaby Rudge* Dickens portrays a wide range of people who commit criminal acts. This spectrum goes from Barnaby whose mental handicap makes him incapable of understanding the nature of his actions, to Hugh the "dreadful, idle, vagrant fellow ... half gypsy" whose acts are conditioned by society's ignorance and neglect, to Old Rudge the bogey who stalks in graveyards at night. Thus while employing the Mark of Cain school of criminal portraiture with some of the characters, in *Banaby Rudge* Dickens also shows individuals made into criminals by abuse, prejudice, and the arbitrary application of inhumane laws.

Coincident with sharing features with Newgate fiction, Dickens built *Barnaby Rudge* as an historical novel. As noted above, the novel treats the real events of the Gordon riots and it also introduces real people — pointedly Lord George Gordon who was connected with the outbreak of anti–Catholic rioting in 1780. The issues of civil disorder and military intervention, however, carried more than historical interest for British readers in 1840. The previous year saw Chartist riots in Birmingham and troops firing on a crowd of demonstrators at the Westgate Hotel in Newport. The horrors of the Gordon riots coupled with the fresh news of civil disorder abroad in the land moved Dickens for the first time to comment in print on the role of government in public order — and that meant commenting about the police too. Thus in *Barnaby Rudge* he writes about the rioters as a "vast throng, sprinkled doubtless here and there with honest zealots, but composed for the most part of the very scum and refuse of London, whose growth was fostered by bad criminal laws, bad prison regulations, and the worst conceivable police." Rather than commenting on how to improve the nation's police, however, in the novel Dickens only expresses the generalized fear of the British public about the police becoming domestic spies. To that end he makes one of the most loathsome characters in the novel, Gashford, end by taking up the despicable trade of the spy:

> He subsisted for a time upon his traffic in his master's secrets; and, this trade failing when the stock was quite exhausted, procured an appointment in the honourable corps of spies and eavesdroppers employed by the government. As one of these wretched underlings, he did his drudgery, sometimes abroad, sometimes at home, and long endured the various miseries of such a station. Ten or a dozen years ago — not more — a meagre, wan old man, diseased and miserably poor, was found dead in his bed at an obscure inn in the Borough, where he was quite unknown.

Along with both the Newgate features and the historical nugget of the Gordon Riots, Dickens blended in gothic elements as essential ingredients in *Barnaby Rudge*. Both the Newgate features and historical facts, of course, were scary enough — the hangings, the suffering of the condemned, the red tide of riot and destruction in themselves surely exist to evoke terror as well as pathos. Indeed, the action of the novel even starts off on a Lyttonish dark and stormy night:

> The evening with which we have to do, was neither a summer nor an autumn one, but the twilight of a day in March, when the wind howled dismally among the bare branches of the trees, and rumbling in the wide chimneys and driving the rain against the windows of the Maypole Inn, gave such of its frequenters as chanced to be there at the moment an undeniable reason for prolonging their stay....

Along with the atmospherics in the novel, Dickens gives periodic glimpses of the sinister highwayman and his blind emissary instead of telling readers up front that they are Old Rudge and Stagg. And this is because he was going to use a murder mystery as one of the plot threads in *Barnaby Rudge*. In the first chapter Dickens has one of the hayseeds at the Maypole Inn give readers a succinct version of the local village mystery that occurred decades ago:

"But, that morning, Mr. Reuben Haredale was found murdered in his bed-chamber; and in his hand was a piece of the cord attached to an alarm-bell outside the roof, which hung in his room and had been cut asunder, no doubt by the murderer, when he seized it."

"That was the bell I heard."

"A bureau was found opened, and a cash-box, which Mr. Haredale had brought down that day, and was supposed to contain a large sum of money, was gone. The steward and gardener were both missing and both suspected for a long time, but they were never found, though hunted far and wide. And far enough they might have looked for poor Mr. Rudge the steward, whose body — scarcely to be recognised by his clothes and the watch and ring he wore — was found, months afterwards, at the bottom of a piece of water in the grounds, with a deep gash in the breast where he had been stabbed with a knife. He was only partly dressed; and people all agreed that he had been sitting up reading in his own room, where there were many traces of blood, and was suddenly fallen upon and killed before his master."

Fifty-six chapters later the murder is solved: Old Rudge, the steward, killed both his master and the gardener whom he dressed in his clothes when he disposed of his body to throw off pursuit. But nobody figures this out. Instead the murderer has lurked in the neighborhood for years and keeps returning to the scene of his crime where Providence delivers him up to justice:

"Villain!" cried Mr. Haredale, in a terrible voice — for it was he. "Dead and buried, as all men supposed through your infernal arts, but reserved by Heaven for this — at last — at last — I have you. You, whose hands are red with my brother's blood, and that of his faithful servant, shed to conceal your own atrocious guilt. — You, Rudge, double murderer and monster, I arrest you in the name of God, who has delivered you into my hands. Nay. Though you had the strength of twenty men," he added, as he writhed and struggled, "you could not escape me or loosen my grasp to-night!"

The way in which Dickens handled murder in *Barnaby Rudge* seems in line with his treatment in *Oliver Twist* — conscience and Providence do the heavy lifting and human agents just do the clean-up work. But there are more than hints that he wants to engage his readers in thinking about what is going on — to try to figure some things out themselves. There is, for example, this instance of giving readers leading questions to ponder:

"Who is this ghost that is only seen in the black nights and bad weather? How does he know, and why does he haunt this house, whispering through chinks and crevices, as if there was that between him and you, which neither durst so much as speak aloud of? Who is he?"

"You do well to say he haunts this house," returned the widow, faintly. "His shadow has been upon it and me, in light and darkness, at noonday and midnight. And now, at last, he has come in the body!"

"But he wouldn't have gone in the body," returned the locksmith with some irritation, "if you had left my arms and legs at liberty. What riddle is this?"

"It is one," she answered, rising as she spoke, "that must remain for ever as it is. I dare not say more than that."

"Dare not!" repeated the wondering locksmith.

"Do not press me," she replied. "I am sick and faint, and every faculty of life seems dead within me.—No!—Do not touch me, either."

On one hand, technique like this is a basic part of the toolbox of the serial novelist. But viewed from another perspective it can become something different. Poe saw it that way.

Barnaby Rudge fascinated Poe. It's where he found his raven and he wrote about Dickens' novel in *The Saturday Evening Post* in May 1841 and did a long review in *Graham's Magazine* in February 1842. In both articles he argued that Dickens was consciously doing something remarkable to his readers in the novel and that his technique in treating the murder mystery in *Barnaby Rudge* corresponded to what modern readers would call detective story technique. In the first review Poe emphasized that close and precise reading of Barnaby's speeches yields clues to the mystery:

> Now these incoherences are regarded by Mr. Chester simply as such, and no attention is paid them; but they have reference, *indistinctly*, to the counsellings together of Rudge and Geoffrey Haredale, upon the topic of the bloody deeds committed; which counsellings have been watched by the idiot. In the same manner almost every word spoken by him will be found to have an under current of meaning, by paying strict attention to which the enjoyment of the imaginative reader will be infinitely heightened.

In the longer piece in *Graham's* Poe expands his discussion of the writer-reader relationship and the use of implanted clues — "But the reader may easily satisfy himself of the validity of our objection. Let him *reperuse* 'Barnaby Rudge,' and, with a pre-comprehension of the mystery, these points of which we speak break out in all directions like stars, and throw quadruple brilliance over the narrative." And he goes on to argue that even if he slipped in calling Mrs. Rudge a widow, Dickens demonstrated technical precision — or played fair — in his initial presentation of the facts of the murder:

> Now, when, at page 10, we read that the body of "*poor Mr. Rudge, the steward, was found*" months after the outrage, &c. we see that Mr. Dickens has been guilty of no misdemeanor against Art in stating what was not the fact; since the falsehood is put into the mouth of Solomon Daisy, and given merely as the impression of this individual and of the public. The writer has not asserted it in his own person, but ingeniously conveyed an idea (false in itself, yet a belief in which is necessary for the effect of the tale) by the mouth of one of his characters.

Determining how much Poe projected his own aims in composing "The Murders in the Rue Morgue," published the month before his first article on

Barnaby Rudge, on to Dickens' intentions is, of course, a vain pursuit. Perhaps the most that can be safely said about the novel's place in the development of detective fiction is that it represents the continued pull of Newgate fiction on Dickens' work and that it is his first use of a murder mystery as both a structural element and as a purposeful attempt to engage readers' (and purchasers') curiosity and engagement with his text.

The Third Murderer

Dickens published *Martin Chuzzlewit* in nineteen installments beginning in January 1843. A lot of the contemporary comments about the novel concerned Dickens' portrait of Young Martin's sojourn in America and almost none of them had to do with the treatment of crime in the book — even though it plays a significant role in plot of the last half of the novel and even though the book both contains a trenchant statement on the police as well as Dickens' first professional detective character.

Up until the brief comments on the police in *Barnaby Rudge* Dickens had not written much about them. In that novel he saw both the necessary role of the police in maintaining civil order and the potential danger of the police to civil liberties. In *Martin Chuzzlewit* Dickens more or less acknowledged that one of the proper roles of the police was serving as a guard against the criminal underworld. Thus in spite of exaggerated urban legends, he tells his readers, there was real danger in the city:

> Tom's evil genius did not lead him into the dens of any of those preparers of cannibalic pastry, who are represented in many standard country legends as doing a lively retail business in the Metropolis; nor did it mark him out as the prey of ring-droppers, pea and thimble-riggers, duffers, touters, or any of those bloodless sharpers, who are, perhaps, a little better known to the Police.

But this was simply a passing reference; a more detailed portrait of the police as a profession comes with Jonas Chuzzlewit's arrest for murder at the end of the novel. There the police arrive to take him before a magistrate and one of their number is a distant relation of the Chuzzlewits, named, appropriately, Chevy Slyme. Slyme has joined the force simply in order to embarrass his family:

> Look here at me! Can you see the man of your family who has more talent in his little finger than all the rest in their united brains, dressed as a police officer without being ashamed? I took up with this trade on purpose to shame you. I didn't think I should have to make a capture in the family, though.

Thus, even 15 years after the establishment of the Metropolitan Police Dickens' view of the profession hardly held it up for praise.

The case is perhaps a bit more complicated with the issue of spying. In *Barnaby Rudge* it is connected with the degradation thrust upon the reptilian Gahford at the end of the novel. In *Martin Chuzzlewit* it's not as clear-cut. In the novel Dickens pays a fair amount of attention to creating the character of Mr. Nadgett who is presented as the domestic spy (i.e. private detective) in action. It that novel, however, the writer pays little attention to the moral implications of spying on other people and presents Nadgett if not as a positive character then at least as an interesting and effective one. He is the investigator hired by Montague Tigg (or Tigg Montague) to do background checks for his Anglo-Bengalee Disinterested Loan and Life Insurance Company Ponzi scheme, and thus claims the title as one of the first (and perhaps the first British) private detectives portrayed in fiction. Nadgett sees everything: "Indeed Mr. Nadgett's eyes were seldom fixed on any other objects than the ground, the clock, or the fire; but every button on his coat might have been an eye: he saw so much." And as he sees things and records what he sees in his notebooks no one notices him:

> The secret manner of the man disarmed suspicion in this wise; suggesting, not that he was watching any one, but that he thought some other man was watching him. He went about so stealthily, and kept himself so wrapped up in himself, that the whole object of his life appeared to be, to avoid notice and preserve his own mystery. Jonas sometimes saw him in the street, hovering in the outer office, waiting at the door for the man who never came, or slinking off with his immovable face and drooping head, and the one beaver glove dangling before him; but he would as soon have thought of the cross upon the top of St. Paul's Cathedral taking note of what he did, or slowly winding a great net about his feet, as of Nadgett's being engaged in such an occupation.

In the plot of the novel Nadgett collects information which seems to prove to Tigg and to Jonas that Jonas murdered his father and he also goes on to collect evidence to prove that Jonas followed and murdered Tigg, the proprietor of the Anglo-Bengalee Disinterested Loan and Life Insurance Company. And these cases connect him with both Dickens' old-fashioned handling of crime and his new use of it in *Martin Chuzzlewit*.

Describing Jonas setting out to murder Montague Tigg, Dickens is at his most orotund:

> Did no men passing in the dim streets shrink without knowing why, when he came stealing up behind them? As he glided on, had no child in its sleep an indistinct perception of a guilty shadow falling on its bed, that troubled its innocent rest? Did no dog howl, and strive to break its rattling chain, that it might tear him; no burrowing rat, scenting the work he had in hand, essay to gnaw a passage after him, that it might hold a greedy revel at the feast of his providing? When he looked back, across his shoulder, was it to see if his quick footsteps

still fell dry upon the dusty pavement, or were already moist and clogged with the red mire that stained the naked feet of Cain!

Not only does he portray Jonas as the nightstalker, he also attaches the wrenchings of a guilty conscience on him. And Dickens tells readers that in Jonas' case, evil is self-destructive: "But the fatality was of his own working; the pit was of his own digging; the gloom that gathered round him was the shadow of his own life." To this point there is perhaps an elaboration of what he did with Bill Sikes or Old Rudge but not much more — except that Dickens chose to do something more with Jonas' character and crimes.

In *Martin Chuzzlewit* Dickens again used techniques that would later be identified as part of the detective story writer's tool kit — especially devices such as tantalizing (or engaging) readers with unanswered questions and enigmatic situations. Here is the beginning of the unraveling of the cause of Anthony Chuzzlewit's death:

> "Mr. Westlock! I don't wish to be overheard. I have something very particular and strange to say to you; something that has been a dreadful weight on my mind, through this long illness."
> Quick in all his motions, John was turning round to desire the women to leave the room: when the sick man held him by the sleeve.
> "Not now. I've not the strength. I've not the courage. May I tell it when I have? May I write it, if I find that easier and better?"
> "May you!" cried John. "Why, Lewsome, what is this!"
> "Don't ask me what it is. It's unnatural and cruel. Frightful to think of. Frightful to tell. Frightful to know. Frightful to have helped in. Let me kiss your hand for all your goodness to me. Be kinder still, and don't ask me what it is!"

Here, however, Dickens is probably working as a serial writer and not as a detective story writer. But he does do something different with crimes and solutions in *Martin Chuzzlewit*. He purposely misleads his readers — along with all of the characters in the novel but one.

After Anthony Chuzzlewit's death Dickens makes several things worthy of his readers' note. First he highlights a change in Jonas' character, one that suggests a guilty conscience. Next he presents a scene in which Nadgett reviews his notebook entries about Jonas with Montague Tigg who immediately begins to blackmail Jonas. Readers are led here to believe that Nadgett collected evidence that Jonas poisoned his dad. As the novel proceeds Dickens brings back Lewsome, recovered from his illness, who reveals that he acquired poison for Jonas and feels responsible for Anthony's murder. He then describes Jonas' murder of Tigg in order to free himself from Tigg's blackmail based on his having killed his father. But then Dickens does something extraordinary — he finishes the narrative of a murder with a surprise. Everyone in the world of the novel, Jonas included, believes that he murdered his father. But in the end of the novel Dickens brings in Chuffey, Anthony's old clerk, who tells the assembled cast that Anthony did not take the poison his son intended to (but did not) give him but in fact died of a broken heart. This pairing of the narrative of a crime with a surprise is substantially different from what Dickens had done in his fiction before this point. To be sure it can still be seen in the context of the technique of the serial novel. It does, however, recapitulate in narrative form the era's obsession with the misleading nature of circumstantial evidence and, consciously or not, it conforms to Poe's reading of Dickens' intent *vis a vis* clues in his last novel, *Barnaby Rudge*.

The Apotheosis of Charles Frederick Field

It took almost ten years after *Martin Chuzzlewit* for Dickens to include another murder plot in one of his novels. And that novel was *Bleak House*, which appeared in monthly installments between March 1852 and September 1853. During those ten years, of course, Dickens was hardly idle: he began writing Christmas books, formed an amateur theatrical company, and published *Dombey and Sons* and *David Copperfield*. But the thing that changed his attitude toward detectives — and perhaps even murder plots — was his magazine *Household Words* which he began publishing in March 1850.

As seen above, in its first year of publication *Household Words* followed the example of *Chambers' Edinburgh Journal* and published a number of pieces on lawyers and on detectives. As these pieces progressed Dickens made Inspector Charles Frederick Field into a star. He first appears in "A Detective Police Party" on September 14, 1850, in which Inspector "Wield" tells the first tale, a narrative which demonstrates dedication to detail and to justice. By May of 1851 Dickens was familiar enough with Field to hire him to keep Bulwer-Lytton's estranged wife away from a benefit performance of Bulwer-Lytton's *Not So Bad As We Seem*. Thus he wrote to the Duke of Devonshire on May 9:

> I have spoken to Inspector Field of the detective police (one of my night-guides and wholly devoted), and have requested him to attend Mr. Wills on both nights in plain clothes. He is discretion itself, and accustomed to the most delicate missions. Upon the least hint from Mr. Wills, he would show our fair correspondent the wrong way to the theatre, and not say a word until he had her out of hearing — when he would be most polite and considerate.

In the next month Dickens ran "On Duty With Inspector Field" (June 14, 1851) in *Household Words*, a piece which casts a heroic light on the detective. The next year he created an amalgamation of Inspector Field and *Martin Chuzzlewit's* Mr. Nadgett in the person of Inspector Bucket in *Bleak House*.

Whereas before *Bleak House* Dickens displayed little confidence in the police — witness Chevy Slyme in *Martin Chuzzlewit*— in *Bleak House* he brings over the same admiration witnessed in the police articles in *Household Words*. Thus Dickens echoes the atmosphere and tone of "The Metropolitan Protectives" (April 26, 1851) in Esther's visit to a police station with Inspector Bucket in *Bleak House*:

> Two police officers, looking in their perfectly neat uniform not at all like people who were up all night, were quietly writing at a desk: and the place seemed very quiet, altogether, except for some beating and calling out at distant doors underground, to which nobody paid any attention.
>
> A third man in uniform, whom Mr. Bucket called, and to whom he whispered his instructions, went out; and then the two others advised together, while one wrote from Mr. Bucket's subdued dictation. It was a description of my mother that they were busy with; for Mr. Bucket brought it to me when it was done, and read it in a whisper. It was very accurate indeed.
>
> The second officer, who had attended to it closely, then copied it out, and called in another man in uniform (there were several in an outer room) who took it up and went away with it. All this was done with the greatest despatch, and without the waste of a moment; yet nobody was at all hurried. As soon as the paper was sent out upon its travels, the two officers resumed their former quiet work of writing with neatness and care.

He also brings Inspector Field over from the *Household Words* articles to *Bleak House*— but those two pieces of journalism provided scant basis for creating a character who plays a significant role in a very large novel. To do that Dickens went back to attributes of Nadgett the private detective in *Martin Chuzzlewit* and also created elements for Bucket not mentioned in the two *Household Words* articles. Significantly, Dickens brought over the emphasis on Nadgett's eyes and applied it to Bucket:

> Mr. Bucket, still having his professional hold of Jo, and appearing to Mr. Snagsby to possess an unlimited number of eyes, makes a little way into this room, when Jo starts and stops.

And just as one is never sure of where Nadgett is going — seemingly waiting for someone who never comes — so Bucket habitually lurks or lounges:

> As they walk along, Mr. Snagsby observes, as a novelty, that however quick their pace may be, his companion still seems in some undefinable manner to lurk and lounge; also, that whenever he is going to turn to the right or left, he pretends to have a fixed purpose in his mind of going straight ahead, and wheels off sharply at the very last moment.

In *Bleak House* Inspector Bucket possesses some of the same sinister, dangerous quality that marks Nadgett in the earlier novel. Thus Jo "is possessed by an extraordinary terror of this person who ordered him to keep out of the way; in his ignorance he believes this person to be everywhere, and cognisant of everything." And Snagsby remembers

Detective Mr. Bucket with his forefinger, and his confidential manner impossible to be evaded or declined; persuade him that he is a party to some dangerous secret, without knowing what it is. And it is the fearful peculiarity of this condition, that, at any hour of his daily life, at any opening of the shop-door, at any pull of the bell, at any entrance of a messenger, or any delivery of a letter, the secret may take air and fire, explode, and blow up — Mr. Bucket only knows whom.

But in *Bleak House* Dickens' detective character is also significantly different from the character who fills the same role in *Martin Chuzzlewit*. For one thing, Bucket is official — Dickens most often introduces Bucket as a detective, an official detective. Next he makes Bucket careful to follow proper form and protect the rights of others. In detaining George, for instance, Bucket informs him of his rights:

"Now, George," says Mr. Bucket, urging a sensible view of the case upon him with his fat forefinger, "duty, as you know very well, is one thing, and conversation is another. It's my duty to inform you that any observations you may make will be liable to be used against you. Therefore, George, be careful what you say. You don't happen to have heard of a murder?

As this passage indicates, along with the sinister side notes and the role that the detective's professional expertise play in the murder plot in *Bleak House*, Dickens makes Bucket a bonhomous, middle-class man: "He is in the friendliest condition towards his species, and will drink with most of them. He is free with his money, affable in his manners, innocent in his conversation." There is a Mrs. Bucket who takes in lodgers and whose society he "highly appreciates." And as with most memorable Dickensian characters, he has an outstanding idiosyncrasy; he plays with his finger:

When Mr. Bucket has a matter of this pressing interest under his consideration, the fat forefinger seems to rise to the dignity of a familiar demon. He puts it to his ears, and it whispers information; he puts it to his lips, and it enjoins him to secrecy; he rubs it over his nose, and it sharpens his scent; he shakes it before a guilty man, and it charms him to his destruction. The Augurs of the Detective Temple invariably predict, that when Mr. Bucket and that finger are much in conference, a terrible avenger will be heard of before long.

Insofar as detective fiction goes, Dickens is most particular in *Bleak House* to provide a few significant details about the way in which detectives work. There is, of course, the emphasis on Bucket's seeing things and being seemingly ubiquitous. Dickens also presents an isolated Sherlockean moment with Allan Woodcourt's prescient observation:

"And so your husband is a brickmaker?

"How do you know that, sir?" asked the woman, astonished.

"Why, I suppose so, from the colour of the clay upon your bag and on your dress. And I know brickmakers go about working at piecework in different places. And am sorry to say I have known them cruel to their wives too."

But the most significant new perspectives on how detectives work are connected to how they gather and evaluate evidence. First Dickens suggests the important role of cash is the detective's job:

> Skimpole reasons with himself, this is a tamed lynx, an active police officer, an intelligent man, a person of a peculiarly directed energy and great subtlety both of conception and execution, who discovers our friends and enemies for us when they run away, recovers our property for us when we are robbed, avenges us comfortably when we are murdered. This active police officer and intelligent man has acquired, in the exercise of his art, a strong faith in money; he finds it very useful to him, and he makes it very useful to society.

Reflecting the changing points of view about evidence, Bucket displays useful skepticism about eyewitness evidence — seen when he parades Hortense before Jo who recognizes the clothes but not the person wearing them. He also displays, for the first time in Dickens, a mastery of scientific evidence — in this case it is ballistics:

> I found the wadding of the pistol with which the deceased Mr. Tulkinghorn was shot. It was a bit of the printed description of your house at Chesney Wold. Not much in that, you'll say, Sir Leicester Dedlock, Baronet. No. But when my foreign friend here is so thoroughly off her guard as to think it a safe time to tear up the rest of that leaf, and when Mrs. Bucket puts the pieces together and finds the wadding wanting, it begins to look like Queer Street.

One of the significant points about *Bleak House*, however, is that in it Dickens included both a story about a detective and a detective story — or at least a detective story in potential. His portrait of Inspector Field in the character of Inspector Bucket is the story about the detective, his professional attributes and his skills. On the other hand, the detective story in *Bleak House* lies in the way Dickens poses questions and reveals their answers in the narrative. Serial fiction more or less runs on posing questions in one issue and answering them in a later one. *Bleak House*, being a very big serially published book, poses lots of questions for readers to ponder — questions such as Nemo's identity, Esther's parentage, and Lady Deadlock's motives, for example. In the normal course of things Dickens gives his readers answers rather directly: all they have to do is wait. Thus, while he supplies readers with questions, they know that sooner or later he will give them the answers. All they have to do is keep on reading. In *Martin Chuzzlewit* Dickens to some extent altered this pattern. Dickens played with his readers' expectations and gave them two answers, first the wrong one and then the right one in the exposition of the crimes at the end of the novel. Nonetheless in that book Dickens couldn't subvert his moral purpose simply for the sake of plotting — he couldn't hide the fact that Jonas is a villain and that evil is self-destructive simply to surprise his readers. In *Bleak House* he did some things differently. For one thing the murderer in the book does not wear the mark of Cain — readers don't know she is a murderer until Bucket reveals that fact. Additionally, in the earlier novel Dickens spent some effort leading readers to believe Jonas a murderer and sprung his second surprise — that Jonas didn't poison his father — very suddenly: Chuffey just blurts it out and everyone's jaw drops. But in *Bleak House* he handles the springing of the surprise in a consciously different manner; he goes about the whole thing more carefully. Chapter 54 becomes Bucket's one-man show in which he carefully lays the groundwork for his surprise, fully conscious that his listeners — including the readers — desperately want him simply to give them the answer:

> "Now, I tell you what," says Mr. Bucket, instantaneously altering his manner, coming close to him, and communicating an extraordinary fascination to the forefinger, "I am damned if I am going to have my case spoilt, or interfered with, or anticipated by so much as half a second of time, by any human being in creation."

And only after laying out the evidence does Bucket reverse his audience's and readers' expectations. Dickens labeled the chapter "Springing a Mine," but perhaps significantly he also described his detective as a card player:

> Thoughtful Mr. Bucket is; as a man may be, with weighty work to do: but composed, sure, confident. From the expression of his face, he might be a famous whist-player for a large stake — say a hundred guineas certain — with the game in his hand, but with a high reputation involved in his playing his hand out to the last card, in a masterly way.

This kind of story-telling was of the sort introduced by Poe in "The Murders in the Rue Morgue." And one of his detective's principle attributes was his skill at playing games.

$106,385.31 or $12.25 Per Word in 2010

It took Robert Bonner, impresario publisher of the *New York Ledger*, two tries to convince Dickens to take £1,000 to write a piece for his family story paper. "Hunted Down" ran in *The New York Ledger* in three installments in August and September of 1859. Later it appeared in Dickens' *All the Year Round*. For that whopping sum of cash Dickens chose to write a crime story, an appropriate subject for a country he saw as obsessed with violence and crime. But he based it on the life of a genuine British criminal celebrity.

Thomas Griffiths Wainewright (1794–1847) held a fascination for a number of mid–Victorian writers: Bulwer-Lytton, for instance, based *Lucretia, or The Children of Night* (1853) in part on his life and career. In "Hunted Down" Dickens, too, built a story on Wainewright and his penchant for forgery and inclination to dispatch his relatives with strychnine — an inclination English courts could not prove and had to make due with transporting him for forgery.

Mr. Sampson, Chief Manager of a life assurance office, narrates "Hunted Down." He says he aims to entertain his readers with a "romance of the real world." Sampson's story concerns the unmasking of a criminal. Julius Slinkton has poisoned one of his wards; her fiancé, Meltham, assumes the disguise of a drunkard and tempts Slinkton to take out an insurance policy on his life. He then warns Sampson; the two of them then save Slinkton's other ward from being poisoned. Sampson finds that Slinkton lives adjacent to Meltham. He visits their lodgings whereupon Meltham throws off his disguise and tells Slinkton that he now has proof that he has been trying to poison him. Slinkton, cornered, takes poison and dies. A year later Meltham dies of grief over the loss of his fiancée.

Except that's not how Sampson tells the story. Until the end of the story as the narrator tells it, readers do not know that Sampson is wise to Slinkton from the beginning, do not know the identity of the disguised man at Scarborough who goes off with Slinkton's ward, and do not know that Beckwith the drunkard is Meltham in disguise. Therefore if manipulating readers' interest in a story connected with crime and solving problems is one of the ingredients of the detective story, "Hunted Down" fills the bill. It fills the bill in another way. Up until *Bleak House* Dickens does not disguise his villains; no one, for example, could identify either Bill Sikes or Jonas Chuzzlewit as other than a villain, and they are complicit in their own ends, as is Old Rudge in *Barnaby Rudge*. Along with this, Dickens includes the theme of evil being self destructive. But not in *Bleak House* and not directly in "Hunted Down." Indeed, in "Hunted Down" Dickens includes a passage that abandons the notion that a criminal's conscience is the way Providence hunts down and exposes crime:

> But there is no greater mistake than to suppose that a man who is a calculating criminal, is, in any phase of his guilt, otherwise than true to himself, and perfectly consistent with his whole character. Such a man commits murder, and murder is the natural culmination of his course; such a man has to outface murder, and will do it with hardihood and effrontery.

If murderers don't identify themselves, someone must: thus readers have Inspector Bucket in *Bleak House* and Meltham in "Hunted Down." By refusing to clearly identify his murderers as the stories unfold, Dickens adopted a new approach to using villains in his narratives, an approach that is very much like that of the detective story. In keeping his criminals under wraps, moreover, he magnified the role of the detective. Indeed, in "Hunted Down" since conscience seems to be out of the picture, Providence has to find a human agent to ensure justice, and that means a detective:

> "That man Meltham ... was as absolutely certain that you could never elude him in this world, if he devoted himself to your destruction with his utmost fidelity and earnestness, and if he divided the sacred duty with no other duty in life, as he was certain that in achieving it he would be a poor instrument in the hands of Providence, and would do well before Heaven in striking you out from among living men."

A Bit of the Supernatural

"To Be Taken with a Grain of Salt" repeats, in miniature, some of Dickens' oldest and probably most fundamental views about crime and justice. It is a short story included in the 1865 Christmas issue of *All the Year Round* built on a frame story concerning the fortunes of Doctor Marigold, an itinerant peddler, and his adopted deaf and speechless daughter. "To Be Taken with a Grain of Salt" is he sixth of eight stories, all of which carry prescription labels (in the context of the overall title, *Doctor Marigold's Prescriptions*). In it a middle-aged bachelor banker tells the story of his involvement with a murder trial. He begins by talking about his interest in "spectral illusions" and then moves from the general topic of murderers ("We hear more than enough of murderers as they rise in succession to their atrocious eminence") to a particular murder described in his morning paper. Shortly after a spectral figure begins to appear to him he receives a summons to serve on the jury in the trial of the murder described in the paper. As the trail proceeds the spectral figure begins to appear among the jurymen and also near the witness box where it pantomimes contradictions to the testimony of defense witnesses. When the murderer is convicted he reveals that a spirit had appeared to him in and placed a noose in his bed at the start of the trial. The story, then, is of the Banquo's Ghost school of justice implicit in Dickens' writing from the time of *Oliver Twist*. It affirms that Justice will ensure the proper functioning of the institutions of society. Indeed, in "To Be Taken with a Grain of Salt" the narrator alludes to sensationalism, jurisprudence, and the Newgate Calendar in order to reject them all and direct the readers to the way in which Providence ensures justice:

Both on the ground already explained, that I wish to avoid reviving the unwholesome memory of that Murderer, and also because a detailed account of his long trial is by no means indispensable to my narrative, I shall confine myself closely to such incidents in the ten days and nights during which we, the Jury, were kept together, as directly bear on my own curious personal experience. It is in that, and not in the Murderer, that I seek to interest my reader. It is to that, and not to a page of the Newgate Calendar, that I beg attention.

An Open Question

Shortly before he wrote "Hunted Down," in 1858, Dickens began doing public readings for profit. In 1868 he undertook a farewell tour in Britain. It may (or may not) be significant for the progress of crime and detection in Dickens' works that on that tour for the first time he added Bill Sikes' murder of Nancy from *Oliver Twist* to the passages he performed on stage.

Dickens began thinking about a new novel in July 1868; he wrote to his friend John Foster "What should you think of the idea of a story beginning in this way?— Two people, boy and girl, or very young, going apart from one another, pledged to be married after many years — at the end of the book." By August he wrote to Foster that he had "laid aside the fancy I told you of, and have a very curious and new idea for my new story. Not a communicable idea (or the interest of the book would be gone), but a very strong one, though difficult to work." Foster, in his biography of Dickens, then goes on say that Dickens did in fact communicate the idea to him:

> The story ... was to be that of the murder of a nephew by his uncle; the original-ity of which was to consist in the review of the murderer's career by himself at the close, when its temptations were to be dwelt upon as if, not he the culprit, but some other man, were the tempted. The last chapters were to be written in the condemned cell, to which his wickedness, all elaborately elicited from him as if told of another, had brought him. Discovery by the murderer of the utter needlessness of the murder for its object, was to follow hard upon commission of the deed; but all discovery of the murderer was to be baffled till towards the close, when, by means of a gold ring which had resisted the corrosive effects of the lime into which he had thrown the body, not only the person murdered was to be identified but the locality of the crime and the man who committed it.

The first installment of The *Mystery of Edwin Drood* came out in April 1870. Before his death on June 9 Dickens had completed six of the planned eight installments of the novel. In the fourth installment, on a stormy night, the title character, Edwin Drood, disappears. Shortly thereafter Mr. Crisparkle spots and retrieves from the waters at the weir a gold watch and a shirt-pin which are identified as Edwin Drood's property. Neville Landless, who had been quarreling with Drood, is arrested and released for want of evidence, and John Jasper, the missing man's guardian, vows to collect evidence necessary to identify and convict the murderer. While Dickens introduces additional characters and drops what may, or may not, be clues to what is going on and how the mystery of Edwin Drood will be explained, these are the only facts we can know. Dickens' death made idle any speculation about what would have happened and who would have done what to whom.

But almost as soon as Dickens was in the ground writers began to finish *The Mystery of Edwin Drood* for him. First off the mark were Americans. Robert Henry Newell, a writer for the *New York World*, led the way with a djinned up a comic version of *Edwin Drood* in "The Cloven Foot" in 1870. Another American journalist, Henry Moreland, believed that

> the author, doing what he believed to be his life-work, had not been entirely reticent as to the scope of that work; and hints had been supplied by him, unwittingly, for a much closer estimate of the bearings of those portions remaining unwritten than he could probably have believed while in life.

And he took those hints he found and supplied a solution to the mystery in *John Jasper's Secret: a Sequel to Charles Dickens's Unfinished Novel "The Mystery of Edwin Drood,"* published in book form in 1872. Two years later another American, Thomas P. James, published a third version of the ending of Edwin Drood based on conversations with the deceased author: *Second Part of the Mystery of Edwin Drood by the Spirit Pen of Charles Dickens Through a Medium* (1874).

The fate of *The Mystery of Edwin Drood* is, perhaps, illustrative of the overall impact of Dickens' work on the history of detective fiction. Regardless of whether he deliberately inserted clues for readers to ponder or how he planned to finish *The Mystery of Edwin Drood*, perhaps its greatest contribution to the history of detective fiction was that Dickens left it unfinished. Rather than discussing the uncompleted novel as a ghost story or one reflecting the author's attachment to the spirit and techniques of the literary gothic — a thread in Dickens going back as far as the "Baron of Grogzwig" in *Nicholas Nickleby* (1838) or "A Confession Found in a Prison in the Time of Charles the Second" (1841) and continuing through "Taken with a Grain of Salt" — readers almost immediately after its publication made it into an artifact to be examined, a puzzle to be completed, and readers made it into the kind of entertainment which writers in the 1920s identified as the fundamental purpose of the detective story. The same might be said for his uses of surprises in the crime plots of *Martin Chuzzlewit* and *Bleak House* — these can be seen as the artful maneuvers of a skilled serial writer who attracted readers by this kind of plotting laid over a traditional, conservative view of the role of Providence in human affairs. And even Nadgett and Bucket, their occupations aside, can be seen as both frightening (and Bucket as made more frightening by his friendliness) and as typical Dickensian characters built on idiosyncrasies of speech, dress, and demeanor. However even as Dickens was creating these plots and characters, publishers and readers in both Britain and the United States were developing an interest in detectives and the detective story. They and their successors, then, looked at what Dickens had done and saw it within that context.

Chapter Five

Collins and the Sensation Novel

When Wilkie Collins met him, Charles Dickens was very much concerned with crime and detectives. In the summer and fall of 1850 Dickens ran his series of articles on police and detectives in *Household Words* and by the next year he had begun work on *Bleak House*, the installments of which began to appear in the spring of 1852. Between the two events, Collins acted the role of Smart, the Valet to Lord Wilmot, in an amateur benefit performance of Bulwer-Lytton's play *Not So Bad as We Seem* in which Dickens played Lord Wilmot. And not long after that Collins, who already had one novel (*Antonia*) under his belt, began writing pieces of *Household Words*.

And over the next 16 years Collins was to change the ways in which fiction appealed to readers and directly and indirectly make what came to be known as the detective novel a standard feature of both British and American literature.

Criminal Excursions

One of Collins' early contributions to *Household Words* was "A Terribly Strange Bed" which appeared in April 1852. The piece runs to almost 7,000 words and is a tale concerning crimes in a Parisian gambling house narrated by a young English swell. The tale begins with narrator looking for more excitement than the fashionable world of Paris affords:

> "For Heaven's sake," said I to my friend, "let us go somewhere where we can see a little genuine, blackguard, poverty-stricken gaming, with no false gingerbread glitter thrown over it at all. Let us get away from fashionable Frascati's, to a house where they don't mind letting in a man with a ragged coat, or a man with no coat, ragged or otherwise."

But what he finds in slumming is hardly what he expected:

I had entered the place to laugh, but the spectacle before me was something to weep over. I soon found it necessary to take refuge in excitement from the depression of spirits which was fast stealing on me.

He finds that excitement in gambling and has an extraordinary run of good luck, so much so that he comes close to breaking the bank. The proprietors give him refreshment and when he becomes sleepy they take him to a bedroom furnished with a canopy bed in which he collapses. Awakening fortuitously, the narrator notices the canopy slowly descending, an action which, in time, would crush him. He escapes, finds the police, returns with them to uncover the death trap and the proprietors' practice of eliminating winners and tossing their bodies in the Seine.

The story contains a some rudimentary police work — when the police arrive they take apart the floor of the house and find the hydraulics that operated the crushing apparatus in the bed, and they also conclude that all of the bodies that have recently shown up in the river, apparent suicides from gambling losses, were really murdered by the gambling house gang. But it's all *ex post facto*. The real purpose of the story lies not in detection or even really in crime but in the fact that it gives Collins the opportunity to present first hand the roller coaster emotional experiences of the narrator. Thus he offers his readers artificial emotional stimulation with the bored young man's disappointment when he does not find diversion by visiting the haunts of the criminal classes, and then he gives him the real thing when he almost dies at their hands. Indeed, there is something reminiscent of the "Pit and the Pendulum" in the narrator's experience as the death-trap descends on him:

I am, constitutionally, anything but timid. I have been on more than one occasion in peril of my life, and have not lost my self-possession for an instant; but when the conviction first settled on my mind that the bed-top was really moving, was steadily and continuously sinking down upon me, I looked up shuddering, helpless, panic-stricken, beneath the hideous machinery for murder, which was advancing closer and closer to suffocate me where I lay.

I looked up, motionless, speechless, breathless. The candle, fully spent, went out; but the moonlight still brightened the room. Down and down, without pausing and without sounding, came the bed-top, and still my panic terror seemed to bind me faster and faster to the mattress on which I lay — down and down it sank, till the dusty odor from the lining of the canopy came stealing into my nostrils.

This heart-stopping excitement — not the narrator or the villains or the police — is all that matters in the story.

In 1854, the year after Dickens published *Bleak House*, Collins made his first real foray into detective territory with "The Lawyer's Story of a Stolen Letter" which was the "Fourth Poor Traveller's" story contained within the framework of *The Seven Poor Travellers* in *Household Words'* Christmas issue for 1854. In the U.S. *Harper's New Monthly Magazine* published the story in February 1855 as "A Lawyer's Story"—and erroneously attributed it to Dickens. The lawyer narrator tells a tale about a potential scandal threatening the up-coming marriage of a young couple, a scandal turning on a letter upon which the prospective bride's father forged a signature. Alfred Davager, one of the deceased father's clerks, gained possession of the letter and proposes to use it to extort money from the wealthy bridegroom-to-be. The groom-to-be turns to his lawyer:

> "Mr. Frank," says I, "you came here to get my help and advice in this extremely ticklish business.... Now, I've made up my mind to act boldly—desperately, if you like—on the hit or miss, win all or lose all principle—in dealing with this matter."

Acting boldly means trying to surreptitiously gain possession of the letter. The one aid afforded the searcher is Davager's cryptic note to himself: "MEM. 5 ALONG. 4 ACROSS." With the aid of a bribed chambermaid, the lawyer gains access to the villain's room and with the help of a carpenter's ruler searches the room until he finds the letter hidden in a slit in the patterned carpet.

For many the title of the story has led to the notion that "The Stolen Letter" was an off-shoot of Poe's "The Purloined Letter." The principal similarity of the two stories lies in the fact that they both center on problem solving—problem solving connected to delicate personal relationships. Indeed, in "The Stolen Letter" Collins spends some time describing problem solving. Thus this passage musing on the cryptic note and the location of the stolen letter:

> It was the measurement most likely of something, and he was afraid of forgetting it; therefore it was something important. Query—something about himself? Say "5" (inches) "along"—he doesn't wear a wig. Say "5" (feet) "along"—it can't be coat, waistcoat, trousers, or underclothing. Say "5" (yards) "along"—it can't be anything about himself, unless he wears round his body the rope that he's sure to be hanged with one of these days. Then it is *not* something about himself. What do I know of that is important to him besides? I know of nothing but the Letter. Can the memorandum be connected with that? Say, yes. What do "5 along" and "4 across" mean, then? The measurement of something he carries about with him? or the measurement of something in his room? I could get pretty satisfactorily to myself as far as that; but I could get no further.

And the story also possesses several references to the need for and use of evidence. While Poe's influence can perhaps be seen in these elements of the story, profit can be gained from also seeing it in the context of the spate of lawyer stories published in British magazines—especially the barrister and attorney stories run in *Chambers'*—in the early 1850s. Thus "The Stolen Letter" can be and perhaps should be seen as Collins' satiric response to all of the contemporary lawyer stories in which he substitutes an openly mercenary lawyer not above breaking and entering for the fastidious and sentimental attorneys who solve problems in the *Chambers'* stories. And Collins' story also demonstrates that for a brief time in the 1850s it was not altogether clear whether the lawyer or the plainclothes policeman or the amateur was going to emerge as the hero of the new detective story.

In 1856 Collins once more combined crime and sensation in "The Diary of Anne Rodway" published in two installments in *Household Words* in July 1856. But this time he added a bit of detective work to the combination he had used in "A Terribly Strange Bed" and instead of terror he used pathos. Anne Rodway is a poor but honest piece-work seamstress who lives and works in a boarding house in London. Her diary briefly recounts the disappointments of her lover who had emigrated to America to seek his fortune and then turns to focus on the predicament of Mary Mallinson, the victim of a cruel stepmother and lost expectations who is struggling to eke out a living as a seamstress. One evening she is brought home by two policemen who have found her, severely wounded, lying in the street. Anne and a friendly physician attend to her, but after lingering a brief time she dies. Before she expires, Anne finds a clue to Mary's injury:

> I took up her right hand, which lay nearest to me. It was tight clenched. I tried to unclasp the fingers, and succeeded after a little time. Something dark fell out of the palm of her hand as I straightened it.
>
> I picked the thing up, and smoothed it out, and saw that it was an end of a man's cravat.
>
> A very old, rotten, dingy strip of black silk, with thin lilac lines, all blurred and deadened with dirt, running across and across the stuff in a sort of trellis-work pattern. The small end of the cravat was hemmed in the usual way, but the other end was all jagged, as if the morsel then in my hands had been torn off violently from the rest of the stuff. A chill ran all over me as I looked at it; for that poor, stained, crumpled end of a cravat seemed to be saying to me, as though it had been in plain words, "If she dies, she has come to her death by foul means, and I am the witness of it."

After a protracted description of the rigors Anne suffers in her attempt to provide Mary with a proper funeral and decent burial with head-stone and all, she accidentally finds the match to the jagged piece of cloth she found in Mary's hand and proof that her death was not an accident. With the help of Robert, her fiancé, now returned from America, Anne identifies Mary's killer:

> Robert agrees with me that the hand of Providence must have guided my steps to that shop from which all the discoveries since made took their rise. He says he

believes we are the instruments of effecting a righteous retribution; and, if he spends his last farthing, he will have the investigation brought to its full end in a court of justice.

They track down the villain, cause his arrest, and testify both at police court and at his trial. He looks the part of a killer:

I could only look at him once. I could just see that he was a giant in size, and that he kept his dull, lowering, bestial face turned toward the witness-box, and his bloodshot, vacant eyes staring on me. For an instant I tried to confront that look; for an instant I kept my attention fixed on him — on his blotched face — on the short, grizzled hair above it — on his knotty, murderous right hand, hanging loose over the bar in front of him, like the paw of a wild beast over the edge of its den.

In the dock he confesses and cries out, asking to be hanged. Anne and Robert receive a surprise visit from Mary's lost brother who leaves them with a gift and the story ends on the morning of Anne's wedding.

"The Diary of Anne Rodway" certainly contains elements of detective fiction. Anne acts as a detective, there is physical evidence as well as discussion of judicial proof, and readers briefly witness an inquest, a police court inquiry, and a trial. All of these, however, are adjuncts to the sentiment in the story. And much of the sentiment — as in Dickens — derives from the fascination with death and its attendant rituals: Anne spends far more time and writes far more about Mary's funeral and grave (from which she picks a flower on her wedding morning) than seeking her killer. Indeed this is what most impressed Dickens when he finished reading Collins' story:

I cannot tell you what a high opinion I have of *Anne Rodway* ... I read the first part at the office with strong admiration, and read the second on the railway coming back here.... My behavior before my fellow-passengers was weak in the extreme, for I cried as much as you could possibly desire ... I think it excellent, feel a personal pride and pleasure in it, which is a delightful sensation, and I know no one else who could have done it [Dickens to Collins July 13, 1856].

Two years after "Anne Rodway" Collins returned to combining sentiment, crime, and detection in "A Marriage Tragedy" which *Harper's New Monthly Magazine* published in February 1858. Set in a frame story told to entertain a bored traveler, "A Marriage Tragedy" is about bigamy at the big house. Narrated by a trusted former servant — and model for Betteredge in *The Moonstone*— the story details the travails of Mrs. Norcross, a widow who unwisely chooses a roué as her second husband. Said roué abandons her using a sailing trip to Sweden as an excuse to leave. Months later Mrs. Norcross receives an anonymous letter alleging that her husband "has married another wife." To investigate this claim the family lawyer sends his clerk—"Don't trouble yourself about the cleverness or the cunning that may be wanted. My clerk has got head enough for two." When he arrives, however, the clerk, Mr. Dark, hardly conforms to the narrator's image of a lawyer's clerk or a detective:

> I had expected, from his master's description, to see a serious, sedate man, rather sly in his looks, and rather reserved in his manner. To my amazement, this practiced hand at delicate investigations was a brisk, plump, jolly little man, with a comfortable double chin, a pair of very bright black eyes, and a big bottle-nose of the true groggy red color. He wore a suit of black, and a limp, dingy white cravat; took snuff perpetually out of a very large box; walked with his hands crossed behind his back; and looked, upon the whole, much more like a parson of free-and-easy habits than a lawyer's clerk.

In Mr. Dark, William, the narrator, finds a shrewd investigator who knows his business:

> Next, what is our business? Not to risk losing a link in the chain of evidence by missing any place where he has put his foot on shore. Not to overshoot the mark when we want to hit it in the bull's-eye. Not to waste money and time by taking a long trip to Sweden till we know that we must absolutely go there. Where is our journey of discovery to take us to first, then? Clearly to the north of Scotland. What do you say to that, Mr. William? Is my catechism all correct, or has your strong ale muddled my head?"

As a result of Mr. Dark's investigations, they have the goods on the absconded husband:

> We can find him, if we want him, by inquiring at Cowes; and we can send to the church for legal evidence of the marriage as soon as we are instructed to do so. All that we have got to do now is to go back to your mistress, and see what course she means to take under the circumstances. Its a pretty case, William, so far an uncommonly pretty case, as it stands at present.

But Mrs. Norcoss, fearing scandal, refuses to take the matter to court. Unaware of this, the bigamist returns home in a brazen attempt to enrich his depleted purse. The day after his visit, however, his room is found to be empty, spots of blood are found there, and Josephine, Mrs. Norcross' French maid, accuses her of having murdered her bigamous husband. But once more Mr. Dark is on the case:

> "But, cunning as she is, I should not be surprised if Mr. Dark and I, together, turned out to be more than a match for her." Mr. Dark! There was something in the mere mention of his name that gave me confidence.

While he has found the missing husband, to avoid further scandal, Dark produces evidence that Josephine is a thief and uses that to convince her to retract her testimony. Mr. Dark and William then proceed back to the hall where the narrative concludes with Dark recounting the details of his investigations to William over a pitcher of ale.

In "A Marriage Tragedy" Collins took on an acutely sensitive topic rife with sentimental opportunities and, uncharacteristically, avoided at least some of them. Certainly choosing William, the naïve, optimistic, devoted servant, instead of the wronged wife as the narrator lessens the pathos potential of the story. But introducing the detective Mr. Dark and his works is the most significant achievement of "A Marriage Tragedy." Supremely confident and avuncular, Dark actually finds joy in what he does — qualities which infect the narrator. And it is also those qualities which set "A Marriage Tragedy" apart from the host of early Victorian lawyer stories which turn on marital difficulties.

Two months after "A Marriage Tragedy" Collins published another story about crime and detectives in an American magazine: "Who is the Thief?" appeared in *The Atlantic Monthly* in April 1858. It is the only one of Collins' early crime-linked stories devoid of sentiment and may be an extension of the good humor attached to law clerk detectives in the earlier stories. "Who is the Thief?" is a comic story told by means of the exchange of letters between Chief Inspector Theakstone of the Detective Police, Sergeant Bulmer of the same force, and Matthew Sharpin probationary detective. When he reprinted the story in *The Queen of Hearts* Collins added the following introduction:

> "Some years since," I continued, "there was a desire at head-quarters to increase the numbers and efficiency of the Detective Police, and I had the honor of being one of the persons privately consulted on that occasion. The chief obstacle to the plan proposed lay in the difficulty of finding new recruits. The ordinary rank and file of the police of London are sober, trustworthy, and courageous men, but as a body they are sadly wanting in intelligence. Knowing this, the authorities took into consideration a scheme, which looked plausible enough on paper, for availing themselves of the services of that proverbially sharp class of men, the experienced clerks in attorney's offices. Among the persons whose advice was sought on this point, I was the only one who dissented from the arrangement proposed. I felt certain that the really experienced clerks intrusted with conducting private investigations and hunting up lost evidence, were too well paid and too independently situated in their various offices to care about entering the ranks of the Detective Police, and submitting themselves to the rigid discipline of Scotland Yard, and I ventured to predict that the inferior clerks only, whose discretion was not to be trusted, would prove to be the men who volunteered for detective employment.

As the letters unfold they tell the story of ex-law clerk Matthew Sharpin who is sent to investigate an apparent robbery of £200 from Mr. Yatman, a stationer. Sharpin suspects Yatman's clerk, Jay, spies on him, follows him, and he and a couple of policemen go shadow Jay and a friend on what he believes to be a sinister mission only to find that Jay is going off to be married. Sergeant Bulmer intervenes and shows in a few minutes that Sharpin was completely wrong, that there was no robbery, and that Mrs. Yatman had abstracted the cash to pay off her milliner. From the first letter readers know that Sharpin is a pompous buffoon and that the experiment of admitting amateurs into the detective business is futile and a burden on the patience of the officials of the Detective Police. Here the apparent crime is not solved by patient and skillful sleuthing but from the superior knowledge possessed by policemen about human behavior.

Also in 1858 Collins published "The Poisoned Meal," which began with two of the five chapters printed as the lead article in *Household Words* on September 18, 1858. It is unlike anything Collins had done before. "The Poisoned Meal" later gained the subtitle "From the Records of the French Courts." The narrative concerns the misfortunes of Marie Franchise Victoire Salmon, a poor serving woman who is unjustly accused, arrested, tried, and condemned to death for using arsenic to poison a member of the family she served. The narrator details each misuse or abuse of evidence, and each misstep and violation of the law by the prosecution — and implies that they are intentional and perhaps the work of an official. It is by mere good fortune that the case manages to achieve national attention and the courts in Paris overturn the unjust verdict. Unlike the anti-capital punishment detective tales found in the *Chambers'* pieces and other mid-century fiction, "The Poisoned Meal," is not so much a protest about capital punishment but one about the misuse of evidence, a theme which the anonymous narrator brings home to readers by addressing question after open question to them about the legitimacy of the evidence used to convict Marie.

That Collins devoted a good deal of time to writing about crime did not entirely go unnoticed. J. Cordy Jeaffreson in his *Novels and Novelists* (1858) wrote:

> It is needless to say that Mr. Wilkie Collins is generally regarded as a man of commanding genius, and one destined to occupy a principal place in the republic of letters. For some time past his writings would lead one to think him as morbidly enamoured of the horrible and revolting as Edgar A. Poe, but we believe that in composing his terrible stories of crime and passion he is only passing through a phase of mental existence, that will be followed by the production of far nobler works than any that have as yet come from his pen [*Novels and Novelists*, 1858].

The year after this appraisal Collins brought together ten stories, including "A Marriage Tragedy," "Who is the Thief?" and "The Diary of Anne Rodway," wrote up a Scheherazade frame story and published them as *The Queen of Hearts* (1859). But during that year he also began a novel which was to contain an element of detection in it, *The Woman in White*.

The Woman in White

Wybert Reeve in *Recollections of Wilkie Collins* recounts learning of a trip to Paris taken by Collins and Dickens in 1856 and Collins' delight when he came upon a copy of Maurice Méjan's *Recueil des Causes Célèbres*: "I found some dilapidated volumes of French crimes, a sort of French Newgate Calendar. I said to Dickens, 'Here is a prize.' So it turned out to be." Relatively quickly he mined the book for material and used one of the cases as the basis for "The Poisoned Meal" in 1858. Then he came upon the cases of Marquise Marie de Douhault, a woman thought to be dead who instead had been imprisoned. That was the opening Collins needed for *The Woman in White*. On November 26, 1859, Dickens ran the first installment of *The Woman in White* in his new magazine *All the Year Round,* and on the same date it appeared in *Harper's Weekly* in the United States.

The plot of *The Woman in White* rests upon marital irregularities and their connection with the transfer of wealth, especially the transfer of wealth to women. As such it is in the tradition of the *Chambers'* barrister and attorney stories — as well as Collins' own "A Marriage Tragedy" and Collins' later book *No Name.* In *The Woman in White* the issues of marriage and the transfer of wealth lead to crimes: characters commit forgery, theft, perjury, kidnapping, false imprisonment, fraud, assault and battery, and miscellaneous other felonies and misdemeanors. Indeed, the principal action of the novel turns on identity theft and false imprisonment — both committed to wrest control of her wealth from Laura Fairlie. Inevitably the crimes in the book connect with righting wrongs and with the conventional machinery of justice. Indeed Collins seems to pay punctilious attention in the book to the role played by evidence in achieving justice. *The Woman in White* is chock full of examples of and talk about evidence. The main issue of the novel, of course, is how to prove that Laura Fairlie is not Anne Catherick and *vice versa*. This task occupies Walter Hartright and Marian Halcombe for a good portion of the book. First there is their search for physical evidence to prove that it is Laura and not Anne who was confined in the asylum. Then follows their search for the testimony of witnesses to confirm the same fact. Collins brings the search for evidence and its evaluation very much to the reader's attention. This occurs both in the form of traditional technique where the reader finds evidence in the narrative with which to evaluate a character's character — Laura's Italian greyhound, for example, hops into Walter's lap but with Sir Percival: "The little beast ... looked up at him sharply, shrank away from his outstretched hand, whined, shivered, and hid itself under a sofa." But more important than this, on the first page Collins tells the reader that he has framed the entire novel in a manner that allows the reader impartial access to evidence:

As the Judge might once have heard it, so the Reader shall hear it now. No circumstance of importance, from the beginning to the end of the disclosure, shall be related on hearsay evidence. When the writer of these introductory lines (Walter Hartright, by name) happens to be more closely connected than others with the incidents to be recorded, he will describe them in his own person. When his experience fails, he will retire from the position of narrator; and his task will be continued, from the point at which he has left it off, by other persons who can speak to the circumstances under notice from their own knowledge, just as clearly and positively as he has spoken before them.

Thus, the story here presented will be told by more than one pen, as the story of an offence against the laws is told in Court by more than one witness — with the same object, in both cases, to present the truth always in its most direct and most intelligible aspect; and to trace the course of one complete series of events, by making the persons who have been most closely connected with them, at each successive stage, relate their own experience, word for word.

It turns out, however, that Collins introduces evidence only as a means to an end — and that end is working upon the reader's emotions. Searching for both physical proof and witness' testimony to prove Laura's identity repeatedly leads the characters (and the reader) only to a mounting series of frustrations which end in the fire that destroys both Sir Percival and the physical evidence of the crime that lay at the basis of all of the other crimes in the book. In the end, Walter's quest to prove Laura's identity ends not with judicial proof but only when he resorts to threats and intimidation rather than detective work. And Collins has practiced the same kind of illusion on the reader in the structure of the novel. While his analogy comparing the structure of *The Woman in White* to testimony before a judge holds insofar as it concerns the unfolding of events, it has nothing to do with the reader's perception of "the truth always in its most direct and most intelligible aspect." From the beginning the reader knows that Sir Percival and Fosco are villains and that Laura is Laura and that Anne is Anne. Thus Collins' pseudo-epistolary technique in *The Woman in White* has more to do with creating suspense than with proving anything.

And *The Woman in White* has more to do with sentiment and suffering than with evidence or justice. Thus Collins began the novel not with the talk about judges and evidence but with the assertion: "This is the story of what a Woman's patience can endure, and what a Man's resolution can achieve." So frustration and persecution reside at the center of the book. And who better to frustrate and persecute than the innocent and powerless? Here Collins presents the travails of two helpless and innocent women — the slightly disabled Anne Catherick rejected by her mother and mousey Laura Fairlie with her spineless nincompoop uncle as a guardian — both of whom he dresses in white. Opposed to them are Sir Percival Glyde and Count Fosco who possess position, power, and wealth which they employ to take power from Anne, Laura, as well as from their would-be protectors, Marian and Hartright. In fact, Collins goes so far as making Count Fosco the spokesman for the doctrine that both human and divine justice are illusions and that evil can prevail and crime can and does pay:

> "It is truly wonderful," he said, "how easily Society can console itself for the worst of its shortcomings with a little bit of clap-trap. The machinery it has set up for the detection crime is miserably ineffective — and yet only invent a moral epigram, saying that it works well, and you blind everybody to its blunders from that moment. Crimes cause their own detection, do they? And murder will out (another moral epigram), will it? Ask Coroners who sit at inquests in large towns if that is true, Lady Glyde. Ask secretaries of life-assurance companies if that is true, Miss Halcombe. Read your own public journals. In the few cases that get into the newspapers, are there not instances of slain bodies found, and no murderers ever discovered? Multiply the cases that are reported by the cases that are *not* reported, and the bodies that are found by the bodies that are *not* found, and what conclusion do you come to? This. That there are foolish criminals who are discovered, and wise criminals who escape. The hiding of a crime, or the detection of a crime, what is it? A trial of skill between the police on one side, and the individual on the other. When the criminal is a brutal, ignorant fool, the police in nine cases out of ten win. When the criminal is a resolute, educated, highly-intelligent man, the police in nine cases out of ten lose. If the police win, you generally hear all about it. If the police lose, you generally hear nothing. And on this tottering foundation you build up your comfortable moral maxim that Crime causes its own detection! Yes — all the crime *you* know of. And what of the rest?"

In addition to these assaults on his characters, Collins folds in technique to work on the reader's complacency and comfort. It's one of the results of the distributed story-telling, in the hiccup caused where one narrator's voice stops and another begins. It's also the reason that Collins works in so many temptations for the reader to make wrong conclusions — take the uncertainty of Anne Catherick's parentage, for instance. And finally it's one of the reasons his narrators pose so many questions which they cannot at that moment answer; in the first narrative, for instance, Walter Heartright poses forty questions in chapter 4, a 3,500-word section.

Define Sensation

It is hardly a secret that *The Woman in White* immediately became a blockbuster best seller on both sides of the Atlantic as soon as its installments began appearing. At the same time that the novel achieved heady popularity among readers it also prompted a number of writers to follow Collins' example and yet others to begin to think about contemporary literature and the place of these new kinds of novels therein. First off, a number of people in the early 1860s saw the evolution of a genre which the publication of *The Woman in White* helped them classify (sometimes pejoratively) as "sensation novels." Thus this piece from *The Living Age* in 1863 tries to explain what this class of fiction does:

> Sensation writing is an appeal to the nerves rather than to the heart; but all exciting fiction works upon the nerves, and Shakespeare can make "every partic-ular hair to stand on end" with anybody. We suppose that the true sensation novel feels the popular pulse with this view alone — considers any close fidelity to nature a slavish subservience injurious to effect, and willingly and designedly draws a picture of life which shall make reality insipid and the routine of ordi-nary existence intolerable to the imagination. To use *Punch's* definition in the prospectus of the *Sensation Times,* "It devotes itself to harrowing the mind, mak-ing the flesh creep, causing the hair to stand on end, giving shocks to the nerv-ous system, destroying conventional moralities, and generally unfitting the public for the prosaic avocations of life."

In the best-known of these early definitions, Margaret Oliphant in her essay "Sensation Novels" in *Blackwood's Magazine* 1862 both tagged *The Woman in White* as a "sensation novel," and singled out what she thought made it the best example of the form:

> A writer who boldly takes in hand the common mechanism of life, and by means of persons who might all be living in society for anything we can tell to the con-trary, thrills us into wonder, terror, and breathless interest, with positive per-sonal shocks of surprise and excitement, has accomplished a far greater success than he who offers the same result through supernatural agencies, or by means of the fantastic creations of lawless genius or violent horrors of crime.

On top of describing Collins' work as a novel designed to stimulate the reader's emotions, early on critics defined a subset of sensation novels as "enigma nov-els" and pasted that label too on *The Woman in White*. The first definition of the enigma novel appeared in *The Spectator* (December 28, 1861) in which the anonymous writer began his essay:

> We are threatened with a new variety of the sensation novel, a host of cleverly complicated stories, the whole interest of which consists in the gradual unravel-ing of some carefully prepared enigma. Mr. Wilkie Collins set the fashion, and now every novel writer who can construct a plot, thinks if he only makes it a lit-tle more mysterious and unnatural, he may obtain a success rivaling the "Woman in White."

Two years later in "Old Recollections and Modern Contrasts" (*Dublin Uni-versity Magazine* April 1863) the writer specifically connects Collins — and the enigma novel — to Poe:

Three kinds of novels are just now in fashion: the enigma novel, the class novel, the sensation novel. The great living master of the enigma novel is Mr. Wilkie Collins. He is unrivalled at a charade in three volumes. In "No Name" as in the "Woman in White," he has puzzled the public admirably. Yet, after all, he is a poor imitator of Edgar Poe. There is more originality in any one of Poe's short tales — "The Purloined Letter," for example — than in Mr. Collins's most complicated construction. Both writers put a tale together as a skilful lockmaker does a difficult lock; the various parts fit into each other with wonderful accuracy, and the keenest intellect cannot find a way through the difficulty.

In the same year yet another term was coined which critics applied to books about crime and criminals:

From vice to crime, from the divorce-court to the police court, is but a single step. When fashionable immorality becomes insipid, the materials for sensation may still be found hot and strong in the "Newgate Calendar"; especially if the crime is of recent date, having the merits of personality and proximity to give it a nervous as well as a moral effect. Unhappily, the materials for such excitement are not scanty, and an author who condescends to make use of them need have little difficulty in selecting the most available. Let him only keep an eye on the criminal reports of the daily newspapers, marking the cases which are honoured with the especial notice of a leading article, and become a nine-days' wonder in the mouths of quidnuncs and gossips; and he has the outline of his story not only ready-made, but approved beforehand as of the true sensation cast. Then, before the public interest has had time to cool, let him serve up the exciting viands in a réchauffe' with a proper amount of fictitious seasoning; and there emerges the criminal variety of the Newspaper Novel, a class of fiction having about the same relation to the genuine historical novel that the police reports of the "Times" have to the pages of Thucydides or Clarendon [*The Quarterly Review* 1863].

Not only does this review define the newspaper novel as a subset of the sensation novel, it goes on to give readers yet another subset of the form:

Of particular offences, which are almost always contemporary and sometimes personal, undoubtedly the first place must be given to Bigamy. Indeed, so popular has this crime become, as to give rise to an entire sub-class in this branch of literature, which may be distinguished as that of Bigamy Novels. It is astonishing how many of our modern writers have selected this interesting breach of morality and law as the peg on which to hang a mystery and a denouement. Of the tales on our list, no less than eight are bigamy stories: — "Lady Audley's Secret," "Aurora Floyd," "Clinton Maynyard," "Recommended to Mercy," "The Law of Divorce," "The Daily Governess," "Only a Woman," "The Woman of Spirit," all hang their narrative, wholly or in part, on bigamy in act, or bigamy in intention, on the existence or supposed existence of two wives to the same husband, or two husbands to the same wife ["Sensation Novels," *The Quarterly Review*, 1863].

Whether sensation novel, enigma novel, or newspaper novel, it's clear that the success of *The Woman in White* served as inspiration for publishers and for new writers on both sides of the Atlantic to add crime, marital difficulties, evidence, and detection to their novels centered on suffering women. First there was Ellen (Mrs. Henry) Wood. To the adultery of Lady Isabel and its attendant travail in *East Lynne* (serialized in the *New Monthly Magazine* beginning in 1860), she added a subplot concerning the murder of George Hallijohn which involves a number of references to evidence but largely turns on accident and coincidence. But in the early 1860s even more than Wood or even Collins the principal sensation writer who used crime and detectives in her work was Mary Elizabeth Braddon.

Mary Braddon Makes Her Mark

The same year the run of *The Woman in White* ended in *All the Year Round* and *Harper's,* Mary Elizabeth Braddon began to play her part in making the detective a popular figure in the novels of the 1860s when the first of the 27 episodes of her first novel, *The Trail of the Serpent,* began to be published in Beverley, Yorkshire. In the sensation line *The Trail of the Serpent* has it all: it begins with the murder of a sick child followed quickly by another murder, a suicide, the conviction of an innocent man, imprisonment in an asylum, a super-sized villain, a forced marriage, two foundlings, false identity, poisoning, a mother's sorrow, and more. *The Trail of the Serpent,* like other sensation novels, predicates it structure on a pattern of crime at the beginning and evidence presented to prove guilt at the end of the novel — with a lot of harumscarum material stuffed in between. Most significantly, however, *The Trail of the Serpent* introduces a police detective as one of its principal characters. From the beginning of the novel Joe Peters, a provincial detective, knows that Richard Marwood is innocent, saves him from the hangman by suggesting an insanity defense, helps him escape from the madhouse, goes to London in the capacity of a private detective, sees through the assumed identity of the villain, visits the crime scene (albeit more than eight years later) and with a band of Marwood's chums discovers the physical evidence necessary to free the wronged innocent and bring his uncle's killer to justice. Although clearly not of his class, Marwood depends upon Peters to figure things out, for Peters possesses both acumen and sympathetic psychological insight:

> Now, what a detective officer's good at, if he's worth his salt, is this 'ere: when he sees two here and another two there, he can put 'em together, though they might be a mile apart to anybody not up to the trade, and make 'em into four. So, thinks I, the gent isn't took aback at bein' arrested; but he is took aback when he hears as how his uncle's murdered.

But Braddon also gives her readers a detective who has overcome a significant difficulty:

> It was a compressed mouth with thin lips, which tightened and drew themselves rigidly together when the man thought — and the man was almost always thinking: and this was not all, for when he thought most deeply the mouth shifted in a palpable degree to the left side of his face. This was the only thing remarkable about the man, except, indeed, that he was dumb but not deaf, having lost the use of his speech during a terrible illness which he had suffered in his youth.

While limited to finger spelling, Peters achieves the admiration of his fellow police officers by solving crimes and rises through the ranks — even before bringing the master villain, Jabez North, to justice. And along his jaunty attitude he picks up a foundling whom he adopts and a plucky wife — all surely reminiscent of Dickens. None of this, however, is artfully or subtly done, and the breakneck pace of the action and the stereotyped characters remind readers of the kind of simplistic, non-stop thrills that would be found in American dime novels in later decades.

Hot on the heels of her first novel Braddon wrote the book that was to make her famous — *Lady Audley's Secret.* The first episodes appeared in John Maxwell's *Robin Goodfellow* in July 1861 and when that magazine folded the final chapters appeared in the *Sixpenny Magazine*. Switching from the larger-than-life male villain she used in *The Trail of the Serpent*, here Braddon gave her readers a really bad woman to ooh and ah over. Lady Audley's secret is that, in truth, she is not Lady Audley but Lucy Graham Talboys, a young woman who, apparently abandoned by her husband, jumps at the chance to move up in the world by marrying Sir Michael Audley. Except George Talboys isn't dead but has slunk off to Australia to make his fortune. Upon returning to England with said fortune, George and his friend Robert Audley find his father-in-law and son but are told that his wife is dead (which she is decidedly not). Robert takes George to meet his uncle and his new wife, but they keep on missing meeting the new wife. And then George goes missing and Robert takes it upon himself to find out what happened to his friend. This opens up the search for evidence:

> I do not think that the woman who bears my uncle's name, is worthy to be his wife. I may wrong her. Heaven grant that it is so. But if I do, the fatal chain of circumstantial evidence never yet linked itself so closely about an innocent person. I wish to set my doubts at rest or — or to confirm my fears. There is but one manner in which I can do this. I must trace the life of my uncle's wife backward, minutely and carefully, from this night to a period of six years ago.

And in this Robert plays the role of the detective:

> "Circumstantial evidence," continued the young man, as if he scarcely heard Lady Audley's interruption — "that wonderful fabric which is built out of straws

collected at every point of the compass, and which is yet strong enough to hang a man. Upon what infinitesimal trifles may sometimes hang the whole secret of some wicked mystery, inexplicable heretofore to the wisest upon the earth! A scrap of paper, a shred of some torn garment, the button off a coat, a word dropped incautiously from the overcautious lips of guilt, the fragment of a letter, the shutting or opening of a door, a shadow on a window-blind, the accuracy of a moment tested by one of Benson's watches — a thousand circumstances so slight as to be forgotten by the criminal, but links of iron in the wonderful chain forged by the science of the detective officer; and lo! the gallows is built up; the solemn bell tolls through the dismal gray of the early morning, the drop creaks under the guilty feet, and the penalty of crime is paid."

But Robert is no detective officer. Indeed Braddon — and other sensation writers — realized that the character of the official detective might be inimical to the purposes of the sensation novel. She puts one of the reasons rather bluntly in *Lady Audley's Secret*:

He had dropped away from his old friends. How could he sit among them, at social wine parties, perhaps, or at social little dinners, that were washed down with nonpareil and chambertin, pomard and champagne? How could he sit among them, listening to their careless talk of politics and opera, literature and racing, theaters and science, scandal and theology, and yet carry in his mind the horrible burden of those dark terrors and suspicions that were with him by day and by night? He could not do it! He had shrunk from those men as if he had, indeed, been a detective police officer, stained with vile associations and unfit company for honest gentlemen.

But it is not only that the police detective is "unfit for the company of honest men." The purpose of *Lady Audley's Secret* lies in using crimes and apparent crimes to titillate and surprise the readers rather than to permit them to observe the business of finding and rationally evaluating evidence; it is to stimulate rather than to satisfy the reader's curiosity:

But there is the skill which carries a story through a steeple-chase of incidents, and never let the reader's curiosity flag. By artful suggestions we are made to believe that the woman whose illness, death, and burial seem authentically proved, is still living in triumphant wickedness. Who was buried in her name? And how was the substitution effected? Here is one mystery. Then for another, there is the sudden disappearance of a man: what has become of him? Is he dead — murdered? If so, how, and by whom? By simply hinting these things, and by never allowing the reader to be present at the scenes thus suggested, the author is master of our curiosity, and can take his own time and means for gratifying it. When the explanations of these mysteries are given, it is true that they turn out absurdly incredible; but by that time you have finished the book [*Cornhill Magazine* 1863].

Robert Audley, of course, figures Lucy's imposture out — hardly much of a surprise since the reader pretty much knows what is going on relatively early in the novel. The really "absurdly incredible" revelation at the end of the novel, however, is that George Talboys did not really die when his wife tipped him down the well in the first third of the book but climbed out and took himself back to Australia without telling anyone. Thus Braddon both satisfies readers by revealing the truth of Lady Audley's past and her incarceration in a mad house and then she gives them the surprise of George's survival. While her use of surprise at the end of *Lady Audley's Secret* seems to approximate those found in Dickens and later in *The Moonstone,* it lacks the kind of careful preparation that would make the laying of clues an essential part of the detective story.

Collins in the Meantime

In the early 1860s Wilkie Collins had hardly been idle. In March 1862 installments of *No Name* began to appear in *All the Year Round. No Name* like *The Woman in White* rests on issues concerned with marriage and the transfer of wealth — here illegitimacy which becomes identity theft. Unlike the woman as victim in the earlier novel, in *No Name* Magdalen Vanstone takes it upon herself to retrieve her lost inheritance. While there are no real detective issues in the novel, Collins does introduce Sergeant Bulmer from "Who is the Thief" as a very minor character. Two years after chronicling Magdalen Vanstone's disguises and plots, in November 1864 the first installment of *Armadale* appeared in *Cornhill Magazine* and later that year in *Harper's New Monthly Magazine* in the U.S. In *Armadale* once more Collins was concerned with identity — the two principal characters bear the same name — and a larger than life villain *à la* Count Fosco from *The Woman in White*. This time, however, in the mode Braddon and Wood brought into fashion, his larger-than-life villain is a woman, one Lydia Gwilt who is willing and able to commit most crimes in order to possess Allan Armadale's fortune. While Collins inserts an exciting episode in which a murder is narrowly averted, *Armadale* has very little to do with detectives or detection. Indeed while Collins does introduce a private detective and uses the detective's report as a plot device, the narrator expresses loathing toward both the man and his profession:

> No ordinary observation, applying the ordinary rules of analysis, would have detected the character of Bashwood the younger in his face. His youthful look, aided by his light hair and his plump, beardless cheeks, his easy manner and his ever-ready smile, his eyes which met unshrinkingly the eyes of every one whom he addressed, all combined to make the impression of him a favorable impression in the general mind. No eye for reading character, but such an eye as belongs to one person, perhaps, in ten thousand, could have penetrated the smoothly

deceptive surface of this man, and have seen him for what he really was — the
vile creature whom the viler need of Society has fashioned for its own use. There
he sat — the Confidential Spy of modern times, whose business is steadily enlarg-
ing, whose Private Inquiry Offices are steadily on the increase. There he sat — the
necessary Detective attendant on the progress of our national civilization; a man
who was, in this instance at least, the legitimate and intelligible product of the
vocation that employed him; a man professionally ready on the merest suspicion
(if the merest suspicion paid him) to get under our beds, and to look through
gimlet-holes in our doors; a man who would have been useless to his employers
if he could have felt a touch of human sympathy in his father's presence; and
who would have deservedly forfeited his situation if, under any circumstances
whatever, he had been personally accessible to a sense of pity or a sense of
shame.

So in *Armadale* Collins moved decidedly away from finding evidence and
solving crimes as the core of his novels and into the same world being exploited
by the women writers of the early 1860s, the world of sensation.

Expert Witnesses

Almost coincident with the publication of *No Name*, in the fall of 1862
Charles Felix published the first episode of *The Notting Hill Mystery* in the
journal *Once a Week*. Whoever Charles Felix was, he pretty clearly patterned
his serial on two of the most remarked upon features of *The Woman in White* —
its narrative "told by more than one pen, as the story of an offence against
the laws is told in Court by more than one witness" and the character of the
larger-than-life villain, Count Fosco. In its narrative technique, *The Notting
Hill Mystery* out–Collinses both *The Woman in White* and *The Moonstone* in
that except for thin framework providing minimal background it is largely
an epistolary novel which calls upon the reader to piece the story together.
That framework is supplied by one Ralph Henderson who, like Nadgett in
Martin Chuzzlewit, is a private enquiry agent for a life assurance company.
The body of the short novel consists exclusively of letters and depositions
submitted as testimony regarding (1) the background and fate of the Bolton
sisters (one of whom had been stolen by gypsies), and (2) their deaths occasioned by poison. The letters build a case that Baron R**, a charismatic practitioner of mesmerism (as well as expert chemist and physician), was
responsible for poisoning both his wife and her sister in order to possess their
inheritance as well as the value of the life insurance in question. On one hand
The Notting Hill Mystery has plenty of sentimental potential — not one but
two sisters being slowly poisoned, a loving husband falsely accused of murdering his wife, as well as mesmerism and the Baron's influence over both his

wife and her sister, which perhaps served as at least partial inspiration for George du Maurier's, the book's illustrator, novel *Trilby* (1894). On the other hand, instead of focusing on its sentimental potential, *The Notting Hill Mystery* focuses on forensic matters and invites readers' participation in solving the crimes. Felix is careful about citing the dates and nature of the sisters' symptoms and, in fact, calls readers' attention to them. Indeed *The Notting Hill Mystery* is the first in the genre to present readers with a floor plan to ponder in their musings on how the crimes were committed. Felix also pays particular attention to supplying them with expert testimony regarding poisons by providing letters from physicians and chemists containing citations from one of the founders of forensic science, Alfred Swaine Taylor (probably from his *On Poisons in Relation to Medical Jurisprudence and Medicine*, 1848). Simultaneously, however, as the testimony unfolds Felix also invites skepticism by having witnesses subtly inform his readers that their observations may, or may not, be faulty. Thus Dr. Marsdon's letter regarding the lack of evidence of poison in the analysis of the contents of one of the sister's stomachs:

> I trusted to those of the Baron, because I knew him to be an expert practical chemist, and in the daily habit of such operations. My own share in them was limited to the observation of results, and their comparison with those pointed out by Professor Taylor. I did not take any special pains to ascertain the purity of the chemical tests employed, or of their being in fact what they were assumed to be. That is to say, when a colourless liquid with all the apparent characteristics of nitric acid was taken from a bottle labeled "Nit. Ac." I took for granted that nitric acid was being employed. Similarly, of course, with the other chemical agents. It never occurred to me to do otherwise.

Perhaps because of its attention to problem solving as opposed to sentiment, *The Notting Hill Mystery* did not make a lot of noise — it was not reprinted after 1865 and was not printed in the U.S. until 1976.

Back to Braddon

In 1862 at the same time that *The Notting Hill Mystery* hit the streets, Braddon checked in with the second of her bigamy novels, *Aurora Floyd*, published serially in *Temple Bar*. The motivating problem of the book is that the young, beautiful, and rich Aurora Floyd while in finishing school in France went off and married a rotter. She leaves him — and pays him off to gain her freedom. Back in England she is courted by two upstanding, love-stricken men who both propose marriage. And she marries John Mellish on the condition that he not inquire into her secret. The rotter husband, James Conyers, returns to England, takes a job as trainer of Mellish's racing horses, and begins

once more to extort money from Aurora. Then he's found shot dead and
Aurora's past comes to light — along with some authorial comment about the
state of England's divorce law:

> Had she, upon the discovery of the first husband's infidelity, called the law to
> her aid — she was rich enough to command its utmost help, though Sir Cresswell
> Cresswell did not then keep the turnpike upon such a royal road to divorce as he
> does now — she might have freed herself from the hateful chains so foolishly
> linked together, and might have defied this dead man to torment or assail her.
>
> But she had chosen to follow the counsel of expediency, and it had led her
> upon the crooked way through which I have striven to follow her. I feel that
> there is much need of apology for her.

Although in *Lady Audley's Secret* Braddon had characterized detectives
as "stained with vile associations and unfit company for honest gentlemen,"
in *Aurora Floyd* she returned to using the detective as the one who solves the
problems of the carriage trade. Three quarters of the way through the novel
she introduces Joseph Grimstone "of Scotland Yard and Ball's Pond" and the
rest of the book is pretty much his. From his first appearance Grimstone puts
the rich folks on notice: "If Mr. Mellish is prepared to act on the square, I'm
prepared to act with him, and to accept any reward his generosity may offer.
But if he or any friend of his wants to hoodwink Joseph Grimstone, he'd
better think twice about the game before he tries it on — that's all." And he
lets them know that as a professional he knows what he's doing:

> "Well, sir, I've had a hard day's work," the detective answered, gravely, "and per-
> haps neither of you gentlemen — not being professional — would think much of
> what I've done. But, for all that, I believe I'm bringin' it home, sir; I believe I'm
> bringin' it home."

And in fact the rich folks — as well as the narrator — watch him with awe:

> There was something almost miraculous in the manner in which Mr. Joseph
> Grimstone contrived to make himself master of any information which he
> wished to acquire; and before noon on the day after his interview with Mr.
> Dawson, the gardener, he had managed to eliminate all the facts set down above,
> and had also succeeded in ingratiating himself into the confidence of the dirty
> old proprietress of that humble lodging in which the softy had taken up his
> abode.

Braddon, however, makes it clear that money helps to motivate Grimstone:

> Now the truth of the matter is that Mr. Joseph Grimstone was not, perhaps, act-
> ing quite so conscientiously in this business as he might have done, had the love
> of justice in the abstract, and without any relation to sublunary reward, been the
> ruling principle of his life. He might have had any help he pleased from the
> Doncaster constabulary, had he chosen to confide in the members of that force;

but as a very knowing individual who owns a three-year old which he has reason to believe "a flyer" is apt to keep the capabilities of his horse a secret from his friends and the sporting public while he puts a "pot" of money upon the animal at enormous odds, so Mr. Grimstone desired to keep his information to himself until it should have brought him its golden fruit, in the shape of a small reward from government and a large one from John Mellish.

Be that as it may, Braddon has Grimstone solve the complex crime problem she contrived for him. He finds a brass button at the scene of the crime and takes it to a "medical practitioner" where he learns:

> The stains upon it were indeed that which the detective had supposed, blood; and the surgeon detected a minute morsel of cartilage adhering to the jagged hasp of the button; but the same surgeon declared that this missile could not have been the only one used by the murderer of James Conyers. It had not been through the dead man's body; it had inflicted only a surface wound.

Patient research enables him to identify the owner of the waistcoat from which the button was torn. But more importantly — much in the manner that later detective story writers would offer endless variations on a clever theme — Braddon took Dickens' use of pistol wadding as a clue in *Bleak House* and turned it into the murderer's use of a button from his vest as wadding for the pistol ball that killed Conyers.

In a piece entitled "Newgate Novels" run in *Every Month* in July 1864 the writer decries the recent influx of novels featuring detectives, and among the perpetrators singles out Mary Braddon:

> Detectives are becoming very prominent just now, and Miss Braddon has found unlimited auxiliaries in such personages for her plot. The whole of "Henry Dunbar," from beginning to end, is a series of chapters on those human ferrets; and of course the doings of the detective assume the most romantic hues and "cries." The ordinary duties of the detective are generally surrounded with a large degree of pictorial superstition, but when examined are found to be commonplace enough. Detectives are very useful scavengers, and are used by police authorities with a view merely for the exercise of particular, mean, contemptible cunning. Anyone sufficiently deficient in manliness to accept of the duties is very eagerly enrolled.... He gets paid, and loathed at the same time!

Braddon's detective in *Henry Dunbar* (1864) is Mr. Carter whose character contradicts that of the reviewer:

> If I had been a happy man, with no great trouble weighing upon my mind, and giving its own dull color to every event of my life, I think I might have been considerably entertained by the society of Mr. Carter, the detective. The man had an enthusiastic love of his profession; and if there is anything degrading in the office, its degradation had in no way affected him. It may be that Mr. Carter's knowledge of his own usefulness was sufficient to preserve his self-respect. If, in the course of his duty, he had unpleasant things to do; if he had to

affect friendly acquaintanceship with the man whom he was inviting to the gallows; if he was called upon to worm out chance clues to guilty secrets in the
careless confidence that grows out of a friendly glass; if at times he had to stoop
to acts which, in other men, would he branded as shameful and treacherous, he
knew that he did his duty, and that society could not hold together useless some
such men as himself— clear-headed, brave, resolute, and unscrupulous in the
performance of unpleasant work — were willing to act as watchdogs for the protection of the general fold, and dire terror of savage and marauding beasts.

A Plurality of Detectives

Carter, however, is only one of the many detectives featured in novels
of the early 1860s. Ellen Wood went into the detective business shortly after
East Lynne and introduced Mr. Butterby in *The Channings* (1862):

> Mr. Butterby puzzled Helstonleigh. He was not an inspector, he was not a ser-
> geant, he was not a common officer, and he was never seen in official dress. Who
> was Mr. Butterby? Helstonleigh wondered. That he had a great deal to do with
> the police, was one of their staff, and received his pay, was certain; but, what his
> standing might be, and what his peculiar line of duty, they could not tell. Some-
> times he was absent from Helstonleigh for months at a time, probably puzzling
> other towns. Mr. Galloway would have told you he was a detective; but perhaps
> Mr. Galloway's grounds for the assertion existed only in his own opinion. For
> convenience-sake we will call him a detective; remembering, however, that we
> have no authority for the term.

And in the next year in *The Castle's Heir* she gave her readers Detective
Blair:

> A Telegraphic despatch went up to London in the course of the following day. It
> was sent by Lord Dane, and received by the head police-office in Scotland Yard.
> On the morning after, Bruff informed Lord Dane that a gentleman, a stranger,
> was at the castle, asking to see him.
> As the reader may surmise, it was one of the chief detectives, come down in
> obedience to the demand of Lord Dane. He bore about him no outward signs of
> his profession; was in plain clothes, and a free-speaking, agreeable man,— one
> who had received a liberal education, and was well read. His name was Blair.

The year 1863 also saw Albany De Fonblanque's portrait of a detective
in *A Tangled Skein*:

> The good woman made a few shillings a week by the sale of this class of litera-
> ture; but her main profit was not from thence. She had a lodger. Her parlors
> were let to a Mr. Sampson Lagger, a gentleman of irregular habits and varying
> appearance. Sometimes he was a slim gentleman, closely buttoned up in a frock
> coat. Sometimes he was a stout gentleman in an Inverness cape. Sometimes he
> was a young gentleman, apparently from the country, smoking a cigar. Some-

times he was an old gentleman in spectacles; but always a merry, kind-spoken gentleman, with a great thirst for information upon all sorts of topics. He had a latch-key, had Sampson Lagger, and came in and out without question. Little Helen gave it as her opinion, that he was doing low comedy business at some theatre, and did not always change his dress when he came home at nights ; and, truly, Mr. Lagger played many parts, but upon a stage larger than that of Covent Garden or the Britannia. Sometimes he would come in regularly, every evening, at nine, for a fortnight, and then would pack up two shirts and a pair of socks in a clean pocket-handkerchief, and not be seen again for a month.

In 1864 James Payn who began as a contributor to Dickens' *Household Words* and ended as editor of *Chambers' Journal* added to the growing number of police detectives in sensation novels with his *The Lost Sir Massingbred* (begun in *Chambers'* January 2, 1864) in which he introduced a fictionalized portrait of John Townshend (1760–1832) perhaps the most celebrated Bow Street Runner. Indeed,

there was scarcely a more public character than Townshend, or better known both to the classes whom he protected, and to that against which he waged such constant war. His personal appearance was itself sufficiently remarkable. A short squab man, in a light wig, kerseymere breeches and a blue Quaker-cut coat, he was not, to look at, a very formidable object. But he possessed the courage of a lion, and the cunning of a fox. The ruffians who kept society in terror, themselves quailed before *him*. They knew that he was hard to kill, and valued not his own life one rush, when duty called upon him to hazard it; that he was faithful as a watch-dog to the government which employed him, and hated by nature a transgressor of the law, as a watch-dog hates a wolf. When Townshend fairly settled himself down upon the track of an offender, the poor wretch felt like the hare whose fleeing footsteps the stoat relentlessly pursues; he might escape for the day, or even the morrow, but sooner or later his untiring foe was certain to be up with him. In those early days, when the telegraph could not overtake the murderer speeding for his life, and set Justice upon her guard five hundred miles away, to intercept him, and when the sun was not the slave of the Law, to photograph the features of the doomed criminal, so that he can be recognized as easily as Cain, thief-catching was a much more protracted business than it is now; nevertheless, it was at least as certain.

When any considerable sum was sent by mail-coach, whether by the government or by London bankers, to their provincial agents, it was not unusual to employ Mr. Townshend as an escort. Nor was it altogether unexampled for him to be sent for, as in the present instance, to unravel some domestic mystery; although he was perhaps the first police-officer who had been so employed, the father of all the Fields and Pollakies of the present day. He was on intimate terms, therefore, with many great people, and an especial favorite with the court, his professional services being engaged at all drawing-rooms and state occasions.

And in 1866 Annie Edwards introduced Inspector Wickam in her novel *Archie Lovell*:

Mrs. Sherborne started up to her feet; her horror at the sickening sight she had been newly forced to look upon; her grief— and very real grief it was — at the confirmation of her fears; every conflicting emotion of her heart swelled up in the one overwhelming terror of her being in the presence of a detective. This mild, middle-aged gentleman to whom she had talked so freely, and who had lionized the city, and given her his arm so pleasantly, a detective! One of that dread force who with a lightning glance, a seemingly careless question, can worm out all secrets from the human breast, and deliver men up, whether dukes or beggars, to the dread retribution of justice. A detective: and to realize what Mrs. Sherborne felt it must be recollected that her belief in the infallible, almost omniscient, sharpness of the corps was the purely popular one: derived principally from weekly serials, and holding as much resemblance to the real defective officer of every-day life as the popular Jesuit, the malignant, fanatical fiend of Protestant stories, does to the pleasant *poco curante* gentlemen of the Society of Jesus, who sit beside you at a dinner party.

Indeed, during the decade of the 1860s the detective became almost a standard character in English novels. In addition to the above, there was Detective Meadows in Harriet Maria Gordon's *Guilty or Not Guilty* (1864), Detective Smart in John Saunder's *One Against the World* (1865), Detective Bales in *The Tallants of Barton* by Joseph Hatton (1867), Private Detective Barton in Henty's *All But Lost* (1869), and Detective Green in Charles Reade's *Hard Cash* (1869).

Sensation Crosses the Atlantic

It wasn't just in Britain that what might be called the School of Collins absorbed the interest of the reading public in the early 1860s; the same thing was going on in the United States. As noted above, serial versions of Collins' novels appeared in *Harpers' Weekly* and their publishing house issued Braddon's *Aurora Floyd* in 1863. In that same year Dick and Fitzgerald of detective "notebook" fame printed book versions of *Lady Audley's Secret* and *Henry Dunbar*, and, as in Britain, a play based on *Lady Audley's Secret* hit the boards in the U.S. During the Civil War the same books were published in the Confederacy: Braddon's *Aurora Floyd* was published in Richmond in 1863 as was Ellen Wood's *East Lynne* in 1864 while *Lady Audley's Secret* was published in Mobile in that same year.

In 1865 Erastus Beadle, the man who invented the dime novel, wanted to move up in the world by publishing a magazine patterned on *Harper's*, and thus *Beadle's Monthly* was born — to last only three years. Perhaps because *Harper's* had published the serial versions of Collins' sensation novels in the United States, Beadle turned to Metta Victor (aka Seeley Register), one of his house writers, and in January 1866 began printing episodes of *The Dead Letter*, a novel originally published in 1864 (see "The House of Beadle and Adams": www.ulib.niu.edu/badndp). While decidedly of the sensation persuasion, *The Dead Letter* gives the murder mystery and detectives a more central role than in the works of any of the English sensation writers. The murder of Henry Moreland, the fiancé of Eleanor Argyll, its repercussions on the Argyll family, and the protracted search for the murderer form the substance of the novel from the discovery of the body in chapter two until the exposure of the murder conspiracy at the end of the book. To be sure Victor adheres pretty closely to the motto of the genre as stated by Collins with reference to *The Woman in White*: "This is the story of what a Woman's patience can endure, and what a Man's resolution can achieve." Thus Victor runs the beatification of Eleanor throughout the novel — from the pathos of her suffering over the loss of her husband-to-be to this:

> But that flitting vision of Eleanor was as if a saint had looked down at me out of its shrine. I saw, then, that she was no longer of this world, as far as her hopes were concerned. My once strong passion had been slowly changing into reverence; I had grieved with her with a grief utterly self-abnegating, and when I saw that her despair had worked itself up to a patient and aspiring resignation, I now felt less of pity and more of affectionate reverence. I would have sacrificed my life for her peace of heart; but I no longer thought of Eleanor Argyll as of a woman to be approached by the loves of this world.

Victor also added the pathos of Lessy Sullivan's story as well as the undeserved suffering of the narrator Richard Redfield, a diminished, American version of Walter Hartright from *The Woman in White*. She also added a detective — a detective who uniquely fit the both the letter and the spirit of the sensation novel.

Contemporary British sensation writers, even Dickens, present their detectives as coming from a separate, lower class than their heroes and heroines. They stress their reason, their adroitness, their practicality, and their work ethic — things not entirely conspicuous in the leisure-class main characters. Victor does something different. Her detective, Mr. Burton, plays a significant role in the novel. But he's no ordinary detective. When Renfield goes to New York to find a detective he learns that Burton is the chief's right-hand man, and even before they are introduced he feels something extra about Burton: "I felt a magnetism emanate from him, as from a manufactory of vital forces; I felt, instinctively, that he was possessed of an iron will and indomitable courage." Burton does all that contemporary detectives do — he gathers material evidence, understands the underworld, has agents for shadowing, and he's a chirography expert:

By the way, Richard, you are not aware of my accomplishment in the art of reading men and women from a specimen of their handwriting. It is one of my
greatest aids in the profession to which I have devoted myself. The results I
obtain sometimes astonish my friends. But, I assure you, there is nothing marvelous in them. Patient study and unwearied observation, with naturally quick
perceptions, are the only witchcraft I use. With moderate natural abilities, I
assert that any other person could equal me in this art (black art, some of my
acquaintances regard it,) by giving the same time to it that a musician would to
master an instrument.

But there is more. He has access to other worlds through his daughter Lenore:

You hear my Lenore singing now — has she not a sweet voice? I have told you
how delicate her health is. I discovered, by chance, some two or three years
since, that she had peculiar attributes. She is an excellent clairvoyant. When I
first discovered it, I made use of her rare faculty to assist me in my more important labors; but I soon discovered that it told fearfully upon her health. It
seemed to drain the slender stream of vitality nearly dry.

And it was his tragic past which made Burton a detective. Formerly a merchant, he was burned out of his business by rich and powerful adversaries.
Gaining evidence of their perfidy — as well as proof of the fallibility of the
courts — Burton made himself a detective:

Burning with a sense of his individual wrongs, he could not look calmly on and
see others similarly exposed; he grew fascinated with his labor of dragging the
dangerous secrets of a community to the light. The more he called into play the
peculiar faculties of his mind, which made him so successful a hunter on the
paths of the guilty, the more marvelous became their development.

The last act of Burton's tragedy comes at the end of the novel, after his successful solution to Moreland's murder. There Renfield tells readers:

The saddest affliction which has fallen upon us since the loss of our father, is the
death of Mr. Burton. Alas! he has fallen a victim, at last, to the relentless pursuit
of enemies which his course in life raised up about him. The wicked feared him,
and compassed his destruction. Whether he was murdered by some one whom he
had detected in guilt, or by some one who feared the investigations he was making, is not known; he died of poison administered to him in his food.

The Moonstone

Being indirectly responsible for a small library of sensation stories
grounded in crime and introducing characters who either are or act as detectives, in 1867 Collins turned to writing what would become the best known
book of the genre, *The Moonstone* which ran in *All the Year Round* from January

4 to August 8, 1868. Sensation novel, enigma novel, newspaper novel, and perhaps even detective novel, in many ways *The Moonstone* is a *tour de force* both showing off Collins' talents and acting as a summary of the different strains of the novel he began when he wrote *The Woman in White*. The sensation parts of *The Moonstone* are easy to spot. Collins adds a fair amount of gothic machinery with the curse attached to the jewel plus the wandering Indians and then he layers in the pathos of Rosanna Spearman as well as Rachael's mute suffering — serving as another helping of "what a Woman's patience can endure" from *The Woman in White*. Likewise the enigma elements stand out to anyone who has finished the book. Readers recognize how artfully they have been manipulated at almost every turn — the narrators, for instance, never say the diamond is stolen, but rather that it's lost; and Collins fastidiously presents the dinner party so that when reread Dr. Candy's absence from the table can be noted — along with the varying state of Franklin's nicotine dependence. And at the end of the novel all of the questions raised (and called to readers' attention) receive answers — logical, consistent answers.

The newspaper novel features are also apparent. The first one is the plot centered on a diamond from India. Collins derived the notion of the diamond from the publicity surrounding the Koh-I-Nor diamond, which on March 29, 1849, the Treaty of Lahore (which ended the Sikh wars) ceded to the Queen of England and the gem was brought to England amid great secrecy and was presented to her on July 3, 1850. Along with the diamond came the tradition that it carried with it a curse from which only women possessors are exempt. Collins added to this bit of contemporary news echoes of one of the most talked-about murder cases of the era. On June 30, 1860, the body of four-year-old Francis Saville Kent was discovered in a privy on the grounds of his family's home in Road (Rode) Somerset. Inspector Jonathan Whicher, one of the original Scotland Yard detectives, was called in. Part of the evidence he used to cause the arrest of the boy's half sister, Constance Kent, involved an inventory of the laundry and a missing night-dress hypothetically stained with blood. Constance, however, was released without trial and Whicher was blackguarded by the press. After residing in convents in France and England, five years later she confessed to the murder and was sentenced to life imprisonment. From this Collins derived Rosanna Spearman and the hidden nightdress as well as Sergeant Cuff.

Finally there is the issue of whether *The Moonstone* is, as T.S. Elliot put it in his 1928 introduction to the Oxford World's Classics edition of the novel, "the first, the longest, and the best of modern detective novels." The novel, of course, has to do with detectives both amateur and professional. On the professional side Collins reprises the Dupin-Prefect pairing from Poe with the ham-handed Superintendent Seegrave and the methodical and professional Sergeant Cuff:

A fly from the railway drove up as I reached the lodge; and out got a grizzled, elderly man, so miserably lean that he looked as if he had not got an ounce of flesh on his bones in any part of him. He was dressed all in decent black, with a white cravat round his neck. His face was as sharp as a hatchet, and the skin of it was as yellow and dry and withered as an autumn leaf. His eyes, of a steely light gray, had a very disconcerting trick, when they encountered your eyes, of looking as if they expected something more from you than you were aware of yourself. His walk was soft; his voice was melancholy; his long lanky fingers were hooked like claws. He might have been a parson, or an undertaker, or any thing else you like, except what he really was. A more complete opposite to Superintendent Seegrave than Sergeant Cuff, and a less comforting officer to look at for a family in distress, I defy you to discover, search where you may.

Collins makes Gabriel Betteredge, Lady Verinder's house-steward, the spokesman for the amateur detectives who look for the lost diamond in the novel:

Do you feel an uncomfortable heat at the pit of your stomach, sir? and a nasty thumping at the top of your head? Ah! not yet? It will lay hold of you at Cobb's Hole, Mr. Franklin. I call it the detective-fever; and I first caught it in the company of Sergeant Cuff.

The inhabitants of Lady Verinder's house treat Cuff as a celebrity and follow his patient inquiries with interest, but neither he nor Betteredge nor Franklin Blake unaided by coincidence can figure out what happened to the diamond. Thus the detectives in *The Moonstone* participate in the solution but do not actually solve the novel's principal problem themselves.

Whereas in the *Woman in White* Collins connected his narrative technique with the law and the use of evidence ("As the Judge might once have heard it, so the Reader shall hear it now. No circumstance of importance, from the beginning to the end of the disclosure, shall be related on hearsay evidence"), in *The Moonstone* he makes no reference to the narrative technique in his Preface and at the beginning of the first narrative Franklin Blake justifies assembling the story entirely on domestic grounds ("The memories of innocent people may suffer, hereafter, for want of a record of the facts to which those who come after us can appeal. There can be no doubt that this strange family story of ours ought to be told"). And when he explains the reason for the dispersed narratives to Betteredge, Blake says that the arrangement is a lawyer's idea, but he does not connect it to the law or the use of evidence:

"We have certain events to relate," Mr. Franklin proceeded; "and we have certain persons concerned in those events who are capable of relating them. Starting from these plain facts, the lawyer's idea is that we should all write the story of the Moonstone in turn — as far as our own personal experience extends, and no further."

In fact, in his Preface Collins says nothing about problem solving or detection but rather stresses sensation as the basis of *The Moonstone*: "The attempt made here is to trace the influence of character on circumstances. The conduct pursued, under a sudden emergency, by a young girl, supplies the foundation on which I have built this book." In other words, perhaps, the action exists because Rachael persists in refusing to tell anyone what she witnessed the night the diamond disappeared.

While the novel may have a number of official and amateur detectives in it and has a complicated series of human events to unravel, perhaps the spirit of the piece is what makes it what historians call a detective novel. First of all, especially from the Victorian point of view, it moves away from the tawdry and disturbing subject matter of the wildly popular sensation novels of Braddon and Wood — thus it is not about adultery or bigamy or even about a capital crime. Additionally, an argument can be made that *The Moonstone*, at least in part, is a comic novel — Collins crafted the Betteredge sections as well as those narrated by Miss Clack largely as comedy. What this does is make Collins' enigma narrative much more light-hearted so that readers view it in the same light and admire the writer's adroitness in creating a puzzle with missing pieces — much in the same manner that Poe intended his readers to respond to "The Murders in the Rue Morgue."

America Sensationized

As noted above, Collins' influence crossed the Atlantic before *The Moonstone* hit the streets. Metta Victor brought the sensation novel focused on solving a crime to American readers in 1864 with *The Dead Letter* followed in 1869 by *The Figure Eight*—although the latter does not include a professional detective among its characters. For the next decade readers in the United States would encounter an increasing number of detectives in novels that were both like and unlike the books being proffered up by Braddon and Wood in Britain during the same decade. Emma Dorothy Eliza Nevitte Southworth, Canadian born Mary Agnes Fleming, and Charles Dimitry clearly belong to the school of sensation practiced by Braddon and Wood. In spite of their American origins, their plots often take place in England with complicated relationships among the same set of unemployed rich folks as seem in Old World sensation novels. The main characters in Southworth and Fleming treat detectives with marked condescension in spite of their utility. Southworth introduced Spry the detective in *A Noble Lord* (1872) and Sims the detective in *Allworth Abbey* (1876). Detective Masters and Mr. Limmerick, "the famous London Detective," make cameo appearances in Dimitry's *The House in Bal-*

four-street (1868). In 1873 Fleming made detective Davis part of the cast in *A Wonderful Woman*— but he, like the other fictional detectives, is decidedly part of the below-stairs crowd:

> "I suppose you're nearly out of patience by this time," his lordship began, "but Davis's report was unusually lengthy and interesting this evening; Davis's incli-nation for port wine was even more marked than usual. The lower orders, as a rule, if you observe, *have* a weakness for port wine, the thicker and sweeter the better. Davis is a clever fellow, and a skilled detective, but no exception to this rule."

In each case the detective character is an incidental feature in a plot based on the harrowing vicissitudes attendant on the course of true love. While prof-fering plots strung one way or another on lovers' travails, some American writers took the sensation novel out of the countryside and set their books in the city and made modern urban complications the potholes and roadblocks on the road to true love. In 1875 A.G. Riddle's *Alice Brand, A Romance of the Capital* found plot complications in the riot of political intrigue and corrup-tion of post Civil War Washington and included General Baker, the head of the Secret Service — "a detective by instinct and habit. The only distinction that he can perhaps recognize between criminals and others is, that the first may be hunted, and he is a born hunter as well." In *Going and Son* by Monk (1869) corrupt business practices and financial speculation underlie the trou-bles in the novel — along with something new and uniquely American — police corruption. In *Going and Son* the view of detectives begins with the same motive for distaste found in some British fiction:

> I have been playing the part of a detective policeman, and can assure you that my boyish admiration for the pursuit has been entirely done away by this night's work. I would not steal my way into a man's confidence, and then, saving myself from moral perjury only by a mental hair's breadth, betray him to the retribution he merited, no, not for all the riches of the world!

And ends with open sarcasm about the current state of law enforcement:

> They ciphered away while their victims did not dream it possible for a detective police officer to join hands with crime, and give the protection of his shield to the swindler. And Mr. Stump is not alone, in Mulberry street. He has many associates who do not intend to starve their families on twelve hundred dollars a year. And yet, the newspapers are beginning to inform the tax-payers, and the public generally, that our police excel the European civil guardians, and that the Metropolitan force is composed of as able and honest a body of men, as can be found anywhere.

Bessie A. Turner's *A Woman in the Case* (1876) uses a detective as the romantic lead and opposes him both with a corrupt Chicago detective and a New York police force riddled with incompetence and corruption:

The Mayor was saying to me only a few days ago, that with all our "modern improvements" he thought there was really less security on the public streets now than there was then. It seems harder to get the right kind of men on the force. Politicians boss the whole job, and it's simply impossible to move on the works of some of the worst criminals in the city, with success. They know all about our purposes about as soon as we do who make them.

The incompetence of detectives became one of the features of Mansfield Tracy Walworth's *Beverly: or, The White Mask* (1872) where a befuddled master detective is constantly one step behind the masked avenger who sets things right. O'Dare the private detective acts as a paid assistant to the avenger hero in *Tekel; or Cora Glencoe* (1870) by Henry A. Bragg; and the detective in W.P. Tenny's mystical religious novel *Coronation* (1877) insists on pursuing Cephas in spite of his patent virtue and sanctity.

In 1878 Anna Katherine Green's first novel *The Leavenworth Case: A Lawyer's Story* served as a summary of the repercussions Wilkie Collins' works caused in American fiction. Her publisher was hardly coy about connecting Green with Collins. In their house magazine Putnam introduced the novel this way:

> This is also a powerful novel, but its power depends upon very different qualities; there is good portrayal of the several characters, who stand out clearly and with individuality; but the special force of the author appears in the construction and elaboration of the plot, which in its capacity for holding absorbed the attention of the reader, reminds one of Wilkie Collins at his best. The "Leavenworth Case" is the kind of a book the reader will be tempted to burn midnight oil over [*Putnam's Library Companion* Sept 30, 1878].

The blurb in Putnam's standard ad for *The Leavenworth Case* went even further:

> Wilkie Collins, in his best period, never invented a more ingeniously constructed plot, nor held the reader in such suspense until the final denouement. The most blasé novel-reader will be unable to put aside 'The Leavenworth Case' until he has read the last sentence and mastered the mystery which has baffled him from the beginning. [*N. Y. Evening Express*].

Following Collins' lead, *The Leavenworth Case* divides readers' attention between empathy for the mute suffering of the Leavenworth cousins and the search for and interpretation of evidence on the part of the lawyer-narrator, Everett Raymond, and Ebenezer Gryce, the detective. As in *The Moonstone*, nineteenth-century notions about social position and gender permit the women in the novel, Eleanore and Mary Leavenworth, to refuse to testify about their secret knowledge about their uncle's murder. This both prolongs the search for Horatio Leavenworth's murderer and, in turn, justifies all of the other action in the novel — as well as the novel itself. It also permits

extended descriptions of the mute suffering of the women. Thus this portrait
of Eleanore:

> Sitting in the light of a solitary gas-jet, whose faint glimmering just served to
> make visible the glancing satin and stainless marble of the gorgeous apartment, I
> beheld Eleanore Leavenworth. Pale as the sculptured image of the Psyche that
> towered above her from the mellow dusk of the bow-window near which she sat,
> beautiful as it, and almost as immobile, she crouched with rigid hands frozen in
> forgotten entreaty before her, apparently insensible to sound, movement or
> touch; a silent figure of despair In presence of an implacable fate.

With her amateur and professional detectives Green follows the English pattern of emphasizing the disparity in social status between the police officer
and the moneyed class. In this, however, it is the detective himself who realizes
(and accepts) the social strictures under which he operates. Thus Gryce's
extended conversation on the subject with Raymond:

> "Mr. Raymond," cried he at last, "have you any idea of the disadvantages under
> which a detective labors? For instance now, you imagine that I can insinuate
> myself into all sorts of society perhaps, but you are mistaken. Strange as it may
> appear, I have never by any possibility of means succeeded with one class of per-
> sons at all. I cannot pass myself off for a gentleman. Tailors and barbers are no
> good; I am always found out."
> ...
> "I have even employed a French valet, who understood dancing and whiskers,
> but it was all of no avail. The first gentleman I approached stared at me, real
> gentleman I mean, none of your American dandies, and I had no stare to return;
> I had forgotten that emergency in my confabs with Pierre Camille Marie Make-
> face."
> ...
> "Just so," he replied, "now I can't. I can enter a house, bow to the mistress of
> it, let her be as elegant as she will, so long as I have a writ of arrest in my hand
> or some such professional matter upon my mind, but when it comes to visiting
> in kid gloves, raising a glass of champagne in response to a toast — and such like,
> I am absolutely good for nothing." And he plunged his two hands into his hair,
> and looked dolefully at the head of the cane I carried in my hand. "But it is
> much the same with the whole of us. When we are in want of a gentleman to
> work for us, we have to go outside of our profession."

Nonetheless, Green puts the official detective very much in charge of the murder investigation — indeed the first chapter in the last section of the book
("Problem Solved") is entitled "Mr. Gryce Resumes Control." And with the
investigation of Horatio Leavenworth's murder Green is as punctilious as
Collins about presenting her readers with conundrums concerning real and
imagined evidence. *The Leavenworth Case* literally presents the reader with
bits of physical evidence — as in the *Notting Hill Mystery,* Green includes room
drawings and she also inserts facsimile letters in her narrative. Following just

about every other detective writer in the nineteenth century she repeatedly mentions circumstantial evidence (in fact using the term as the title of chapter VIII) along with the admonition that circumstantial evidence "is not truth." Indeed part of Green's strategy in *The Leavenworth Case* is one character's discovery of material (like Hannah's confession) and another's discrediting it.

Contemporary reviewers often praise Green's careful construction of her first novel — even when bound up with misogyny:

> To believe that the "Sword of Damocles" was written by the author of "The Leavenworth Case" is quite as difficult as it was to realize that "The Leavenworth Case" came from a woman's pen. The logical clearness, the distinct portraiture, the sense of nothing omitted and nothing superfluous, which made the earlier novel remarkable, are wanting in this [*The Critic,* June 4, 1881].

And they use it to connect her with Collins. Unlike Collins' works, however, *The Leavenworth Case* was not a serial novel. That was one of the things that made a difference. So did making the detective policeman's role trump that of the amateur. These contributed to the fact that Green became one of the first writers to have her books consistently labeled — and read — as "detective novels."

The year after Green's debut with *The Leavenworth Case,* Donnelley, Gassette & Loyd in Chicago published *Shadowed by Three,* by Lawrence L. Lynch. Other titles followed under the Lynch name — *The Diamond Coterie* (1882), *Dangerous Ground or the Rival Detectives* (1884), *Madeline Payne, the Detective's Daughter* (1884), *Out of the Labyrinth* (1885), and *A Mountain Mystery, or the Outlaws of the Rockies* (1886). The title page of the first book announced Lynch as "Ex-Detective," but by the time of *Dangerous Ground* Lynch became "Of the Secret Service." Actually Lawrence Lynch was neither detective nor of the secret service — "he" was Mrs. Emma Murdoch van Deventer, whose name appears on reprints and her books published in the 1890s.

From the beginning her publisher pushed the Lynch books as belonging to the school of Wilkie Collins — thus this 1882 ad for *Shadowed by Three*:

> But do not imagine that this book is a "detective story" in the sense those words are generally understood, for it is not. But it *is* a powerfully constructed novel of the school of "The Woman in White," "The Moonstone," "Foul Play," etc. with the added great advantage that its author is thoroughly familiar with, and master of, the varied and entrancing material he has so skillfully woven into his vivid and richly colored story.

And, sure enough, at the center of the Lynch books reside the patented sensation novel motifs — the persecuted woman, the misdirected inheritance, etc. Indeed, leaning toward Old Sleuth and Cap Collier, her detectives are paragons. Thus this from *Madeline Payne, the Detective's Daughter*:

Lionel Payne had entered upon the study of law, but circumstances threw in his way certain mysteries that had long been puzzling the heads of the foremost detectives, and the young law student discovered in himself not only a marked taste for the study of mysteries, but a talent that was remarkable. So he gave up his law studies to become a detective. He rose rapidly in his new profession, giving all the strength of his splendid ability to the study of intricate and difficult cases, and became known among detectives, and dreaded among criminals, as "Payne, the Expert."

And they laugh at danger:

Well, to tell the truth, I quit simply because I wanted a change and because I had overworked. I have been knocked on the head with a jimmy, stuck in the ribs with a bowie, and perforated in divers places with bullets since you "sailed away in a gallant bark," and neglected your friends for five long years [*Shadowed by Three*].

But the Lynch books possess an element (albeit a small one) of realism absent in most other detective stories of the period. In *The Diamond Coterie* there is this assessment of the American judicial and police systems:

If there is anything in all our dispensations of law and order that is calculated to strike astonishment to the heart and mind of a foreigner, it is our off-hand way of conducting a police investigation. In other countries, to be a magistrate, a notary, means to be in some degree qualified for the position; to be a constable, means to possess a moderate allowance of mother wit, and a small measure of "muscular christianity"; and to discover a crime, means to follow it up with a thorough and systematic investigation. Such is not our mode. With us, to hold office, means to get a salary; and to conduct an investigation, means to maunder through some sort of farce, which gives the criminal time to make good his escape, and to permit the newspapers to seize upon and publish every item, to detail every clue, as fast as discovered; all this being in favor of the law-breakers, and detrimental to the conscientious officers of justice.

The mixture of romance, detective genius, and a pinch of realism achieved significant popularity: the "Lynch" books were published in Chicago, New York, and in London, and *Shadowed by Three* came out in editions in 1879, 1883, 1885, 1887, 1890, and 1892.

Sensation and Detectives

For almost two decades amateur and professional detectives joined the expected cast of characters in sensation novels in Britain and the United States. There were a lot of them. The detectives, however, were hardly the heroes of these books. This is the case in part because of class prejudice — a point markedly made by Green. But they perform functions essential to the purpose of the sensation novel. A principal premise of the sensation novel (and one thing that makes it quintessentially Victorian) is admiration for patient, even heroic suffering — the antithesis to using reason to solve problems. Collins and his followers discovered that they could maintain the readers' admiration for the heroine's mute suffering — thus, for instance, Rachael Verinder's or the Levenworth cousins' refusals to tell what they know — and provide them with a reward in the shape of a happy ending by bringing in an amateur or professional detective to gather evidence and use reason to solve the problem, and thereby help unwind the complications of the plot. But using a detective to solve problems was not entirely a safe proposition. By implication, arrest, trial, and punishment should follow the discovery of criminal acts, and that means publicity, and scandal — avoidance of which is one of the principles of the genteel world and one of the motives of the mute suffering of the main characters. And letting the machinery of civil justice take over also does not let providence have the last word and effect its own justice. In sensation novels, however, those three things — arrest, trial, and judicial punishment — rarely occur. Usually providence — sometimes in the form of acts of nature and sometimes in the form of guilt and suicide — intervenes to reestablish justice, or sometimes, as in *The Dead Letter*, families are permitted to enact private justice before providence takes over. All of this, inevitably, limits the role of the detective as an officer of the law. In practice it means that almost all detectives in sensation novels, even those identified as members of a police force, act as private detectives, responsible to their employers and not to the courts or the law. Thus, while they use the search for, discovery, and evaluation of evidence as a significant motif, it is in order to enhance suspense as opposed to being a demonstration of the uses of reason. Furthermore, because sensation novels rarely disguise guilty characters from their readers, they create suspense not in identifying the criminal but in the tension between the readers' knowledge about who is good and who is evil and minutiae required by the world of laws and courts to demonstrate those truths.

Chapter Six

Magazines and Family Story Papers

Detectives' notebooks and sensation novels account for only a small fraction of the hundreds of pieces of detective fiction published in the middle years of the nineteenth century. Those other detective stories appeared in magazines, family story papers, dime novels, and newspapers — to say nothing of the burgeoning number of plays with detectives in them that hit the boards following the immense success of Tom Tayler's *Ticket of Leave Man* (1862). Almost none of this material was available before the advent of digital archives of magazines and newspapers which now allow us to assemble a far more accurate picture of the formative years of the detective story, in this case the detective story in the United States.

Main-line Magazines

In the 1850s, just as in the previous decade, American readers witnessed a proliferation of magazines. As before, special interest groups continued to publish their own periodicals as a service (or appeal) to their members, and new literary magazines sprang up — a few of which, like *The Atlantic* (founded by Emerson, Longfellow, Holmes, and Lowell in 1857), became staples of the American intellectual scene. A larger and broader literate population made a difference in the American publishing industry, as did the impact of railroads and postal regulations on distribution of reading material. Perhaps the largest difference in the mid-nineteenth century was the influence of advertising — used most prolifically, as will be seen later, by family story papers and newspapers. Book publishers, however, were hardly sitting on their hands: at mid-century a number of American publishing houses began their own magazines in order to promote their authors as well as to keep their presses going between runs of books. Thus Harper's launched *Harper's New Monthly Magazine* in June 1850 followed by *Harper's Weekly Magazine* in 1857; G.P. Putnam came out with *Putnam's Magazine* in 1853; and a bit over a decade later Lippincott inaugurated *Lippincott's Magazine of Literature, Science and Education*, and Appleton published *Appleton's Journal of Literature* in 1869. The next year saw the first issue of *Scribner's Monthly*.

With their new magazines, the Harper brothers not only got in on the ground floor of transatlantic detective fiction, it could also be argued that they helped to build that floor. In its first two years of publication detective fiction was one the staples of *Harper's New Monthly Magazine*. First came reprints of some of *Chambers'* series of stories from Recollections of a Police Officer. The first was "Villainy Outwitted" which appeared in *Harper's* on November 1850—a quick turn around and new title for "Recollections of a Police-Officer: Legal Metamorphosis" published in *Chambers' Edinburgh Journal* on September 28, 1850. Next, "The Robber's Revenge" came out in *Harper's* in January 1851—taken from "Recollections of a Police-Officer: The Revenge" in *Chambers'* November 9, 1850, issue. As did *Chambers* in its early years, *Harper's* ran stories about lawyers in tandem with stories about detectives. Thus three lawyer pieces reprinted from *Household Words* ran in *Harper's Monthly's* first year of publication: "The Gentleman Beggar: An Attorney's Story" (October 1850); "History and Anecdotes of Bank Note Forgeries" (November 1850); and "Mistakes in Personal Identity" (December 1850). Another *Household Words* crime story appeared in *Harper's* two years later with "Fashionable Forger" (January 1852). More than from Dickens' magazine, however, the *Monthly's* editors turned back to *Chambers'* for lawyer stories. Thus in the early 1850s *Harper's* ran *Chambers' Journal's* stories "Jane Eccles" (April 1851), "The Chest of Drawers" (August 1851), "Edward Drysdale" (June 1852), "The Incendiary" (September 1852), "Dark Chapter" (October 1852), and "The Temptress" (January 1854). These later made their way into the notebook collections *Experiences of a Barrister* published in New York in 1852 and *Diary of a Law Clerk* published in London in 1857. But more important than all of this, while *Harper's Monthly* ran the lawyer stories, in 1852 they also began the serial publication of a novel that would combine both problems of the law and lawyers with a narrative about a detective — Charles Dickens' *Bleak House*, which ran in the magazine from April 1852 until October 1853. While episodes of *Bleak House* continued, *Harper's* also printed a handful of other stories about detectives and crime. Thus, Henry Mills Alden's "Crime Detected — An Anecdote of the Paris Police" appeared in May 1852 followed in July by one of Wilkie Collins' early forays into crime fiction: "A Terribly Strange Bed" lifted from *Household Words* (April 1852). The September issue contained "Reminiscence of a Bow Street Officer" appropriated from the July

1852 number of *Tait's Edinburgh Magazine*, which begins with musings on the contemporary interest in detectives:

> It was not near so much the fashion in my time as it is now to let all the world know how the secret and silent machinery of justice did its business.

and

> Fifty years ago thief-taking had not grown into a science, and there was then much more uncertainty in the practice even of sciences than there is at present.

While in its first years of publication detective stories — along with ghost stories — claimed considerable space in *Harper's New Monthly*; in the early 1850s the big-name British writers Dickens, Bulwer-Lytton, and Thackeray were the real star attractions — and the only ones who consistently had their names attached to their works. While the editors continued to glean occasional detective pieces from British journals — pieces like "The Reprieve; Or, the Wild Justice of Revenge" (August 1854) taken from June 1854 issue of *The Dublin University Magazine* — there appears to have been a move to make the magazine become more literary, and in practice this meant seeking out known writers. The first step of this new direction appeared in the February 1855 number of *Harper's* with the publication of "A Lawyer's Story" by "Charles Dickens." The story, however, was not by Dickens but one with superficial resemblance to Poe's "The Purloined Letter" written by Wilkie Collins and originally appearing in "The Fourth Poor Traveller" from "The Seven Poor Travellers" printed in the Extra Christmas Number of *Household Words* for December 1854. Another detective story by a prominent figure was "Mysterious Occurrence at Lambeth" in *Harper's* August 1855 number, a narrative by G.P.R. James, British Counsel at Norfolk, about a skeptical and persistent amateur who solves a murder, frees innocents, and discovers treasure. In September 1856 "An Alibi" appeared, a piece in which a young lawyer frees a lovelorn young man presumed guilty because of circumstantial evidence, a story attributed to Henry Mills Alden who would become editor of *Harper's* in 1863. In 1858 the editors made up to Collins for their name goof with "A Lawyer's Story" by printing "A Marriage Tragedy" in February, not only with Wilkie Collins' name attached to it, the magazine also announced that it was "Written Exclusively for Harper's Magazine." *Harper's Magazine's* last detective story of the 1850s seems to indicate a turning point for the publisher. Probably inspired by "The Button," and other stories about an unnamed New York detective run in *Harper's Weekly* in 1857–8, "The Costly Kiss: A New York Detective Experience" (April 1859) takes place in the U.S. — the only other *Harper's* detective story of the 1850s set in the U.S. is "An Alibi." More importantly, while lawyers or amateurs do the detecting in all of the earlier *Monthly* pieces, the hero-narrator of "The Costly Kiss" is an official, professional New York City detective, and the plot does not center on saving a wrongly accused innocent but on arresting a dissolute young man for the mundane crime of robbing the till and spending the cash on debauchery.

The number of detective stories published in *Harper's Monthly* in the 1860s perceptively dwindled. There were only five: "The Boldero Murder" (May 1860), "The Pigot Murder" (December 1864), "Mr. Furbush" (April 1864), "The Pond House Murder" (1864), and "In the Maguerriwock" (August 1868). The authors of most of these, all Americans, possessed considerable literary credentials. F.B. Perkins who wrote "The Boldero Murder" wrote a biography of Dickens, J.T. Headley (who wrote "The Pond House") was Secretary of State of the state of New York, and Harriet Prescott Spofford whose "Mr. Furbush" and "In the Maguerriwock" chronicle the activities of the same hero, was a budding novelist whose first detective story appeared in *The Atlantic Monthly*. Credentials, however, were no guarantee of quality. In "The Boldero Murder" the demand that the lawyer-narrator tell "some moral, entertaining, and instructive story" results in a hum-drum narrative about a surprise witness revealing evidence of a gruesome murder. "The Pond House" likewise is a lackluster account of an amateur detective searching for evidence to exonerate a friend and save his romance. C. Davis, author of "The Pigot Murder," however, did something a bit different: for the second time in *Harper's* the story features a middle-class police detective:

> I had been eight years on the special detective force in Philadelphia when that trouble about Joe Myers turned up. Joe was an old chum of mine: the only red-headed fellow I ever did trust.... The fact is, whatever success I met with there is due to a succession of lucky chance — hits, as I may say, at discoveries in my line of business, rather than to any astuteness of mine. That troubled me but little; it was enough that I did succeed; at the end of the eight years had a snug marble-slabbed brick house out on Green Hill, which my wife had as prettily fitted up as any of the old blooded nobs in town.... Next to Pike (the chief) I had the best salary on the staff; and no man on the force was so often called on for fancy jobs; and they always pay well.

It follows the narrator's persistent (and successful) search for evidence to save his friend.

Harriet Prescott Spofford's two stories are also a cut above the rest. "Mr. Furbush," which preceded an episode of Collins' *Armadale* in the April 1864 *Monthly*, turns on the police detective's interpretation of a photograph, but most importantly goes beneath the surface of the detective's character:

> A detective has perhaps no right to any pity; but for a moment Mr. Furbush would gladly have never heard of the More murder as he saw in the long, slow rise and fall of the bosom this woman's heart swing like a pendulum, a noiseless

pendulum that ceases to vibrate. Her eyes wavered a moment between him and
the table, then, as if caught and chained by something that compelled their gaze,
glared at and protruded over the sight they saw beneath them. Her own hand —
her own executioner. A long shudder shook her from head to foot. Iron nerve
gave way, the white lips parted, she threw her head back and gasped; with one
wild look toward her husband she turned from him as if she would have fled and
fell dead upon the floor.

"Hunts up," said Mr. Furbush to his subordinate, coming out an hour or two
later, and the two found some congenial oyster-opener, while the Chief
explained how he had gone to get his wife's spoons from the maid who had
appropriated them and taken service elsewhere. Mr. Furbush made a night of it;
but never soul longed for daylight as he did, he had a notion that he had scarcely
less than murdered — himself; and good-fellow as he must needs be abroad that
night, indoors next day he put his household in sackcloth and ashes.

At the end of "Mr. Furbush," disheartened, the hero leaves the police
force, but in the sequel, "In the Maguerriwock," published four years later,
he has become a private investigator, and the story opens:

> MR. FURBUSH was waited upon one morning by a client, and requested to take
> charge of a case that was rather out of his usual beat, as he said. And though its
> being a good instance of mysterious disappearance, with almost nothing to start
> from, gave it an immediate interest to his inquisitive mind, yet the investigation,
> being located upon an almost uncivilized region of the frontier forest, made it a
> much less agreeable study than was the same line of cases when they could be
> worked up in the pleasant purlieus of the city, and involved no greater hardships
> than attendance at the opera-houses and in the drawing-rooms of fashionable
> ladies.

Even as *Harper's Monthly* began to carry fewer detective stories, the publisher's other magazine began to take up some of the slack. *Harper's Weekly*
hit the streets in 1857 and by 1860 had achieved a circulation of 200,000.
One of the features that gave impetus to those numbers was that on November
26, 1859, *Harper's Weekly* began to publish episodes of Collins' *The Woman
in White*. But the font of all sensation novels was not *Harper's Weekly's* first
foray into crime and detection. In its first year of publication the *Weekly* published "The Grammercy Park Mystery" (? 1857), a light-hearted tale involving
a pet monkey and not a thief, and J.B. Armstrong's "A Police-Officer's Seven
Thousand Miles' Chase" (January 3, 1857) in which the detective, acting on
behalf of a number of banks, spends 71 days "traversing, by sea and land, near
fourteen thousand miles" to bring a forger back to Ohio only to discover that
the felon's friends repay some of the banks' losses and that

> he was mysteriously released from prison one night before trial, and he disap-
> peared to rejoin his family, it is to be hoped, a wiser and better man. Sympathy
> for his broken-hearted young wife, doubtless, had much to do with his release.

More importantly, on July 25, 1857, the *Weekly* established a new direction in detective fiction with "How Bob the Bolter's Prisoner Escaped," a tale told by a veteran New York detective about the capture of an escaped jewel thief. The next year the same casual, confiding narration by a New York detective characterizes "The Button" (October 16, 1858), subtitled "An Experience of a New York Detective, Related by Himself"; and "A Detective Experience" (December 4, 1858), a story about catching professional criminals. As noted above, "The Costly Kiss" in *Harper's Monthly* echoes the tone and intent of these stories, and all three of the *Weekly's* stories had a continued life when they were included in Ward and Lock's 1860 collection *The Detective's Note-Book* (where the setting changes to Britain) and in Dick and Fitzgerald's *Strange Stories of a Detective or The Curiosities of Crime.*

The focus of the *Weekly* shifted in April 1858 with "The Culprit Judge." The story comments on a flawed system of justice when a prosecuting attorney discovers and exposes a judge in league with counterfeiters. "The Pet of the Law" in the *Weekly's* February 27, 1858 issue exemplifies a consistent, realistic — sometimes even cynical — point of view toward justice and law enforcement in the *Harper's Weekly* stories of the 1850s. Hence this sentiment expressed by the thief-narrator of "The Pet of the Law":

> Many persons suppose that we detest the police, and look upon them as our bitterest enemies. On some occasions, I admit, we find them troublesome; but, generally, we consider them as wholesome checks upon the increase of unskillful thieves, who diminish the profits without adding to the credit of the profession. The ordinary police force is not a very highly paid, highly educated, or highly intelligent class; and any man who knows his business can easily avoid coming in contact with them.

During the Civil War years *Harper's Weekly* ran fewer detective stories than in its inaugural years, and these tended to be imports. One was "The Case for the Prisoner" (November 1863) nicked from the October 10, 1863, number of *All the Year Round*. In February 1865 "An Australian Detective's Story; or, Murder Will Out" (December 24, 1864) ran, a piece originally printed in *Once a Week* (December 24, 1864). Three months later another story lifted from *Once a Week*, "Who Did it?" came out in the *Weekly*. Perhaps because of the publication of these imports, the first detective story in *Harper's Weekly* after the end of the War, "After Those Seven Thirties" (July 1865), begins with a reflection on detectives in England and America:

> Well, Sir, there is a certain amount of interest attaching to the commonest jobs in our line, as you say. But the detective system in this country ain't what it is in Old England: it's younger, you know. There is some smart fellows among us, though; not that I'm one of 'em. I'm modest, I am. But I'll tell you how I done up that Osdell job, if you care to hear it. I dare say it'll sound simple enough to you, Sir. It does to me.

Published in August 1866, "The Murders at Sunset Canyon" has a decidedly American setting — Mariposa, California. In it the lawyer-narrator exposes a disguised murderer, and in so doing indicates that the detective character was on the way to becoming a cliché:

> In my professional capacity I had had to deal with numerous specimens of these gentry, and my present visitor's entire bearing was that of the Detective par excellence. Every word he uttered was given with that premeditated terseness which he would have displayed in the witness-box, while confronting the criminal whom he had hunted down to justice; he accompanied himself with explanatory gestures, and that keen, restless, half-evil green eye of his would dance about in his head from one object to another as he spoke till you thought that it could have no interest in the owner's words, while at the same time it appeared wonderfully wide-awake.

At the end of 1867 and beginning of 1868 the editors of the *Weekly* returned to trolling in British waters for their detective stories and came up with "Making Up for It" in December 1867 from *Tinsley's Magazine* and "Eleven Thousand Pounds" in February 1868 from *The Leisure Hour* (December 1, 1867). The next year witnessed *Harper's Weekly's* biggest catch: Wilkie Collins' *The Moonstone* began its American publication in it on January 4, 1868. The decade of the 1860s, however, ended with a final story which seems to reflect Harper's changing corporate attitude toward detective stories implied in the contents of both the *Monthly* and *Weekly*. "Loaf the Bootblack," published in the *Weekly* in January 1869, is a response to the wildfire popularity of Horatio Alger's 1867 *Ragged Dick* (Chapter 11 of which is "Dick as a Detective") and suggests a reassessment of the purpose, audience and literary merit of the detective story — rather than being informative, literary, or clever, the Horatio Alger connection suggests that the detective story is straight forward, adolescent, and moral. Interestingly, nothing called a detective story appeared in *Harper's Monthly* in the decade of the 1870s.

In addition to Harper's magazines, from the 1850s onward detective stories appeared sporadically in a number of other American magazines. In February 1850 *The Eclectic Magazine of Foreign Literature*, giving credit to *Chambers'*, reprinted both "Legal Metamorphoses" (December, 1850) and "The Revenge" (February 1851) from the Recollections of a Police-Officer series. In July 1851 *The Living Age* printed "The Metropolitan Protectives" copied from *Household Words* (April 26, 1851), and in August 1857 *Putnam's Magazine* published a light-hearted detective story set in America, "Another Glimpse at My Hotel"; and in the publisher's anthology *Stories for the Home Circle* (1857) included "The Left-Handed Glove; or Circumstantial Evidence." In April 1858 *The Atlantic* came out with Wilkie Collins' detective spoof, "Who is the Thief?" then printed Harriet Prescott [Spofford's] first published story, a tale of felony in Parisian court circles, "In a Cellar" (February 1859); and in December 1862 ran the anonymous "One of My Clients" which begins with a meditation on crime and detection:

> After a practice in the legal profession of more than twenty years, I am persuaded that a more interesting volume could not be written than the revelations of a lawyer's office. The plots there discovered before they were matured,— the conspiracies there detected
> "Ere they had reached their last fatal periods,"—
> The various devices of the Prince of Darkness,— the weapons with which he fought, and those by which he was overcome,— the curious phenomena of intense activity and love of gain,— the arts of the detective, and those by which he was eluded,— and the never-ending and ever varying surprises and startling incidents,— would present such a panorama of human affairs as would outfly our fancy, and modify our unbelief in that much-abused doctrine of the depravity of our nature.

Shortly after its founding, *Appleton's Journal of Literature* published "The First Case" (October 1869) about not one but two cases solved by professional detective Robert Blaisdell, M.D., followed by "A Safe Investment" (June 1870), and "Miss Whitelake's Diamonds" (January 24, 1874). During its twelve-year life, *The Galaxy* delivered four detective stories: Edward Gould Buffum's "A Case of Mistaken Identity" (February 1868); Gaston Fay's "How Lamirande Was Caught" (March 1868); W.L. Alden's "A Fourfold Alibi" (February 1873); and Frances T. Richardson's "Zizi, the Little Detective" (July 1877). "A Case of Mistaken Identity," set in San Francisco, ends with this comment on detectives and Providence:

> Was it "chance" alone which directed the steps of the Vigilance detectives to Jim Stuart's burrow, among the sand-hills? Was not the life of an innocent man, even of one so poor and humble as Berdue, worth more than that of "many sparrow"; and are we not assured that the Guide, and Governor, and Orderer of all things, suffers not one of these to fall to the ground without His notice?

Late in the 1870s *Scribner's Monthly* published "The Documents in the Case" (September 1879). This piece by Brander Matthews (who would become one of the first academic proponents of the detective story) and J. Bunner presents readers with a pile of newspaper clippings, pawn tickets, telegrams, and correspondence from which lawyers are to find the clues to discover the whereabouts of a missing heiress. Finally, *The Literary World, a Monthly Review of Current Literature* included "Monsieur Lecoq" (June 5, 1880) along with a footnote citing Estes & Lauriat's 50 cent edition of Gaboriau's novel as its source.

But it was not only main-line literary magazines that occasionally ran detective stories in the second half of the nineteenth century; they also occasionally appeared in special interest periodicals. Hence "Aunt Janet's Diamonds" came out in *The Ladies' Repository* (February-March 1860); "The Boy Detective" popped up in *The Yale Courant* (December 1885); "Incident in the Life of a California Detective" came out in the *Overland Monthly and the Old West Magazine* (February 1884); "My Veiled Client" (October 1885), and Liston Hardy's "A Tangled Web" (November 1887) appeared in *Arthur's Home Magazine*; and a piece about a detective nabbing a disguised murderer on the Dover Express starting from London Bridge Station, "A Romance of a Railway Carriage" (January 1870), was published in *The Locomotive Engineer's Monthly* printed in Cleveland, Ohio.

The Huddled Masses Yearning to Read

In 1850 *Harper's New Monthly Magazine* cost 25 cents an issue or three dollars a year. Twenty years later, in 1870, *Putnam's Magazine* appeared at a cost of 30 cents an issue or three dollars a year. Even at the end of the century it would have been a stretch for a working-class individual to buy, let alone subscribe to, one of the publishers' magazines. Data about wages in mid-century America is difficult to find, but in 1897 *The Encyclopedia of Social Reform* cited these as average wages for working-class men in 1891:

> Common and agricultural laborers, sums varying from $2.50 per day in Montana to 75 cents in the Carolinas and $1.25 in New York; masons, from $4.50 and $5 in Colorado and California to $2.50 in North Carolina and $2.50 and $3.36 in Pennsylvania; carpenters in New York, $3.50; bricklayers and their helpers, $4 and $2.50 respectively; locomotive engineers, $3.77; firemen, $1.96.

With wages like these it was unlikely that working people would or could splurge on one of the publishers' magazines. Additionally, the publishers' magazines inclined toward being "literary" and intellectual — the best case in point being *The Atlantic Monthly*, founded by an academe of New England notables. The contents of the December 1851 *Harper's Monthly* illustrate the presumed audience of the journal: they included essays on "American Arctic Expedition" and "Pleasures and Perils of Ballooning"; stories including "The Bow Window: An English Tale," and "The Expectant — a Tale of Life"; a Monthly Record of Current Events; and Literary Notices (including a review of *Moby Dick*). Given the leisure — which is a stretch — and the extra 30 cents, this kind of reading was unlikely to be the kind of thing a mechanic, or his wife, or his children would choose to pick up. But, as opposed to the beginning of the century, the mechanic, his wife, and their children could read — in 1852 Massachusetts passed the first compulsory school attendance law, followed by New York in 1853.

In response to what was becoming a gigantic potential market, enterprising publishers in both Britain and the United States came out with a dizzying variety of cheap publications. There were inexpensive weekly and monthly magazines that featured fiction and poetry, there were family story papers — containing fiction and poetry but published in a newspaper format — there were cheap, yellow paper-backed novels that sold for a nickel or a dime, and there were newspapers. The cheap monthly magazines published in the U.S. included *Gleason's Monthly Companion, Arthur's Home Magazine, The Ladies Repository, The Home Monthly, Ballou's Dollar Monthly,* and the short lived *Beadle's Monthly* (in which *The Dead Letter* was to appear). Among the mass of family story papers in the U.S. were *Brother Jonathan, Saturday Night, Saturday Courier, The New York Ledger, Omnibus, The New York Fireside Companion,* and a number with patriotic titles like a *The Flag of Our Union, The True Flag, Uncle Sam, The Yankee, The Yankee Blade, The Star Spangled Banner,* and *The Flag for the Free.* These were echoed in Britain with publications like *The Family Herald, The London Journal, Reynolds's Miscellany,* and *Cassell's Illustrated Family Paper.* Although cheap editions of novels were available earlier, the official start of the dime novel in America was Irwin and Erastus Beadle's reprinting on June 9, 1860, of a prize story run earlier in *The Ladies Companion* which became *Malaeska, the Indian Wife of the White Hunter* by Mrs. Ann S. Stephens, the first of hundreds of novels and novellas that would become known as "dime novels."

All of these publications trumpeted that they were cheap. Thus this announcement from the *Courier* in 1839:

> 32,000 subscribers!!
> Extending from the LAKES TO THE OCEAN, and combining all interests and classes of the people of our Republic. It is the LARGEST and CHEAPEST Journal in the World! [cited in *Villains Galore*].

In the February 1856 issue of *The Ladies Repository*, the editors singled out Maturin M. Ballou for the popularity the cheapness of his publications:

> "Ballou's Pictorial Drawing Room Companion," "The Flag of our Union," and "Ballou's Dollar Monthly Magazine." The aggregate number of these magazines is over two hundred thousand copies per week.
>
> These are truly papers for the people. They are the cheapest and most interesting papers published in the country. Mr. Ballou has an eye to the wants of the public, and he has spared no expense in his endeavors to place the Pictorial and Flag at the head of the weekly issues. The Dollar Monthly contains more reading than any of the two dollar magazines, and is of that class which cannot fail to interest and amuse the general reader.

These weeklies, monthlies, and family story papers sought to differentiate their purpose from the high-brow literary magazines of the day. They not only emphasized their pricing, they also made it clear that their purpose was to provide literature as entertainment. Thus in the U.S. *Frank Leslie's Ten Cent Monthly* (1864) was "Devoted to Light and Entertaining Literature," *Town and Country* (1866) aimed "to supply a superior entertaining literature," *The Sapphire* (1866) provided "A rich repository of entertaining literature," *Demorest's Magazine* (1867) contained "useful and entertaining literature," *The Model Parlor Magazine* (1867) promised "A constant succession of artistic novelties, with other useful and entertaining literature," *The Western Monthly* (1869) boasted that it was "A periodical of solid and entertaining literature," and the masthead of Beadle's *Saturday Journal* announced that it was "A Popular Paper for Pleasure and Profit" (1871). Indeed in the 1860s the growth of inexpensive literature directed to non-traditional readers with entertainment as its purpose saw a new twist added to the age-old arguments about the purpose and morality of literature: the argument of critics was that it wasn't literature *per se* that was bad, but cheap literature that was bad, and, like a literary Gresham's Law, cheap literature drove out good literature. It was an argument that the Chambers brothers in Britain sought to counter by using statistics:

> CHEAP LITERATURE : THE GOOD IT HAS EFFECTED.— The Messrs. Chambers, of Edinburgh, having made a careful investigation into the changes effected in the British book trade by the introduction of a cheap literature, state that it has driven into obscurity the sale of books of a grossly demoralizing tendency. They give the following summing up of a classification of the cheap periodical trade. In 1859–60. Works of an improving tendency, monthly circulation, 8,043,000, a large portion of which are religious, but not sectarian periodicals, including those of the London Religious Tract Society, temperance, useful, educational, and entertaining literature. Works of an exciting nature, but not positively immoral, monthly circulation, 1,500,000. Works Immoral, and opposed to the religion of the country, monthly circulation probably under 80,000 [Cited in *Godey's Lady's Book and Magazine* July 1861].

It was in this context that the detective story put down roots — especially in the United States. And the most influential figures in making that happen were Maturin M. Ballou with his *Flag of Our Union* and *Ballou's Monthly Magazine*, Robert Bonner with his *New York Ledger*, George Monro with his *New York Fireside Companion*, and the purveyors of dime novels, especially Frank Tousey.

Ballou's Detective Agencies

Maturin M. Ballou was a prolific writer and publisher. In 1854 he bought out Frederick Gleason with whom he had co-founded *Gleason's Pictorial Draw-*

ing-Room Companion and changed its name to *Ballou's Pictoral Drawing-Room Companion*. The same year he also acquired Gleason's interest in *The Flag of Our Union*, at the time perhaps the largest circulation family story paper in the country. The next year he founded "the cheapest magazine in the world," *The Dollar Monthly Magazine*—which would become *Ballou's Monthly Magazine*. Before and during his publishing ventures Ballou was a prolific writer — often writing under the pseudonym of Lieutenant Murray (Twenty Cent Novelettes by "Lieutenant Murray" offered as premiums by *Ballou's Monthly*, for instance, included such titles as *The Outlaw, or the Female Bandit; The Cabin Boy, or Life on the Wing; The Poisoned Barb*; and *The Highwayman*).

Almost from the beginning Ballou included detective stories in *The Dollar Monthly*. One of the earliest was "Mag Durfries" which appeared in his *Monthly* in May 1855. In it Breton, a Parisian plainclothes policeman, aided by the beggar Mag Durfries, escapes death and captures a notorious criminal:

> Berton added new laurels to his fame as a police agent, and soon after this adventure was promoted for his bravery and success in taking the cunning and desperate rogue who had so long been a scourge to the city and neighborhood. He was somewhat bruised and lamed after his fearful night's work, but this kind of thing was a part of his profession, and he expected rough treatment at times.

And Breton also returns Mag to middle-class respectability and reunites her with her long-lost daughter. Next Ballou turned to the detective story as amusement with two stories set in the U.S. in the *Monthly*: "A Mysterious Burglar" (August 1855), a somnambulism story, followed by a tale about a rube and a pickpocket in "Mr. Snickers' Misadventure" (January 1856). "Murder Will Out" by Darius Blackburn in July 1858 follows a new course. It begins with an English detective's observation that

> Lord bless you, sir! we detectives see so many things in our line of business, that we could furnish a dozen story-tellers with better materials than they could trump up, if they harassed their brains till doomsday.

and proceeds through his narration about the "curious murder in Bermondsey." At the denouement the narrator observes that

> The murder was now literally out; the body was identified, as was Dr. Parkman's in Boston, partly by some artificial teeth, and a reward of five hundred pounds offered for the arrest of the Mannings.

This identifies the piece as a story roughly based on a real crime — as was "The Mystery of Marie Roget" — in this case it draws on details taken from the forensic evidence given at the trial of Dr. John Webster for the murder of George Parkman on November 23, 1849, in Ballou's home town of Boston.

In "My Mysterious Neighbors" (January 1859) reprinted in the *Monthly* from Ballou's family story paper, *The Flag of Our Union* (October 30, 1858), a woman overhears fellow boarders' suspicious conversations, reports them to the police, and "officer Webb, a competent detective" arrives to arrest the couple for murder.

After this miscellany of detective stories, in April 1859 *Ballou's Monthly* did something different; it carried a story entitled "A Curious Stratagem" which begins with

> I had been some years connected with the Detective Bureau (so the thief-taker commenced his story), and had naturally arrived at a great degree of proficiency in the calling at the time when the strange matter occurred which forms the basis of my story.

In the narrative the French detective, M. Guillot, tells of how he tracked down and penetrated the disguise of a notorious criminal. While humdrum enough, "A Curious Stratagem" is important because it introduces the first of Ballou's series detectives, and it was followed in the *Monthly* by another Guillot story, "The Guest Chamber of the Inn at St. Ives" (December 1859). "The Guest Chamber" is a knock off of Wilkie Collins' 1852 murder machine plot in "A Terribly Strange Bed." The authorship of the Guillot pieces, however, is at best muddy. The first story credits James F. Franklin and the second names James Franklin Fitts as the author. And although Ballou added "Original" above their titles, given the epidemic plagiarism of the period, even that can be questioned, especially because a French detective very much like Guillot had already appeared in *The New York Ledger* in "Assassin of Castellane: from the Records of a French Policeman" (June 12, 1858). Ballou's stories, however, do introduce one of the earliest series detectives to appear in the U.S. and add a new voice to Ballou's detective stories — instead of the deferential, lower-middle class voice of the English detective in "Murder Will Out," the narrator Guillot is a sought-after hero who is proud of his profession and eager to share his triumphs.

While the last of the Guillot pieces was running in *Ballou's Monthly* in December 1859 he published "The Robbery of Plate" in *The Flag of Our Union* and then reprinted it in the *Monthly* in February 1860. In it readers meet Benson, the detective officer:

> His great coat was buttoned up to the neck, around which a heavy muffler was wound. Upon his head a heavy fur hat rested, from beneath the rim of which a pair of sharp, ferret-like eyes glowed on me, appearing to take in my whole character, history and business at a single glance. The man's features seemed familiar to me, and I soon recognized him as a noted detective officer, who lived in Philadelphia. He had succeeded some two years before in bringing some famous counterfeiters to justice, one of whom selected me as his counsel.

Benson diverts the lawyer-narrator on a trip from Albany to New York City by telling him "about the queerest case happened about a year ago in Philadelphia," and filling him in on detectives' tradecraft — "the reason why detectives are often wonderfully successful in the detection of crime is *that they take notice of the smallest things*." In July of the same year, with "Original" again above the title, Ballou published "The Car Acquaintance" by Mrs. Caroline Orne, a story about the apprehension of a robber based upon the discovery of a tiny scrap of the criminal's correspondence.

After a two-year hiatus, in 1862 Ballou got back into the detective business with a vengeance with a year-long string of stories in the *Monthly* that would arguably become the most popular detective stories in the country for a decade at least. Ballou appears to have recognized what he had on his hands — but only after the first few stories ran. The series began with "The Masked Robbers: A Leaf from a Detective's Note-Book: By Percy Garrett" and superscribed as "Original" (April 1862). The second story, "The Mysterious Advertisement" (July 1862), lacks an author's name and is credited to "A New York Detective." Then Ballou returned to attaching Percy Garrett to "The Knotted Handkerchief" (July 1862). At that point he must have recognized that he had created a brand and attached "By A NEW YORK DETECTIVE" to the following nine stories in the series: "The Club Foot" (August, 1862), "The Struggle for Life" (August 1862), "Stabbed in the Back" (September 1862), "The Coiners" (September 1862), "The Lottery Ticket" (October 1862), "The Accusing Leaves" (November 1862), "The Bowie Knife Sheath" (December 1862), "A Night of Peril" (December 1862), and "Mr. Sterling's Confession" (January 1863).

In the first New York Detective story the detective is known only by the pseudonym of Mr. Clark, but in the second the writer attached the name James Brampton to the detective hero, a name which continues in the other stories. The stories (mostly told in the first person) repeat several details about Brampton's life, principally that family misfortunes caused him to leave his medical studies, that he is immensely successful as a consulting detective, and that he is happily married — several of the stories begin with the detective and his wife sitting near the hearth of the Brampton family home. Connected to the hero's medical background, a number of the stories turn on physiology or pharmacology — "The Struggle for Life" and "The Knotted Handkerchief." Related to this, apropos to the emphasis on minutiae in the stories Ballou ran in the *Dollar Monthly* in 1860, the majority of the Brampton stories center on the discovery of tiny bits of physical evidence, evidence overlooked by others like the almond tree leaves in "The Accusing Leaves," or the fingermarks in "The Bowie Knife Sheath." While two of the stories ("The Club Foot" and "Mr. Sterling's Confession") depend on the traditional subject of wills and estates, a third of the Brampton tales ("The Accusing Leaves," "The Bowie Knife Sheath," and "The Knotted Handkerchief") are about murder. In three of the stories ("The Struggle for Life," "The Night of Peril," and "The Coiners") the hero confronts physical danger and several of the stories are peripatetic — Brampton travels to the South and to the Mid-West. A majority of the stories, however, center on demonstrating the innocence of a person wrongly accused because of misinterpretation of circumstantial evidence.

As seen earlier, Dick and Fitzgerald snatched up Ballou's New York Detective stories, added a miscellany of others — including "The Silver Pin" — and published them as *Leaves from the Note Book of a New York Detective* (1864). Whether based on the originals in *Ballou's Dollar Monthly* or on the Dick and Fitzgerald volume, the New York Detective stories were widely printed and reprinted in newspapers and magazines across the United States for the next decade. Indeed they turn up in the strangest places, and fewer could be odder than the appearance of "The Masked Robbers" under the title of "The Maimed Hand" in the *Illuminated and illustrated business directory of Boston for 1870.*

The next series detective in *The Flag of Our Union* appeared after the war. The paper's new editors (James R. Elliott, William Henry Thomes and Newton Talbot) and prolific southern writer and translator James D. M'Cabe, Jr., combined the character of the expert French detective from the Guillot stories with the energetic New York Detective character and debuted a new series hero in four stories about French detective M. Eugene Laromie published in 1866: "The Tell-Tale Eye" (*Flag*, January), "An Official Blunder" (*Flag*, April), "Seventy Miles an Hour" (*Flag*, June), and "A Little Affair" (*Monthly* October). The series begins with a science fiction twist with Laromie discovering a murderer with the help of a photographer friend who undertakes to prove "...that the last impression made upon the eye of a dying person ... [was] retained a certain time after death. That being the case, he thought it possible to obtain a photographic likeness of impression...." The third story, "Seventy Miles an Hour," uses another marvelous machine, this time the locomotive, and centers on the excitement of a railroad chase at unheard of speeds. In fact, all of the stories contain a varieties of excitement, and in "A Little Affair" M'Cabe introduces Laromie to his readers as an action hero:

> M. Eugene Laromie had passed through some wonderful adventures in the exercise of his profession, and had been nearer death than most men care to be. His success in ferreting out and bringing to light crimes of all kinds had won him the bitter enmity of all offenders, both political and criminal, in the city."

M'Cabe wrote two more detective stories. In the first, "A Lady's Glove" in *Ballou's Dollar Monthly* (August 1866), one of the most distinguished families in New York City calls in Officer Hale to find the stolen De Villiers diamonds. Hale is "a well-known man in the great city of New York. In all the detective force of that city, whose exploits have made them so famous, none bears a higher reputation for skill, sagacity and bravery, than he." He finds the thief and returns the gems. The second M'Cabe story, "An Amateur Detective," appeared in *The Flag of Our Union* (October 12, 1867). Like "Loaf the Bootblack" published in *Harper's* the next year, "An Amateur Detective" reflects the impact of Horatio Alger's boy heroes on popular fiction by focusing on a boy hero who finds a robber the professional New York detective cannot.

While 1866 was largely M'Cabe's year, Caleb Russet's "The Detective's story" appeared in *The Flag* in April 1866. It introduces a problem of funds taken from a safe which is solved by detective John Smith:

> He seemed specially adapted to his calling. Being liberally educated, with a polished address, endowed with extraordinary conversational powers, and the art of pleasing, together with a thorough knowledge of human nature, he was eminently qualified to fill almost any sphere in society; but, stimulated by a love of adventure, and a tolerably fair income, he was well content to remain in his present position.

For the rest of the decade of the 1860s, however, the editors of *The Flag* published very little detective fiction and the same was the case with *Ballou's Monthly*. On June 1, 1867, "A Detective's Story," a very short piece about an English detective solving a murder in Paris, ran in *The Flag of Our Union*. And on June 1, 1867, *The Flag* provided an even more exotic setting than Paris with "In the Cellar," a piece set in the Australian gold fields. With another set of editors, during the next two decades detective stories became a rarity in *The Flag of Our Union*. In the 1870s "An Evening with a Detective" (September 1870) takes place in Carlisle, Pennsylvania and starts off with musing on detectives' acumen:

> If there is anything more calculated to sharpen a man's wits, and keep him continually on the lookout than the detective business, I don't know what it can be. A few years of the life that we in this peculiar business have to lead makes it a man's second nature to be watchful without seeming to be so at all, and to take notice of what is going on even when not engaged on any particular "lay," as the rogues say. I have two little stories to tell which will illustrate this.

"The Diamond Cross" (January, 1876) is a caper story in which the criminal gets the best of the detective: "To be taken in by a male sharper is bad enough, but to have yourself and your profession laughed at by a woman, is too much for a detective, proud of his sagacity, to bear with equanimity."

Creating Demand

While Ballou's publications could post circulation figures unheard of twenty years earlier, there were two family story papers in the 1860s and 1870s that dwarfed even the numbers that *The Flag of Our Union* could put up: *The New York Ledger* and *The New York Fireside Companion*. In each case reaching an immense, largely new readership was a result of Barnamesque showmanship and canny, nationwide marketing. Thus late in the century George Monro's son John commented on his father's use of serial novels in special issues to bump up the circulation of *The New York Fireside Companion*:

> We do not publish them regularly, nor any set number, but we run them quite frequently between September and June. And the editions vary all the way from one million to four or five. You see these specials are really merely sample copies. They contain fifteen or twenty chapters of some regular story, which is just about to be run in the regular weekly. We begin the story at its beginning in the special, as we do in the weekly, but give about three times the installment in the former than we do in the latter. Indeed, if we find that the story is going to be especially popular, by means of selecting small type we give even more, say thirty chapters, or half the story that has appeared in the regular editions, indicating at the end the number in which the continuation can be found. People who have begun to read the story in the special are generally desirous to finish it, and since the end is only to be found in the regular editions, they must buy these. Once buying it they are very apt to continue, for the various stories in the regular editions are likely to fasten their attention. In the specials, you know, we never publish anything except that one installment of one story [*Printer's Ink*, January 5, 1898].

While Bonner, too, used teasers to bring new readers, his novel promotions became the talk of the new advertising profession. Thus, in *Sunshine and Shadow in New York* (1868) Matthew Hale Smith praised his unique promotional endeavors at the *Ledger*:

> Mr. Bonner knows how to reach the public. He pays liberally, but intends to have the worth of his money. He does not advertise twice alike. The newspapers are afraid of him. His advertisements are so queer and unusual, that when they make a contract with him, they have no idea in what shape the advertisement will come. Sometimes it is in the shape of a fragment of a story; sometimes the page will be nearly blank, with two or three little items in it. In his peculiar style of advertising he often gives great trouble to the editors of the leading papers. Sometimes an entire page is almost blank. Sometimes a few small advertisements occupy the corner, giving the sheet a peculiar appearance, which attracts attention. Said an editor, "I had rather publish one of your horses in the centre than have such a looking sheet." But Mr. Bonner's purpose was answered by one insertion, and the contract was withdrawn.

As shown in an earlier chapter with his extravagant pay for one short story from Dickens, Bonner made it a *Ledger* policy to seek out and pay top dollar for well-known writers' and public figures' contributions to his paper. His contributions to the growth and development of the detective story, however, are, at best, problematic.

The New York Ledger

In 1855 Bonner, who had risen from printer to owner of the *Mercantile Ledger*, changed the name of the paper to *The New York Ledger*, and changed its character and its intended audience. Within a short time he made it one of the most popular publications in the United States. Almost from the start the *Ledger* featured stories about crime; the first was "The Two Nephews," a physician's account of preventing murder by poison (with the aid of a stomach pump), run on April 26, 1856. In the 1850s and early 1860s two well-known writers, Emerson Bennett and Sylvanus Cobb, Jr. (who Bonner lured away from Ballou's employ), wrote most of the stories about crime and detectives to appear in the *Ledger*; in the late 1860s and 1870s Amy Randolph, Mary Kyle Dallas, and Judge Clark joined Cobb as the *Ledger's* crime fiction regulars.

Publishing an average of five crime stories per year, superficially at least, in the early years the *Ledger* followed the lead of *Chambers' Edinburgh Journal* and the notebook publishers by adding an authenticating phrase about their sources to the titles of its crime stories: thus, for instance, "Helen Montressor, or Judge Remsen's First Client" (May 31, 1856); "The Bank Vault: From a Lawyer's Notebook" (August 22, 1857); "Finding a Criminal: From the Notes of an English Detective" (January 9, 1859); "The Colonel's Will: A Lawyer's Story" (January 30, 1858); "Assassin of Castellane: From the Records of a French Policeman" (June 12, 1858); "A Hunt on the Highway: From the Record of a Sheriff" (March 26, 1859); "The Silent Witness: From a Lawyer's Diary" (January 26, 1861); and "Resting Powders: From the Diary of a Physician" (September 28, 1861). From the beginning, however, crime stories in the *Ledger* differed considerably from those in contemporary magazines, story papers, and newspapers — for one thing, they were clearly and no doubt purposefully provincial. Big cities rarely serve as the settings for the crime stories in the *Ledger*. "Resting Powders" takes place in Lancaster, Pennsylvania; "The Disguised Robber" (August 8, 1857) is set in Lawrenceberg, Indiana; "The Murderer's Ordeal" (August 10, 1861) occurs in California; "The White Perfumery Bottle" (October 13, 1860) is set in Alexandria, Virginia; "Unexpected Evidence" (June 26, 1858) is set in Kentucky; "The Sheriff's Story" (May 30, 1863) takes place "on the Wabash"; and "Arresting a Murderer" (July 17, 1865) happens in Texas. Indeed, rural Mississippi serves as the setting for a number of *Ledger* crime stories: "An Unexpected Witness" (October 11, 1856); "The Two Fingered Assassin" (June 20, 1857); "Retribution, or Rodden the Gambler (April 6, 1861), and "The Horse Detective" (March 30, 1861). In line with the predominately small town or rural settings of the stories, one of the more popular crimes in *Ledger* stories is the murder of travelers in wild places between small towns: see "A Sick Robber" (August 9, 1858); "Unexpected Evidence" (June 26, 1858); "The Trained Horse" (January 4, 1862); "The Sheriff's Story" (May 30, 1863); "Hidden Crime Revealed" (January 14, 1865); and "A Strange Affair" (April 1, 1865).

Through the 1860s stories in the *Ledger* that feature professional detectives are decidedly in the minority and those few that appear tend to take place outside the U.S.— typically in Britain; thus, for example, "Finding a Criminal: From the Notes of an English Detective" (January 9, 1858); "Mysterious Robberies A Detective's Story" (March 1, 1862); "Catching a Burglar" (August 16, 1862); and "The Jewel Thief: A London Detective's Story" (August 13, 1864). By extension, crime stories in the *Ledger* set in America typically do not feature professional detectives as heroes, but instead rely on physicians and lawyers — the most common learned authorities in small towns — and sheriffs. Because of their expertise, physicians expose poisoners in "The Two Nephews" and "Resting Powders"; "The Pen Knife Blade," which turns on a dissection, is subtitled "A Leaf from a Surgeon's Diary." More common, especially in Cobb's stories, are lawyer heroes. Thus not only do the pieces with authenticating tags in their titles cited above feature attorneys, they frequently appear as heroes in other *Ledger* stories through the 1860s (see "Important Evidence, A Lawyer's Story [June 9, 1866]; "A Juror's Testimony" [September 8, 1866]; etc.). Perhaps the most important of the *Ledger* lawyer stories of the 1860s is the anonymous "A Defence Without Evidence" which focuses on judicial rules of evidence in righting a circumstantial wrong. Sheriffs and deputy sheriffs play the detective's role in "A Camp Adventure" (September 24, 1859), "A Hunt on the Highway" (March 26, 1859), "The White Perfumery Bottle" (October 13, 1860), and "The Sheriff's Story" (May 30, 1863).

Just as the *Ledger* ran stories which were aimed at appealing to rural and small town readers, its crime stories were largely conservative and focus not on the detective's methods but on the plot as an example of the working of Providence. The world of the crime stories in the *Ledger* is largely one in which it is easy to discern the nature of people. Bad people mostly look bad:

> She was a tall, dark, saturnine woman, with coarse, masculine features, black, sharp, sunken eyes, and with nearly as much beard on her face as her husband ["Hidden Crime Revealed"];

or

He was a dark looking man, thirty years of age, and not such a one as I should have ever chosen as a companion. The darkness of his skin was in all probability caused by exposure in traveling; but then there was a darkness deeper than this which was apparent at least to me ["The Two Nephews"].

It is a world in which physiognomy is accepted as science:

I was always fond of the science of physiognomy. From my youth up, I was noted for my proclivity for reading the character of a man from his face; and I finally became such an adept in the art, that I could occasionally guess the very thoughts of the individual whose countenance I was studying ["The Murderer's Ordeal"];

He was of very dark complexion, with straight, black hair, scanty black beard, and small, piercing black eyes, and I could not help believing that not many generations back there had been an Indian parent in the family. In general outline his head had what we commonly term the female form, but not so in local developments. The ears were broad and thin, standing out from the mastoid process in a peculiarly cautious manner; the seat of the perceptive faculties, directly over the eyes, was very prominent, while the reflective group was sadly deficient. And this slope of deficiency continued on, cutting off almost entirely the dwelling places of benevolence and veneration, leaving the summit of the skull at the seat of self-will and self-esteem. His nose, in profile, was of the Hebrew or commercial mould; but when seen in front view it was found to be too thin for any great work; yet it was the most emphatically money-getting nose. His voice was, if I may use the expression, a sort of button-hole voice — low, oily and insinuating. His vocal organs were never intended for any great range of power, but were made for use in corners and closets, and for producing tones that would not startle even a mouse if he desired to entrap the tiny marauder. I saw his handwriting, and I found it to be as delicate and regular and finely traced as the most perfect copperplate impressions that are to be found in our copy-books. It was one of those entirely mechanical, negative hands which indicate a character so secretive that only an expert physiognomist can read it ["The Apothecary's Compound"];

And in some cases detectives hardly need physiognomy or evidence:

I felt sure that if I could once get my eye upon the murderer, I should know him. There is something in the very look and bearing of a man who has done a murder, as palpable to me as the color of the Ethiop. I can see it written on his face, though how I cannot tell. It may be an intuitive perception, or it may be from long habit in hunting rogues ["Finding A Criminal"].

And if their experience with evil doers does not suffice, detectives can rely on other powers:

...though, as matters eventually turned out, I have reason to believe my steps were directed thither by the mysterious workings of an Overruling Providence.
I felt, however, that Providence was directing me in its own mysterious way, and that it was my duty to pursue the investigation, leaving the result to a Higher Power ["Murder Will Out" December 3, 1864].

Indeed, in the background of many of the *Ledger* crime stories resides the belief in nature as an actively moral phenomenon. Thus when humans cannot sort out guilt, animals do it for them. In "The Horse Detective" (March 30, 1861), for example,

> Thus it was, that a noble and affectionate animal, with a wonderful intelligence, not only pointed out the murderer of his master, but the very spot where the terrible crime had been committed, thus being the instrument, in the hands of Providence, of retributive justice ["The Horse Detective" March 30, 1861].

Ledger stories begin with the same motifs found in most contemporary fiction — inheritance, robbery-murder, somnambulism, etc. — but they tend to avoid plots associated with big cities and commerce (e.g. counterfeiting and embezzlement) that were beginning to emerge in magazine and newspaper fiction. Additionally, romantic love becomes a significant feature of a growing number of *Ledger* stories at mid century. "The Torn Newspaper" (October 30, 1858) and "The Murder at Cedar Glen" (November 19, 1864) both center on love triangles; "A Strange Adventure" (June 4, 1864) turns on love versus class prejudice, as does "Who is the Thief?" (December 31, 1864) which is a fully articulated love romance going from falling in love, ritual death with false accusation, to marriage after the perpetrators reveal themselves.

Another New Audience

Flag of Our Union and *The Ledger* were refined literature compared to what George Munro' *Fireside Companion* carried. Here is a passage that reflects on the quantity and quality of the *Companion's* contents:

> *From a St. Louis Exchange.* Last week copies of the Fireside Companion were gratuitously circulated on the streets of St. Louis. The occasion of this seeming generosity was the beginning of a new story, entitled "The Giant Detective in France; or, the Beautiful Mystery of Paris," by "Old Sleuth," author of "Prince of Detectives," etc., etc., etc. Here is the opening sentence:
>
> A giant's arm cut the air like an avenging sword, a giant's fist landed between a pair of fierce, gleaming eyes, and one of the meanest and most contemptible specimens of humanity keeled over like a circus clown, turning a back somersault, and immediately there followed the explanation in most excellent English:
>
> "Take that, you swarthy-faced scoundrel! and learn to keep your hands off a helpless maiden."
>
> (Here we may suppose that the author pauses in his writing and gives a wild and blood-curdling snort, of the old Bowery pattern, while his eyes gleam with the fire of consuming ferocity.)
>
> A glance at the opening chapters of this story indicates that it is a sample of sensational literature run mad, and it is noticed here only as a specimen of a very

vicious form of current fiction. The traditional Ledger story which has made Robert Bonner a millionaire, though open to severe censure on its absolute merits, is infinitely better and purer than the style of sensational trash that is given to the public through the columns of some of the younger story papers. Such publications appeal to a depraved taste, and gratify the most brutal longings. The bulk of their patronage comes from the uncultured and illiterate classes, as the newsdealers well know. They diffuse a malign and pestilent influence, and represent a base prostitution of literary art. The sensational literature of America has attained a dangerous growth, and, in its worst forms, is productive of immeasurable mischief [*The Literary News*, February 1884].

This was not the first time censure was cast on Munro and his works and it's not altogether difficult to understand why. The year after his *Fireside Companion* hit the streets it started to run stories about crime and detectives and most of them are lurid, sensational, and quite short. The parade of the *Companion's* crime pieces began with "Medical College Sketches. The Chemist's Story; or Science vs. Murder" (April 18, 1868). Here readers observe the chemist — who is also a police surgeon — finding arsenic in a victim's stomach by means of Marsh's test. But the substance of the story concerns the providential salvation of said chemist after he is bound and faced with the ticking of an infernal machine filled with nitroglycerin. This is a bland preview of a number of *Companion* stories run in the paper's first years centered on threats to their heroes' lives and limbs. Perhaps the most grisly describes the fate of Jack Finall ("A Detective's Story," November 22, 1869):

At this instant a trap door opened in the floor and a curious-looking machine slowly ascended.

It was made of two heavy stone rollers which could be raised or lowered one over the other and both worked with cranks at the side.

Jack was lifted and lashed on a board with his arms extended in front of him and then plank and all was lifted and placed with his feet toward the rollers.

I saw in an instant. They were going to crush him between the rollers.

Close to this was the fate of "Earless Bill the Detective" (February 14, 1870):

"Your time has come," said one of the ruffians, "and you're not the first that has tried to entrap us; but they all disappear very mysteriously, the same as you will. We don't kill you at once," he continued, with a brutal laugh, "but we bleed you to death scientifically."

In its early years *The Fireside Companion* carried a few stories which concerned the discovery of evidence; in "A Detective's Sketch" (August 3, 1869), for example, the lawyer hero finds bits of overlooked evidence to free an innocent man. But the earliest of these stretches the boundaries of mid-nineteenth century propriety — thus "My First Case" (June 27, 1868) combines forensic evidence with a bare breast:

I closed the door and bent over the form of the murdered girl, and drew aside the light waist she wore and bared her breast. *There, right over the heart, scarcely visible, was a small dagger wound.* The blow had been a sure one, and driven with such force that the under part of the hilt was outlined on her fair skin; and there must have been some mark on it, for there were two letters of the sentence that I could see by gazing sharp. The letters were W and S. Strange that no blood had flowed from that wound; but I judged that it had been well washed. I had seen enough; and now all was clear to me.

All of this was a bit too much for anti-vice crusader Anthony Comstock. In what was one of the opening rounds of forcing public debate about the morality of publishing stories about crimes and violence, in 1872, Comstock and the New York police raided Munro's offices and arrested the publisher for publishing indecent material.

Dime Detective Libraries

But lurid or not, short fiction about detectives did not continue to be Munro's bread and butter — nor did the family story paper format for that matter. Serials had always been the big sell in family story papers, but until the 1870s the papers ran a miscellany of serial romances centered on frontiersmen, love romances, and a variety of other Old World themes and heroes — serial fiction often pirated from British sources. But in 1870 Munro discovered that detectives were a draw not only in short fiction but in serials as well; and in April of that year *The Bowery Detective* by Kenward Philip (the name of a newspaper reporter) came out in *The Fireside Companion*. This became Munro's next new thing and he began to regularly feature serial stories about a miscellany of detectives in *The Fireside Companion*: thus appeared *The Broken Dagger: or The Mysteries of Brooklyn* (Winter 1871); *The Boy Detective; or The Chief of the Counterfeiters* (Spring 1871); and *Perils and Escapes of a Detective* (Spring 1871). All of this served as prelude to the introduction of Munro's wildly popular detective, Old Sleuth, whose adventures began in the *Companion* with *Old Sleuth; or, The Bay Ridge Mystery* (beginning May 27, 1872). This was followed by an avalanche of Old Sleuth stories — stories that appeared both in the *Fireside Companion* and in an array of publications which continued to be reprinted until the early years of the 20th century. While Harlan Page Halsey, formerly a director of the Brooklyn Education Board, actually wrote the Old Sleuth stories, in the beginning Munro advertised them as having been written by Tony Pastor — a well-known song-and-dance man and one of the creators of what would become vaudeville. Indeed in his advertising Munro created the fiction that Pastor was his in-house detective story writer.

Thus in 1875 he advertised him as "Author of Old Sleuth, the Detective"; "The Shadow Detective"; "The Lightning Detective," etc. Like its successors, the first Old Sleuth story is a whirlwind of action. There are multiple crimes, past and present; several villains and their minions; chases around the countryside; captures and escapes; amnesia and other convenient illnesses; disguises; virtuous and pure women; a resourceful hero; and a quick nod given to clues and evidence. Old Sleuth the detective, introduced as "a tall, elderly, handsomely dressed, business-like looking man," is in fact the young, energetic, and oh so handsome Harry Loveland. Thus *The Bay Ridge Mystery* and all of the other Old Sleuth stories are quintessential melodrama.

Others, of course, were quick to notice the success of the new detective hero and the popularity of the format of the continuing story. Erastus Beadle's family story paper *The Saturday Journal* took to detectives soon after its creation in March 1870. Albert Johannsen in his *The House of Beadle & Adams and its Dime and Nickel Novels: The Story of a Vanished Literature* traces two decades of their history:

> The first Beadle detective story was written by Albert Aiken as a serial for the *Saturday Journal* and began June 10, 1871, in No. 65. Another by the same author began in No. 119, June 22, 1872, and one by Anthony P. Morris in No. 143, December 7, 1872. There was another by Aiken in No. 167, May 24, 1873, after which none appeared until December 30, 1876, when one by Charles Morris began in No. 355. There were three in 1877, and one in 1878. The next year they appeared in both the *Saturday Journal* and the *Half-Dime Library*. Excluding reprints, there were two in 1879, five in 1880, seven in 1881 and seven in 1882. The flood began the next year with 14 in 1883, and they soon overshadowed the Indian, western, and historical novels.

While brother Irwin Beadle shied away from including detective stories on the list of his Dime Novels, other bottom-feeders in the world of New York publishing saw the potential of moving the manly new detective hero out of the serial contained in the general purpose family story paper or magazine and putting a him between paper covers which contained an adventure "complete in itself, and full of startling and exciting scenes" (ad. for Tousey's Wide Awake Library, 1882). Thus in the 1880s the creation of collections of short books about detectives' adventures published in "detective libraries" came about. The first of these was created by Frank Tousey. Before finding detectives to market, Tousey had published a kaleidoscope of titles — mostly for boys: there were his story papers (*The Boys of New York, The Young Men of America, The Arm Chair*); there were his how-to books (*How To Write Letters, How To Cook, How To Flirt, How To Dance, How To Become Beautiful*); and there were his collections of titles gathered together in "libraries" (The Boys of New York Pocket Library, The Great Wide Awake Library). By 1881

Tousey included a number of detective titles in his general libraries — thus *Denver Dan and the Road Agents*, *Denver Dan and the Counterfeiters*, *Tim Finnegan the Young Irish Detective*, *Ferret the Little Detective*, *Dare Devil Detective*, *The False Detective*, and *Detective Sketches* appeared in his Wide Awake Library. The next year he specialized and published *Old Sleathy, the Government Detective* "by Police Captain Howard" as the first volume in his New York Detective Library. Between 1882 and 1898 Tousey published 801 titles in the New York Detective Library. Among that jumble of titles, some centered on clues (see #7 *The Marked Finger; or the Slightest of Clews*, #8 *The Broken Button*, #16 *A Torn Letter*, #19 *A Piece of Paper*), and some focused on oddity (i.e. #4 *Sam Sly and His Dog Detective*; #26 *The Dwarf Detective*; #31 *The Dandy Detective*; #49 *Dick Dark, the Boss Detective*). Tousey added a faint whiff of detective verisimilitude with many of his authors' names: viz. Police Captain Howard, A U.S. Detective, Alexander Douglas Scotland Yard Detective, Police Captain Williams, and A New York Journalist. Detective Old King Brady was one of the regulars in Tousey's various publishing ventures, appearing first in the New York Detective Library in 1885 ("Old King Brady, Sleuth-Hound" November 14, 1885).

The year after The New York Detective Library appeared, the continued sniping, pilfering, and lawyering about who owned what — especially the word "sleuth"— that went on between the Munro brothers led to the Old Cap Collier Library. In 1873 Norman Munro set up *The New York Family Story Paper* in competition with his brother, George's *Fireside Companion*. A decade later he published *Old Cap Collier, Chief of Detectives, or Piping the New Haven Mystery, by the Author of the Seaside Detective* (April 9, 1883), which became the first number in the Cap Collier Library which would contain over 800 titles before its demise in 1899. While Cap Collier is a paragon among detectives, he is not the only detective featured in the library that bears his name. In his early titles Norman Munro, like Tousey, included adventures of an assortment of odd detectives: thus the Second-Sight Detective, the Young Lady Detective, the Cautious Detective, and the Brooklyn Bridge Detective. He also freely swiped French stories —#14 *Vidocq the French Detective*, #26 *The Greatest Detective in France; or Piping the Mystery of Orcival*, by Emile Gaboriau, #27 *Old Taboret, the Self-Made Detective; or Piping the Larouge Case*, by Emile Gaboriau. While he had been publishing stories featuring or purportedly written by Old Sleuth since the mid–1870s, in 1885 brother George Munro established the Old Sleuth Library with a reprint of the first story — *Old Sleuth the Detective, or The Bay Ridge Mystery*. Unlike the earlier Libraries, however, George Munro's collection contained a significant percentage of stories about the advertised hero; nonetheless the collection still aimed for the same kind of variety as the other libraries. Thus the Old Sleuth collection featured unusual detectives (e.g. #6 *Old Electricity, the Lightening Detective*; #8 *Red Light Will, the River Detective*; #18 *The Lady Detective*; and #23 *The Gypsy Detective*) and stories set in a variety of locales (e.g. #14 *Billy Wayne, the St. Louis Detective*; #21 *Black Raven, the Georgia Detective*; #28 *Mura, the Western Lady Detective*; and #33 *The American Detective in Russia*).

By the beginning of the twentieth century the New York Detective, the Cap Collier, and the Old Sleuth Libraries combined to publish 1,724 titles. That Niagara of fiction about detectives, however, has tended to obscure much of the early history of the detective hero and the detective story in the United States. There was a considerable body of detective fiction printed in the United States before the advent of dime novels and its development bears witness to major changes both in the nature of authors, publishers, and readers and in all of the literary elements of the detective story — its hero, its plot, its setting, its theme, etc. What began as an exploration of a new profession and a new consciousness about the fallibility of Anglo-American law and justice with the potential for riveting storytelling rather quickly became very popular. And that popularity caused publishers and writers to simplify the form in order to appeal to what was becoming a very large and very different reading public.

Chapter Seven

Newspaper Detectives

During the nineteenth century detective stories began to appear, grew, and then prospered in a variety of mediums — periodicals aimed at various kinds and classes of readers as well as in anthologies of short stories and then in novels. But, from the beginning, detective stories also appeared in daily and weekly newspapers — indeed as the century progressed, newspapers helped to establish the genre and can claim a significant amount of credit for creating the modern detective story and making it popular.

Newspapers in the U.S.

Even before Massachusetts passed the first compulsory school attendance laws, a substantial number of adults in the U.S. in the nineteenth century could read. What almost all of them read was their newspapers — publications catering to their localities and frequently also their politics. Daily and weekly newspapers became remarkably accessible in the nineteenth century. By mid-century improvements in transportation allowed the timely distribution of newspapers across the country, and this had more than a bit to do with the meteoric rise in the number of papers in the U.S. In 1850, census figures show that there were 254 daily papers and 1,902 weekly papers in the country; by 1899 that number had risen to 2,226 daily papers and nearly 12,979 weekly papers and another 3,500 published less frequently — which means that a whopping 18,793 individual newspapers were published in America at the turn of the century. Readers in large cities could choose from a long list of papers, with New York boasting 50-some dailies near the end of the century. And from coast to coast every small community had its own paper or even competing papers. Thus there were titles like *The Wellsboro* [PA] *Agitator, The Marion* [OH] *Weekly Star, The Badger Workman* [Neillsville, WI], *The Freeborn County* [MN] *Standard, The Bangor* [ME] *Whig and Courier, The*

Hagerstown [MD] *Torch Light, The* [San Francisco] *Alta Californian, The Alton* [IL] *Daily Telegraph, The Thomas County Cat* [Colby, KS], *The Cedar Rapids* [IA] *Republican, The Columbus* [Nebraska] *Journal, The Tombstone* [AZ] *Daily Epitaph, The People's Vindicator* [Natchitoches, LA], and the *Indian Chieftain* published in Vinita in the Indian Territory that would become Oklahoma.

And they were cheap. For one thing, it was inexpensive to send them through the mails. Since the Revolution, politicians and the American elite had promoted newspapers as ways to spread information and educate the masses, and they supported their publication through generous subsidies of the mails. In 1845, for example, an act of Congress provided for the free distribution of four-page newspapers (or those less than 1,900 square inches) within 30 miles of their printing; in 1851, weekly papers of less than three ounces could be delivered free within the county in which they were printed. For greater distances, Congress set up the delivery charge at less than a cent a copy; for delivery of smaller papers (those of 300 square inches or less) the cost was set at one quarter the rate. Subscribers were required to pre-pay for this delivery; however, as few did, those who complied were offered a 50 percent discount. The biggest boon to newspaper subscribers came in 1874, when Congress reduced the postal rate on papers published weekly or oftener and assessed this charge to the publishers rather than to the subscribers. Thus, by 1880, 2,067,848,209 copies of newspapers were printed annually in the U.S. and of these, 852,180,792 went through the mail (A.M. Lee, *The Daily Newspaper in America*). After the Civil War prices per copy of newspapers ranged from a penny to five cents and yearly subscriptions cost from $6 to $10. While the *New York Times* sold for four cents a copy (reduced to three cents and then a penny in 1898), papers in rural areas often sold for two dollars (or less) per year.

It is a misnomer, however, to call most of the papers published in the U.S. in the middle of the nineteenth century newspapers, because, given the state of communications, national and even local news occupied the smallest amount of space in each issue. Often advertisements for local goods and services from lumber to quack nostrums took up the most space. In *The Central Wisconsin* of July 8, 1858, for instance, each eight-column page contained an increasing percentage of ads: page one had three columns of ads; page two three columns; page three five and a half columns; and on page four ads filled seven out of the eight columns. And in a lot of other small town and rural papers the proportion of ads to copy was the same. These ads, of course, provided revenue for the publishers, but they hardly supplied potential readers with much of a motive to regularly buy and read the paper. The news, such as was available, provided some of that motive for readers, but at mid-century many of the hundreds of local papers attracted readers by providing other kinds of offerings. It is difficult, for example, to find at mid-century a contemporary paper that does not contain at least one poem — providing, one supposes, uplift for readers. And both daily and weekly papers invariably printed a lot of fiction, frequently in sections labeled "Select Stories." Some mid-century papers, in fact, carried more fiction than anything else — except ads. Thus the front page of *The Denton* [MD] *Journal* ("A Family Newspaper Devoted to General Intelligence, Agriculture, Advertising, &c — Independent on All Subjects") for January 10, 1872, contains a poem ("Lay of the Hopeless"), four columns of a story ("Won and Lost" by Eben A. Rexford), two columns of biography of Patrick Henry ("Something New About Patrick Henry"), and a column and a half of miscellaneous, quasi-informational items — "Presence of Mind" and "Voice and Sound" — and a short anecdote: "A little girl was heard to wish she was a boy, 'so she could swear when she dropped her books in the mud.'" And from the 1850s until the end of the century detective stories became a regular part of the fiction newspapers across the U.S. used to attract, entertain, and perhaps even enlighten their readers.

Found Copy

Less than a decade after Poe's Dupin stories, the Recollections of a Police-Officer tales originally run in *Chambers' Edinburgh Journal* from July 28, 1849, through June 5, 1852, became a favorite among American readers. Most of them were published together as a book in New York by Cornish and Lamport entitled *The Recollections of a Policeman* in 1852. In the front matter of the book the publishers noted:

> Some of the tales included in this volume have already appeared in some of our American Magazines, and they proved exceedingly popular. It is believed they deserve a more permanent form — that this collection will gratify those familiar with their merits, and interest and instruct those whose interest is now for the first time directed to them.

This was partly true, as several of the stories had been printed in *Harper's* and in *The Eclectic Magazine*. But before they came out in book form or were printed in the magazines, a number of the Recollections stories had been lifted from *Chambers'* and published in American newspapers. Thus on October 10, 1849, two months after "The Gambler's Revenge — Recollections of a Police-Officer" came out in *Chambers'*, under the heading of "Tales and Sketches" the story took up five of the six columns on the front page of Wellsboro, Pennsylvania's *Tioga Eagle* — without attribution to *Chambers'*. On November 16 of the same year *The Oshkosh* [WI] *True Democrat* published the same story but cited its source. On November 1, 1849, *The Milwaukee Sentinel and Gazette* printed the second story in the Recollections of a Police-Officer series, "Guilty or Not Guilty," which had come out in August in Edinburgh. Indeed before Cornish and Lamport published the first of the so-called detective notebooks, many of the Recollections stories had appeared in American papers from a number of localities — thus "The Pursuit" appeared in *The Fond du Lac* [WI] *Journal* (September 12, 1850); the same story also ran in the *Wisconsin Argus* (October 22, 1850); the *Daily Sanduskian* [OH] printed "The Revenge" (March 18, 1851); "The Gambler," (on December 25, 1851), "Legal Metamorphosis" (on April 24, 1851), "The Revenge" (on May 8, 1851), and "The Twins" (on November 7, 1850) appeared in *The Janesville* [WI] *Gazette,* and "Flint Jackson" was printed in Wellsboro, Pennsylvania's *Tioga Eagle* (January 8, 1852). And it wasn't just *Chambers'* police officer stories that American papers rushed into print: in the 1850s there was a continuing appetite for *Household Words'* police pieces — from the publication of "Two Detective Anecdotes" (cut down from the original three anecdotes in *Household Words*) in *The Watertown* [WI] *Chronicle* (March 26, 1851) to "Tally-Ho Thompson" in *The New Hampshire Statesman* (October 25, 1856) to "Thief Taking in London" in the *Cedar Falls* [IA] *Gazette* (June 20, 1860). Grazing British pastures for crime stories in the 1850s also brought to readers in Wisconsin a piece from *Once a Week* ("The English Highwayman" published in the *Manitowoc* [WI] *Pilot,* December 23, 1850); one from *The Family Journal* ("The Porcelain Button" in the *Fox Lake Gazette,* May 12, 1859); and in North Carolina readers found a story originally printed in *The Liverpool Journal* ("Story of Circumstantial Evidence" in *The Fayetteville Journal* on April 17, 1854).

But it wasn't just British police stories that caught the fancy of American newspaper editors. Indeed the *New York American* carried an English translation of "Vidocq and the Sexton" a full decade before Poe wrote "The Murders in the Rue Morgue." Before mid-century news stories about the French police in general and Vidocq in particular got more press coverage than did news of British police and criminals. Indeed in the mid–1830s the term "Vidocq" meant "detective" to reporters who wanted to be *au courant* in their diction: thus "If the people of Hudson choose, they may have a Vidocq from our Police Office who will soon unravel the plot" (*Huron* [OH] *Reflector,* January 5, 1836). One early example of fiction probably derived from a French source is "The Female Assassin. As related by Prince Canbacers Arch-Chancellor of the French Empire" printed first in *The Rural Repository* (February 2, 1850) and then picked up by the *Janesville* [WI] *Gazette, The Prairie du Chien Patriot, The Wisconsin Democrat, The Sheboygan Mercury, The Wisconsin Statesman,* and *The Elyria Courier.* Several Vidocq stories made the rounds of U.S. papers before the Civil War beginning with "Vidocq and the Sexton," translated for the *New York American* in 1830, "Vidocq's Last Exploit," which appeared first in *The Western Fireside* [Madison, WI] on July 11, 1857; and "Vidocq and the Charcoal Burner of Rouen," which came out in a number of U.S. papers starting, perhaps, with *The Appleton* [WI] *Crescent* on December 29, 1860. And Vidocq tales continued in U.S. papers well into the 1880s: see "Diamond Cut Diamond" ("Translated from the French, for the SUNDAY UNION, by Mrs. N. E. White") in the *Sacramento Daily Record Union*, September 8, 1889. In 1859 and 1860 "Mysterious Deaths at Castellane: From the Records of a French Detective" circulated in American papers including Placerville, California's *Mountain Democrat* (June 25, 1859). Ballou, of course, ran two series of stories about French detectives (some of which were written by an American author) in his magazine in the 1860s and some of these found their way into others' publications. But the most important French writer to make an impact on the Anglo-American detective story in the last half of the century was Emile Gaboriau. And he appeared in the papers before he appeared in books. On March 31, 1867, *The New York Times* ran a five-column synopsis to *L'Affaire LeRouge* ("THE CASE OF THE WIDOW LEROUGE"); "The Jandidier Mystery," a translation of "Une Disparition" from Gaboriau's *Le Petit Vieux Des Batignolles* (Paris 1876), came out in the *Freeport* [IL]*Daily Bulletin* (December 3, 1877) and also ran in the *Wellsboro Agitator* (September 11,1877). On June 24, 1879, "A French Detective Story, How a Skilled Policeman Solved a Murder Mystery," a portion of *L'Affaire LeRouge,* appeared in San Francisco's *Daily Evening Bulletin*. And in the 1870s a number of papers ran a serial entitled *The Parisian Detective* "by Erskine Boyd" which is actually a translation of Gaboriau's *L'Affaire LeRouge*.

The trackless wilderness of plagiarism that characterizes most mid-nineteenth century newspaper and magazine fiction often makes it difficult to separate the original from the purloined in letters. That being said, while before the Civil War detective stories certainly appeared in a lot of American papers, only a trickle of them were original and/or set in the United States. The few stories that seem to be American originals in the 1850s (even if borrowed from other papers) include "The Peddler's Story" in the *Daily State Journal* [Madison, WI], January 10, 1857, which recounts how a Yankee peddler traps a criminal and turns him over to the authorities; "The Odd Glove, or Tricks Upon Travelers by Jeremiah Gyngoo" in the *Horicon*[WI] *Argus,* January 28, 1859, which tells of a trip down the Mississippi during which an innocent is accused and a disguised criminal is captured; and "The Young Widow, A Leaf from a Detective's Portfolio" in the *Wisconsin Patriot*, December 3, 1859, containing the narrative of a New York detective who employs disguise to catch a woman who has been filching jewels from the gentry. While American sources began to fill readers' growing appetite for detective stories after mid-century (and controversy about the lack of international copyright simmered) newspapers in the U.S. continued to dip into British publications for detective stories up to the end of the century in far greater proportion than they printed stories based on French sources. Thus from *Chambers' Edinburgh Journal, The St. Joseph* [MI] *Herald* ran "A Great Jewel Robbery" on August 14, 1869; *The Burlington* [IA] *Hawkeye* printed "Hunting Rogues" on April 4, 1879; *The Decatur* [IL] *Review* ran "How I Got Promoted" on December 20, 1880; *The Indian Chieftain* published "A Mysterious Valise, The Story Told by an Ex-Life-Guardsman" on July 2, 1885; and *The Pittsburg Dispatch* ran "Mrs. Harrington's Diamond Necklace" on July 4, 1891. Several pieces from *Cassell's Family Magazine* show up in American papers in the 1870s: "Who Took it?" in *The Stevens Point* [WI] *Journal* (August 23, 1879) and "A Bank-Note in Two Halves" in *The Waterloo* [IA] *Courier* (September 17, 1879). And in the 1880s editors of several U.S. papers cribbed detective stories from *All the Year Round* (e.g. "The Twin Brothers" in 1889); from *The London Truth* (e.g. "The Great Diamond Robbery in 1888); and from *The London World* (e.g. "The Tidal Train" in 1885).

That one finds fewer imported detective stories in American newspapers after the Civil War, however, had little to do with the sanctity of intellectual property — at least in the beginning. There simply came to be a lot more homegrown detective stories around, and with or without attribution or compensation for the writers, in the last half of the century many of those detective stories became viral and spread from one paper to another across the country. Thus, for example, more than a decade after "The Club Foot" ran in *Ballou's Monthly Magazine* in August 1862 it reappeared in Iowa (*The [Algona] Upper Des Moines,* August 31, 1876), in Greenville and Indiana, Pennsylvania (*The Advance,* August 3, 1876 and *The Indiana Progress,* November 2, 1876) and in Aiken South Carolina (*Aiken Courier Journal,* August 24, 1876). Increasingly, however, instances of the same story reappearing in newspapers across the nation had less to do with freebooting and more to do with the invention of syndication. Shortly after the Civil War Ansel Nash Kellogg imported B.B. Blackwell's process of preset, transportable type and offered to furnish his services to local papers: "Parties can order a certain number of columns of Story Department, or Miscellany, or Agricultural, or Children's Reading, as may suit their tastes." In 1873 in Britain William F. Tillotson created Tillotson's Fiction Bureau to market serial versions of novels to newspapers in Britain and the United States. Most significantly for the detective story, a decade later Irving Bacheller, at first with Kellogg, and then with S.S. McClure, went into the syndication business in the U.S. Because of these new approaches to marketing, in the last quarter of the century newspaper publication often became as lucrative for writers as magazine publication. In the 1870s the syndicates were on the look-out for detective stories, and by the

1880s they were also on the look-out for serial detective novels — thus *Under a Cloud; or Clearing Himself: The Thrilling and Absorbing Story of a Great Crime* syndicated by the A.N. Kellogg Newspaper Company in 1888, and *The Strange Footprint: A Detective Story* syndicated by S.S. McClure in 1889.

During the war years relatively few detective stories borrowed or original appeared in U.S. newspapers; notebook and story paper fiction dominated the early 1860s and in those years Americans saw the publication of *Strange Stories of a Detective, or, Curiosities of Crime* (1863), *Experiences of a French Detective* (1864), *The Diary of a Detective Police Officer* (1864), *The Autobiography of a London Detective* (1864), and *Leaves from the Notebook of a New York Detective* (1865)— as well as stolen versions of their contents published in their daily, weekly, or monthly newspapers. The period was also the heyday of crime and detectives in Ballou's and Bonner's family story papers where readers found fiction about felony in almost every issue. By the end of the 1860s, however, as detective fiction declined in main-line magazines, short stories about detectives published in newspapers — and written for newspapers — began to compete with those in family story papers. Indeed some newspapers went through phases of running what amounted to detective story features: thus *The New Orleans Picayune* ran a number of stories entitled "A Detective's Experience" between 1868 and 1871. Closing in on the next century, original and borrowed detective stories became usual and accepted features in many if not most American newspapers. In 1880, for example, The Westminster Detective Library's partial record lists 36 individual detective stories published in papers across the U.S. including *The Hagerstown* [MD] *Mail, The Long Islander, Palo Alto* [IA] *Reporter, Stevens Point* [WI] *Journal, The Racine* [WI] *Argus, Freeborn* [MN] *County Standard, Janesville* [WI] *Gazette, Indiana* [PA] *Weekly Messenger, The* [New Philadelphia, OH] *Ohio Democrat, The* [Gettysburg, PA] *Star and Sentinel, The Bismarck* [ND] *Tribune, The Oxford* [IA] *Mirror, The Portsmouth* [OH] *Times, The Allen County* [OH] *Democrat, The Dover* [OH] *Weekly Argus, The Waukeshaw* [WI] *Freeman, The Lowell* [MA] *Sun, The Sioux County* [IA] *Herald, The Rocky Mountain* [CO] *News,* and *The St. Louis Globe-Democrat. The Bismarck Journal,* in fact, printed three in 1880: "Circumstantial Evidence" (May 21), "The Wronged Wife" (June 16), and "The Ebony Bedroom" (July 30). And from the 1860s onward, year by year until the end of the century the number of detective stories in American papers increased.

The Spice of Life

And with those numbers came variety — the kind of variety that notebooks, or magazines, or dime novel libraries did not provide. First of all there was length. Not counting stories run in two installments or serial novels, fiction about detectives in U.S. newspapers came in a wide variety of sizes, from under 1,000 words — "Detected by Peculiar Habits" from the *Detroit Free Press* in 1889 ran 927 words — to those running close to 10,000 — "The Stolen Laces" in *The* [Warren, PA] *Ledger*, December 7, 1888, has 9,070 words. While all of these can technically be called detective stories (i.e. narratives that involve a crime and its solution), a number of particular branches of the genre flourished in American newspapers in the last half of the nineteenth century. There were comic pieces that went from farce to satire — from Twain's "Making a Fortune" (*Indiana* [PA] *Democrat*, November 2, 1871) to "A Clever Detective Story" (*Pullman* [WA] *Herald*, March 30, 1889). There were love romances with a thin film of detection added, stories like "C.S.A." in the *Defiance* [OH] *Democrat* (August 16, 1862), or "June's Valentine, How It Won a Lover and Caught a Thief," in the *Elyria* [OH] *Democrat* (February 14, 1889). There were initiation or growth stories exemplified by all of the "My First" titles: e.g. "My First Case" (*Waterton* [NY] *Reunion,* May 9, 1888); "My First Detective Job" ([Colorado] *State Herald*, March 29, 1889), "His First Case: How a Detective Found the Lost Money and a Wife" (*Chillicothe* [OH] *Constitution*, March 21, 1891). There were chase narratives like "Trailing a Thief" (*Pullman Herald* [Pullman, Washington Territory] October 19, 1889). There were courtroom dramas aplenty. There were a few exposes: "A Famous Detective Officer; or, How He Managed" from the *Albany Evening Journal* in 1868. There were pieces whose sole goal was offering melodramas observed by and related by detectives:

> "Then I'll die with you. I, too," he said, turning to me, "am equally guilty. I planned the deed; I helped to execute it; I will not be separated from him."
> "This is strange devotion in a boy."
> "Boy no longer; I am this man's wife," and shaking loose her bright yellow golden curls disclosed the features of one of the most noted, as well as beautiful, decoys in the city — an outlaw's daughter and a murderer's wife ["A Midnight Adventure, A Detective's Experience," *Fort Wayne Democrat*, June 3, 1869].

and

> Years afterwards we ascertained that the real culprit was her son! She had confessed a sin that she had never committed, to give him an opportunity to escape ["A Detective's Experience: A Female Forger, *New Orleans Picayune*, 1869].

There were overtly moral tales:

> "What kind of boys become burglars?" the reporter asked.
> "All Kinds."
> "Do good boys ever get to be thieves?"
> "Yes, when they fall into bad company" ["A Detective's Sermon, *The Lowell* {MA} *Weekly Sun*, September 22, 1883].

And there are even poems. Thus:

> A motive they sought for the terrible deed,
> And found it beyond the least doubt;
> They saw in their quest the miller's strong
> chest
> Wide open and rifled of all it possessed,
> The money bags turned Inside out.
>
> These amateur sleuth-hounds went hunting
> around
> To find of the villain some trace;
> And people looked wise as if the disguise
> Of the villain would fail if it came neath
> their eyes,
> No matter how guiltless his face
> ["Mystery of the Mill," *New York Evening
> World*, June 6, 1890].

Tangentially, there were also newspaper stories that mention places — lot of different places. Thus newspaper readers found stories not only set in the usual places of London, Paris, or New York, but also a lot of stories set in St. Louis, or Cincinnati, or the gold fields of California, or New Orleans, or the backwoods of Kentucky, or Australia, or Mexico, or (most frequently) small town U.S.A.

Something Old

Just because the medium changed from the pseudo-biographical note-book stories of the 1850s and early 1860s to narratives labeled as fiction printed in newspapers, however, did not mean that all of the new stories were fundamentally different from those that began appearing in *Chambers' Journal* in the early 1850s. In some respect, they were not. As in notebook fiction, one of the prominent advertised aims of newspaper stories was to inform readers about the life of the detective. Thus one finds authenticating tags in the titles of lots of the stories. There are the "A Detective's Experience" stories run in the *New Orleans Picayune* cited above, and stories called "A Detective's Story" (versus "A Detective Story") were close to ubiquitous until the 1890s — the title appears, for instance, with different stories in the *Janesville Weekly* (March 4, 1864), the *Tioga* [PA] *County Agitator* (August 14, 1867), the *Allen County Democrat* (November 1874), the *Hagerstown Herald* (January 28, 1886), etc. As in *Chambers'*, moreover, lawyers also sometimes got billing in the titles and subtitles of personal experience detective stories throughout the period: thus "All for a Will: A Lawyer's Story" (*Dubuque Daily Herald*, June 2, 1867),

"An Old Lawyer's Story," (*Burlington* [IA] *Hawk Eye*, July 16, 1874), and "The Lawyer's Secret" (*McCook* [NE] *Weekly Tribune*, February 7, 1884). Newspapers, however, had a significant advantage over the notebooks in creating the illusion of being factual accounts of detectives' experience — they were, after all, newspapers and although fiction was customarily labeled as such, nonetheless detective stories appeared in the same physical place as snippets of real news that was sometimes about crime and detectives. Furthermore, by the late 1860s it became usual for reporters to be introduced into newspaper detective stories as listeners or as narrators (but not actors) in order to authenticate them. Thus:

> An incident in the experience of two men well known in the city of New Orleans, as the most skillful and accomplished detectives in the Southern country, has been related to the reporter ["A Detective's Story," *Cedar Valley* {IA} *Times*, September 17, 1868].

> "It was just before the war," said a detective to our reporter, "that a queer trick was played me by a young fellow accused of forgery ["A Detective's Story," *The Hawaiian Gazette* [Honolulu} December 16, 1868].

> "The detective who arrested that foreign defaulter the other day didn't have much of a clew," remarked a reporter to one of Detroit's ablest detectives. "The peculiar habit the fellow had of placing his finger lengthwise along the side of his nose, in a contemplative manner, was the only thing that gave him away" ["Detected by Peculiar Habits," *Sandusky* {OH} *Daily Register* October 28, 1889].

> "During the month of September, 1889, I was employed on a confidential case in St. Paul, Minn.," said Detective Ainge of the New York, Ontario and Western railway service, to a Herald reporter, "and was one day standing in the Union depot watching for a suspected party, when a train came in well filled with passengers ["Detective Ainge's Story," *The Watertown* {NY} *Re-Union*, January 21, 1891].

Along with the attraction of depicting how detectives work, newspaper fiction in general also shared with notebook fiction a fundamental concern about the workings of the law — particularly the use and abuse of evidence. Superficially just as in the notebooks, the titles of a lot of newspaper fiction underline concerns about evidence. Indeed, titles including "circumstantial evidence" span the period: "A Story of Circumstantial Evidence" (*Fayetteville* [NC] *Observer* April 17, 1854), "Pretty Meggy Heywood: A Tale of Circumstantial Evidence" (*Waukesha County* [WI] *Democrat*, June 21, 1859), "Convicted but Innocent, A Story of Circumstantial Evidence" (*Denton Journal*, September 20, 1873), "Circumstantial Evidence" (*Franklin* [MA] *Gazette*, May 2, 1879), "Circumstantial Evidence" (*Bismarck Tribune*, May 21, 1880), "A Story of Circumstantial Evidence" (*Sioux County Herald* (September 9, 1880), "Circumstantial Evidence" (*Cambridge* [OH] *Jeffersonian*, January 29,

1885), "Saved from the Gallows, or, Circumstantial Evidence" (*The Van Wert* [Ohio] *Republican*, August 23, 1888), and "Circumstantial Evidence" (*Syracuse Standard*, March 1, 1891). Not only do titles introduce the subject of circumstantial evidence, characters in the stories frequently broadcast their divergent views on the subject to the readers. Here's a cross-section:

> It is quite common, and some would think it fashionable, to cry out against circumstantial evidence; while the fact is — and a fact not to be disputed — that no evidence is more reliable.

> Circumstances do not lie; they are trustworthy as far as they go, and the only thing required to render the evidence indisputable is, that no link in the chain shall be lacking ["Circumstantial Evidence," *Bismarck Tribune* May 21, 1880].

> "The first murder case I tried," said one of them, "was stranger than fiction, as you will admit, and is quite as remarkable as any of the cases you have referred to where innocent men have been wrongfully convicted upon circumstantial evidence. It ought to have been reported as an example of the unreliability of the direct and positive testimony of eye-witnesses who tell what they believe to be the truth" ["A Lawyer's Story" {Syracuse} *Sunday Herald*, May 29, 1881].

> In my profession as a detective I have often been asked if I believed in the virtue of circumstantial evidence. In every instance I have replied in the affirmative. While the profession may make a man hard-hearted and anxious to convict, it is nevertheless a certain fact that a complete chain of circumstantial evidence against a criminal will settle his case sooner than half a dozen respectable witnesses. Lawyers can browbeat and confuse, and the veracity of a witness can be slurred or impeached, but when you strike against a circumstance it is not so easy to step over it or explain it away ["A Detective's Story" *Decatur* {IL} *Daily Republican*, December 2, 1887].

> An English lawyer once said that circumstantial evidence would hang the king of England. While that was putting it pretty strong, it is admitted that a chain of circumstantial evidence has often sent men to the gallows. If a circumstance can be explained away, it is but a shadow. If it cannot be explained away, it becomes a menace to the prisoner's life. A witness may be bribed, abducted or impeached. A circumstance is a lion in the path demanding blood ["Evidence Broken," *The Lowell* {MA} *Sun*, February 16, 1889].

Moreover, concerns about evidence, its presence or absence, its interpretation or misinterpretation, form the skeleton of the majority of detective story plots in nineteenth century detective fiction whether in notebooks, magazines, family story papers, or newspapers. And this ramifies beyond the plot framework of these stories.

From the beginning of detective stories, finding and interpreting either human or material evidence, whether to free an innocent wrongly accused or to solve a mystery, depended upon a variety of personal and intellectual qualities which writers used to establish the detective's character and separate him or her from other characters in the world of the narrative. One of those qualities, that of being the indefatigable searcher, goes back to the metaphor included in the name of Samuel Ferret in *Chambers'* Barrister stories in the 1850s. Newspaper fiction clearly followed the tradition of using the term "ferret" as one of the terms that defined what the detective does:

> He knew, Jennings did, how much tougher would be the work of any officer to ferret him out, and bring him back if he were to put thousands of miles of rail and river and unhealthy climate, and lawless places betwixt him and the usual landing places of passengers from England ["The Detective: After a Forger," *The Berkshire County* {MA} *Eagle*, November 7, 1861].

> Proceeding at once to headquarters, after a short consultation with the Chief, I received instructions to go immediately with another officer and endeavor to ferret out the perpetrator of this foul deed ["A Detective's Yarn," *The* {San Francisco} *Golden Era*, October 19, 1862].

> I had performed my self-imposed detective duty with success, and having learned during my journey in secret from my husband much of the cowardice of criminals and the double character of men and women, I found myself fascinated with the idea of ferreting out the guilty and rescuing the innocent ["A Woman of Mystery," *St. Louis Globe-Democrat,* January 26, 1879].

Along the same lines, fictional detectives hunt, they follow scents, and they run down clues — threads that lead them through labyrinths. A lot of detective stories involve sorting out human evidence and therefore center on the hero's ability to read people:

> "Ah, I've a wonderful eye," he used to say. "I can see through and through a man. The human face is an open book to me, and I'm never mistaken in what I read there. And it's not the face alone that I read: I see through a man's behavior. The rogue who tries to look honest; the criminal who tries to look innocent — none of them ever escapes my eye. Yes, sir, I'm a born detective; I never suspect a man without cause. If there were a few men in the police like me there wouldn't be so many undiscovered murders, and if there were a few men in the world like me there wouldn't be so many political humbugs about. Yes, sir, I can see through impostors and rascals of all descriptions, and it's all my eye" ["An Amateur Detective," *The Syracuse Sunday Standard*, September 22, 1889].

Increasingly, however, especially late in the century when quack sciences were being debunked, detectives and detective stories began to pay more attention to minutiae — the tiny bits of evidence others had overlooked. Thus "minute" and "minutely" litter the descriptions of newspaper detectives' discoveries:

> I now felt the importance of examining the footprints of the murderer, carefully and minutely, in order to form some idea of the man himself ["Detecting a Murderer, *Alta Daily Californian*, September 4, 1864].

> Like a true detective Jack examined every article minutely ["A Bank-Note in Two Halves," *Waterloo* {IA} *Courier*, September 17, 1879].

I have known him to look into a room that he had never seen before, and in the evening, when we were sitting together, he would describe that room, down to the maker's name on the clock, as minutely as if he were holding a picture of it in his hand at the time ["Why He Failed," *Lafayette* {LA} *Advertiser*, December 12, 1891].

And, of course, finding and relentlessly following the tiny, hidden clue was the basis of the plots of a lot of newspaper fiction. It leads to stories like those with "button" or "hair" in their titles: thus, for example, "The Matched Button," "Traced by the Buttons," "The Porcelain Button," "Hung by Three Hairs," and "Saved by a Hair."

As in several of the detective notebooks of the 1860s, American newspaper fiction developed a minor thread of stories centered on forensic science — hence forensic stories. Microscopes became part of the office equipment of some detectives — "going to his trunk brought forth a small bottle containing diluted alcohol, in which floated what appeared to be a human cuticle, and putting the same under a microscope looked at it under the light of his study lamp long and carefully ("Found Dead," *Franklin* [Philadelphia, PA] *Gazette*, April 29, 1881), and "Upon submitting them to a microscope he discovered that they were dead — that they had been pulled from a wig. The murderer, then, had concealed his natural hair beneath a wig" ("Hung by Three Hairs," *Lewis County Democrat* [NY] April 14, 1883). Among the things detectives found and interpreted in newspaper fiction was blood, and the examination of blood became pivotal in some stories. Thus:

In an hour we returned, and found Denning with a large microscope and several small vials. I immediately went to my desk, took out Roger Lyon's knife, and handed it to him, asking him to see if there were any pieces of stone in the blood stains which still showed on the knife. He knew my meaning in an instant. And taking a vial he carefully rinsed a portion of the stains with its contents, letting the liquid run upon a glass slide, which he had placed in the sun's rays.

Impatiently we waited and watched for the evaporation of the liquid. It was soon all gone, when he placed the slide in the microscope and turned the powerful sun-glass upon it. On looking in the lens, minute particles of stone, some stained with blood, were plainly visible, thus proving that the knife had been used to cut the stone of the cellar after the blood had stained it ["Saved by a Mark," *The Indiana Progress*, December 12, 1872].

and

I asked to see the blood stained clothing, and I found it to be a single daub of blood on a white vest. It was a curious mark, such as I had never seen before, and when I quietly investigated further, I discovered that the murdered man had been struck on the back of the head and fallen forward on his face. He had very thick hair, and while the blow had crushed the skull, he had bled but little. The blood would not spurt from such a blow. The body had to been lifted, and so how did Graham get that blood stain? Accident gave me the knowledge ["Evidence Broken," *The Lowell Sun*, February 16, 1889].

More than blood evidence, fingerprints held a fascination for newspaper writers in the U.S. well before Mark Twain used them in *Puddin' Head Wilson*, serialized in *The Century Magazine* in 1893–4:

> When I locked up the safe for the night, I spread upon the knob of the door and upon the money drawer, some pale red lead, being careful not to get enough on to be easily noticed. I had left the cash account open, to be closed up in the morning. When I next opened the safe all was as I had left it.
>
> The next night I fixed the knob in the same manner, and on the following morning I found forty dollars gone!
>
> Upon the pocketbook were finger-marks of red lead and when I came to the cashbook, I found the same kind of marks there ["The Left-Handed Thief," *Ft. Atkinson {WI} Standard*, November 28, 1861].

> I procured a ladder and placed it beside the water spout, and made a careful examination of it from the ground up to the library window.
>
> I was soon assured that the murderer had made use of that means to reach the window. The lead was soft and yielding, and it bore the finger marks of the assassin, each finger had made an impression in the metal ["The Left Handed Assassin," *The Coshocton {OH} Democrat*, November 2, 1864].

> The murderers, evidently quitted the premises by the front garden, for their footsteps were discernable close to the iron railings, and on the white stonework which supported them there was the mark of a bloody left hand, the fingers, thumb and ball of the hand being very distinctly marked. As the murderers had evidently wiped their hands on the curtains before quitting the room, it was believed that one of them had wounded his left hand when in the act of cutting the throat of his victim, and hence the bloody imprint on the stone ["Murder Will Out," *Sioux County {IA} Herald*, March 9, 1876].

> Mr. Slater and Mr. Carson proceeded without loss of time to carry out the object of their visit. A smooth tablet had been prepared, with a thin coating of coloring material on the surface, and it was explained to the men that it was desired to obtain from each of them an impression of the thumb of the left hand ["Story of a Thumb Mark," *Wellsboro Agitator*, February 14, 1882].

> Not pretending to notice his discomfiture, I made some jovial remark, and when he brought a cloth to wipe up the ink, I asked him if he had ever noticed the peculiarity of the under part of a person's thumb. He had never heard of it, and entered heartily in the experiment, soon regaining his self-composure. With little trouble I secured one of the pieces of paper on which he had placed his thumb, and we were soon on our way to the theater. I paid little attention to the play, and when it was over rushed home to compare the mark on the piece of paper with that on the block. They were identical; every line and curve was the same. I knew that was proof enough to convict him; and the next day a warrant was sworn out for his arrest ["A Tell-Tale Ink Mark," *Iowa State Reporter*, June 17, 1886].

But often the attraction in newspaper detective stories lies both in the describing the method of finding small, hidden things, and in finding that unexpected clue in an unexpected place — the legacy, perhaps, of Poe's use of the term "outré." This motive on the part of writers led to titles such as "The Fatal Potato" (*The Franklin Gazette*, October 18, 1889) and "The Sexton's Boots" (*Waterton* [NY] *Reunion*, June 18, 1883). The term "Strange" appeared in the 1863 notebook volume *Strange Stories of a Detective*, and terms like "strange," "odd," and "queer" in titles in newspaper fiction also pretty clearly signal that this kind of story will follow the title: e.g. "The Odd Glove, or Tricks upon Travelers" (*Horicon Argus*, January 28, 1869), "Strange Clews to Crime" (*Stevens Point Journal*, January 31, 1880), "A Queer Clue" (*Daily Kennebec* [ME] *Journal*, October 11, 1877). Here fictional detectives need more than persistence and acute vision when confronted with the unconventional. So both notebook and newspaper fiction add the term "sagacity" to the talent of simply being observant to the catalog of qualities that define their detectives:

> The case in all its phases ranks among the most curious and interesting in criminal annals. The slight clew so perseveringly followed, the little incidents which pointed so unerringly toward the culprit, and the sagacity with which these little hints were followed to the end, places the detective art among the most notable and useful of the sciences ["Detecting A Rogue," *The Indiana Progress*, April 29, 1891].

Indeed the term sagacity became so attached to the detective in fiction that Twain used it to describe the police chief in his burlesque piece "The Stolen White Elephant" (1882):

> When I read the first half of that I was more astonished than ever at the wonderful sagacity of this strange man. He not only saw everything in the present with a clear eye, but even the future could not be hidden from him.

Finding things, and assigning (or reassigning) guilt may have formed the center of the detective story — whether in the newspaper or not — but, like earlier fiction, newspaper fiction offered readers something more than the discovery of the solution to a crime. And the titles of the stories suggest what they offered. One of the things that sets detective stories apart as a genre is that they are easily and quickly identified — often before readers begin the first lines of the narrative — by their titles. This is particularly true in newspaper fiction. Of course the stories with the word "detective" in their titles are legion. But added to those, there are "mysteries" ("A New Year's Mystery" *Palo Alto* [Iowa] *Reporter,* March 18, 1876), "affairs" ("A Strange Affair" *The* [Wellsboro] *Agitator*, August 30, 1865), "experiences" ("A Detective's Experience" *The* [Sag Harbor] *Corrector,* October 3, 1868), "romances" ("The Romance of Crackers's

Neck" *Palo Alto Pilot* [Iowa], August 4, 1882), and even yarns ("A Detective's Yarn" *The* [San Francisco] *Golden Era*, October 19, 1862). "Story," of course, is the most common title word — sometimes meaning pseudo biography but increasingly meaning a form of fiction — found in both "A Detective's Story" and "A Detective Story." The words "case" and "adventure" often come into titles. "Case" is a term connected to courts and lawyers and set procedures: etymologically, a case is "a statement of the facts of any matter *sub judice*, drawn up for the consideration of a higher court," or "the case as presented or 'put' to the Court by one of the parties in a suit; hence, the sum of the grounds on which he rests his claim" (OED). Close to being universal in the narrative and dialogue of newspaper stories, the term comes up in titles as well: e.g. "Bicornet's Murder Case" (*Indiana Progress*, October 9, 1879), and "A Possible Case of Circumstantial Evidence" (*Frank Leslie's Illustrated Newspaper*, April 6, 1867). Used less in dialogue and narration, but more often in titles, the word "adventure" comes up a lot. Thus, for example:

> "Thrilling Adventure in a Gaming House" (*The Boston Traveller*, 1856),
> "A Midnight Adventure: A Detective's Experience," (*Fort Wayne Democrat*, June 3, 1869),
> "Rescued: Midnight Adventure in New Orleans" (*Coshocton Age*, January 21, 1870),
> "A Night of Adventure" (*New York Times*, April 21, 1872),
> "A Detective's Adventure" (*M'Kean County Miner*, May 22, 1873),
> "A Mountain Adventure" (*Defiance Democrat*, February 25, 1875),
> "Murder will out: A Gold Digger's Adventure" (*New York Star*, 1877),
> "A Detective's Adventure" (*Indiana Progress*, Dec 11, 1879),
> "A Detective's Adventure (*Daily Evening Bulletin* [San Francisco], July 30, 1881),
> "A Detective's Adventure (*Gettysburg Star and Sentinel*, March 15, 1882), and
> "A Fearful Adventure" (*Sioux County Herald*, Dec 18, 1890).

The term "adventure," to be sure, suggests a plot and atmosphere seemingly quite different from the suggestions raised by the word "case." An adventure is "The encountering of risks or participation in novel and exciting events; adventurous activity, enterprise" (OED). While the term "case" suggests reason, logic, and order, "adventure" suggests a variety of strong emotions — surprise, thrills, fear, horror, and terror. But seemingly antithetical, detective stories (and newspaper detective stories in particular) bring them together and often combine the excitement of thinking, understanding, and intellectual competition with the experience of physical danger. Thus:

> As a consequence he soon grew exceedingly communicative, and entertained the colonel with the most thrilling Scotland Yard narratives, all illustrative of the cleverness of rogues and the superior astuteness of detectives ["A Butterfly," *Sandusky Daily Register*, July 8, 1890].

The Detective Hero

American readers could encounter several kinds of fictional detectives in the last half of the nineteenth century in their newspapers: there were government detectives, private detectives, other professionals (lawyers and physicians) who acted as detectives, and there were amateurs. While the United States became the setting of the majority of the detective stories printed in American newspapers during the period, nonetheless, a few detectives from England, from France, and a sprinkling of other countries as well made their way into the daily and weekly papers. Diminishing in numbers as the century progressed, detectives in stories set in France were usually government agents who reported to Prefects. More numerous, but still a minority, fictional detectives from England came from Scotland Yard — with British private detectives as the rare exception. With all of the stories set in the United States, however, credentialing the heroes — i.e. determining how they were entitled to call themselves detectives or to act as detectives — is not simple or easy. In the 1850s and 1860s, physicians and to a larger extent lawyers served as the heroes of some of the detective stories set in the U.S. — particularly in *The New York Ledger*. Their educations and professions licensed them to act as detectives. Throughout the century papers also printed a small number of stories featuring amateur detectives. In 1883, for example, there was "A Young Woman Detective" (*Stevens Point Journal*, August 11, 1883), "The Little Detective" (*Bangor Whig and Courier*, January 27, 1883), and "Bob Becomes a Detective" (*Newport* [RI] *Mercury*, April 7, 1883). Circumstances and necessity made amateurs, often the least likely amateurs, into detectives.

The majority of newspapers' stories, however, were about professional detectives. Nonetheless, it is still often difficult in newspaper fiction to separate official detectives employed by government entities from employees of private detective agencies or from self-employed private detectives. In a few cases writers deputized their heroes by creating federal government agencies for them: thus "Tea-Chest Tommy, The United States Open Service Detective" (*Daily Leader* [Eau Claire, WI] May 27, 1885), and "A Bit of Good Luck, By a Secret Service Detective" (*Sterling* [IL] *Standard*, June 3, 1886). There is the impressive sounding United States Detective Service:

> With the exception of Mr. Americus Biggerton, Chief of the United States Detective Service, whose men all traced Brashear not only to the place he adopted in his flight, but to the house where even now he lay awaiting a favorable opportunity to quit the country ["Watching a Defaulter," *The Freeborn County Standard*, September 18, 1879].

And there is even a "detective association":

I therefore concluded to lay the matter before the chief of the detective association which, it was alleged, had been successful in bringing many burglars, forgers and other crooked fellows to justice. The chief listened to my story attentively … ["Buggs the Detective," *The Atchison* {Kansas} *Globe*, December 27, 1883].

Even before Ballou's series of stories, the "New York detective" had become a standard figure in notebook, magazine, and newspaper fiction. But whether New York detectives were employed by the New York City Police Department is a vexed issue. In the real world, even relatively late in the century, many jurisdictions in the United States had only rudimentary police forces, and even large cities (including New York) were still trying to figure out how to organize or even establish an official detective division in their police departments. It is not surprising, then, to find that private detective agencies sometimes did the work that later became the sole jurisdiction of official police departments — and that newspaper fiction reflected that fact. Making things harder, while detectives in period stories may sometimes report to or mention a "chief," that term was used to indicate both the executive of a police department and the head of a private detective agency. Likewise, two of the motivators of detective heroes in period fiction — rewards and promotions — applied equally to police officers and agency detectives. Finally, although occasionally a story opens in a detective's "office," it is not necessarily an office in a police station. Indeed, very few detective heroes mention or report to police headquarters and uniformed police officers are conspicuously absent from period fiction. Fundamentally, newspaper detectives act as free agents whether paid by cities or by private clients and being an outsider became one of the defining characteristics of the detective hero whether in magazines, family story papers, or newspapers.

While some newspaper stories do take place in large cities, detectives in a lot of period fiction do not work in or do their work in cities. Indeed, a significant percentage of the period's detective stories take place in small towns. And often, in small towns, when trouble strikes, the first response is sometimes to send off to the city for a detective:

My next proposal is this: Telegraph to Chicago for one of the best bank detectives in the city, and place the case in his hands. A train leaves Chicago at 1 o'clock. It is now shortly after 11. If you commission me to write the dispatches I will guarantee to have both on the train and we can meet here at 3 to consult ["A Detective's Ruse, *Daily Kennebec Journal*, November 16, 1886];

and

Mr. Mansfield caught at the suggestion at once, and telegraphed to the city for a detective. The next train brought one of the best detectives in the city of New York, and he lost no time in setting to work ["A Baffling Mystery, *The Daily Independent* {Monroe, WI} September 29, 1891].

As an outsider, like the other emerging nineteenth-century American hero, the cowboy, the detectives in a lot of the stories are often peripatetic. Thus:

> My firm — a detective agency — had been instructed by the authorities at Mineral Point to depute some one to attend the inquest and to sift the affair to the bottom. An intimation was given me that speedy promotion would follow on my unraveling the mystery, and as I got unlimited discretion concerning my line of action, whether as regards the time I should occupy about the business, the expenses I might incur or the assistance, if any, I should avail myself of, I felt that my professional reputation was at stake and that if another such murder were to be committed ere I had unearthed the guilty parties, the sooner I changed my vocation for some other the better for myself and my employers ["Number Eight," *Waterloo Courier* December 15, 1886].

and

> "It was during such weather as this," continued the detective, "when I was summoned from an important case in some southern town to undertake the highly lucrative (if successful) case of ferreting out this band of criminals. They had given the local authorities no little trouble and the case was getting 'cold' when I took a hand" ["A Detective's Story," *St. Louis Globe-Democrat*, May 18, 1886].

The nature of newspaper fiction, however, eliminates the possibility of heroes being perceived as rootless drifters, partly because being a detective is the hero's dominant characteristic, partly because series heroes in newspaper fiction are extremely rare — and consequently the hero has no life after the end of the story — but more importantly because at the close of the narrative the focus almost invariably shifts from the detective to the solution and then to exonerating innocence and finally, at the end, to assigning guilt and, briefly, describing its punishment.

It goes without saying that almost all fictional detectives whether in newspapers or elsewhere were men. Nonetheless, a handful of stories feature women who choose to be detectives or, more commonly, have the role thrust upon them. "A Woman of Mystery" (*St. Louis Globe-Democrat*, January 26, 1879), centers on "New York's Great Female Detective":

> We shall call her by one of her most familiar names, Mrs. Lucille Benton — the shrewdest detective of all those whose ambition has led them to aspire to that title, while forgetful of their sex and their lack of endurance. While other women have succumbed to the wearing watchfulness, the long, wearisome journeys, the tension of nerve, this woman has not grown old, or weak, or lost her wonderful power of self-control, her matchless vitality, her incredible endurance.

"Clubnose," a story copied from *Chambers'* widely reprinted in 1880, recounts Margaret Saunders' initiative in solving a crime and her appointment as an official detective:

It was a novel and startling proposition, and the inspector was somewhat taken aback by it; however, he faithfully promised to lay the matter before the authorities at Scotland Yard, and let her know the result; with that he and his companion left her. The end of it was that her wish was granted. Margaret Saunders was duly enrolled as a female detective, and a most active and intelligent officer she proved to be [*The Ohio Democrat*, April 29, 1880].

In "The Missing Jewels" (*The Columbus* [NE] *Journal*, September 3, 1882) one Miss Bardulph signs on as a housekeeper in order to find missing jewels, and after she does she refuses the proposal of the scion of the house with the admonition to

"be reasonable Mr. Dorman, for you must be well aware that I am not at all the sort of person whom you ought to marry. And beside," she added, with a quaint little laugh, "I have a profession now, and I must not wed one who knows nothing of the instincts and requirements of my calling."

The handsome young fellow was somewhat agitated by her speech which he considered daring and significant.

"Surely, my dear Anne," he faltered; "you would not wish to become a professional detective?

Less professional, the hero of one of the earliest newspaper stories about a woman acting as a detective, "Brought to Justice" (*Sterling* [IL] *Standard*, June 3, 1866), is the daughter of a murdered officer who is called upon to undertake "a delicate secret service":

One day I was surprised by a message from the Chief. He had conferred many favors upon my mother and myself, for my father had been one of his most trusted men. He had a delicate secret service which he considered me tilted to perform and which he wished to intrust to me. My pride arose in revolt. I could not be a "female detective." Such a dreadful name! But the compensation was liberal, and my father's last words came to me, "You must fill my place"; Could I afford to throw away this chance for a mere whim? Before I left the office I had received my instructions and since then had overruled my mother's objections and conquered my repugnance for the work, for the sake of the support it afforded us.

Rescuing a falsely accused loved one causes Maude Clarkson in "The Girl Detective" (*Allen County Democrat*, July 26, 1877) to disguise herself to get the goods on the real villain. In "The Tell-Tale Key, or a Woman as a Detective" (*Palo Alto Pilot*, May 27, 1875) the hero finds the material evidence to free her wrongly accused husband; and in "An Old Offender" (*Indiana Progress*, September 27, 1877) a detective's wife holds criminals at gun-point:

"Stop where you are, villains! I'll kill the first man who attempts to leave this car without my orders. You two rascals will oblige me dropping into the seats where you now stand, and remaining there until promptly disposed of."

Finally, "A Young Woman Detective" (*Stevens Point Journal*, August 11, 1883) tells of a canny country woman who detects and tells the local authorities how a peddler has been surreptitiously selling moonshine.

Because until the 1880s most newspaper fiction was short fiction, not much space existed for writers to expand upon the natures of their heroes beyond establishing those traits which led them to be successful detectives and to demonstrate them in action of righting the scales of justice. The opportunity to develop the detective's character beyond the hero's function of solving the crime might have been possible if the hero appeared in a series of stories, but, to date, only one series of newspaper detective stories with a continuing hero (Detective Varnoe in "Story of Crime," "The Finger of Providence," "A Double Crime," and "The Poisoner" appearing in 1880 and 1881) has come to light in the U.S. before the 1890s. This was both a blessing and a curse. Newspaper detectives in the U.S. were bracketed by Dupin at the beginning and Sherlock Holmes after 1891: two larger-than-life, eccentric geniuses who always knew the answers and, not surprisingly the type of detective character lampooned by Mark Twain first in "The Stolen White Elephant" (1882) and then with the advent of Sherlock Holmes in "Double-Barreled Detective Story" (1902). During the last quarter of the century there were also dime novel heroes who, in a much less sophisticated way, were larger-than-life individuals. Newspaper heroes while astute and quick-witted, more usually appeared as average people, willing to share a story (and often a cigar) with a reporter or with a friend. While the theme of justice forms an undercurrent in all of the fiction, newspaper detectives rarely act as single-minded avengers, but as professionals who solve problems. Increasingly, however, papers began to provide more extensive descriptions of people and places in their detective stories, but for that they needed more space.

Serials

In 1880 the population of the United States was 50,189,209 — 30 percent larger than the number recorded by the census of 1870. The growth of the size of U.S. cities was even more accelerated, often double the population in the decade after the Civil War. As noted above, the number of newspapers in major and even minor cities grew accordingly. Not only did the number of papers in cities like Cincinnati, St. Louis, and San Francisco increase, the sizes of those papers did as well. Take, for instance, the *Boston Daily Globe*: throughout the 1870s it was an eight-page paper, but by the middle of the 1880s it had become a 12- or 16-page daily. And it wasn't news alone that filled all of those pages. Across the country in the 1880s newspapers added features — they began covering sports, offering Sunday supplements, and soon would add puzzles and comics. While they are best known for the Hearst-Pulitzer competition of the 1890s, in the last quarter of the century papers in most cities across the nation engaged in what amounted to circulation wars. By the 1870s the trend was even apparent to the editor of Reno's *Daily Nevada State Journal* (April 5, 1875):

> The papers of San Francisco are at the present time engaged in a fierce conflict for the leadership and are not leaving a stone unturned to gain a point over their competitors. The *Bulletin* had issued a double sheet every day, and on Sunday a supplement additional; the *Chronicle* doubles itself three times a week; the *Call* issues a double sheet every Sunday, and the *Post* a "doubler" every Saturday.

And fiction played a role in those circulation wars.

Most prominently, there was the serial — the form long used to get the most income from literary efforts and one connected to such diverse titles as *Bleak House* and *The Bowery Detective*. The prospect of spellbound readers waiting for the next installment of a novel held an obvious allure for newspaper editors. With their modest sizes and in the absence of syndication, however, at mid-century few papers in the U.S. possessed the means to publish serial fiction. But the desire was there. This can be seen in a technique Robert Bonner used to attract even more readers to his family story paper: he would allow papers to print several chapters of one of the *New York Ledger's* serials at no cost, but withhold the remainder with the proviso that editors bump their readers to the *Ledger*. Thus *The Rock County* [WI] *Republican* (January 1, 1861) printed several columns of *Moses Oran; or, The Burglar's Nest* which concluded:

> The above is all of this story that will be published in our column. The continuation of it from where it leaves off here can be found in the New York Ledger, the great family story paper, which is for sale at all the stores throughout the city and country.

While in the 1870s the pirated translation of Gaboriau, *The Parisian Detective* "by Erskine Boyd," ran as a serial in papers like the *Defiance* [OH] *Democrat* (Spring 1877), the real beginning of serial detective stories in American papers was in the 1880s. There was a relatively steady stream of them appearing simultaneously in papers across the country with titles such as *A Clouded Life; or, The Red Manse Mystery* (*The Weekly* [NY] *World*, Winter 1880), *The Way of the World* (*Sacramento Daily Union*, Winter 1882), *The Red Band; or, the Mystery of Paris, A True Story of Detective Life in the Seventeenth Century* (*Boston Daily Globe*, Spring 1884), *A Polished Villain* (*Olean* [NY] *Democrat*, Spring 1885), *Dark Days* (*The* [Logansport, IN] *Critic*, Winter 1885), *The Mystic Sign* (Sterling [IL] *Standard*, Fall 1886), *The House on the*

Marsh; or, The Mystery of Alders (Sausalito [CA] *News*, Fall 1886), and *189-H-981 The Tale of a Bank Note, A Detective Story* (*Boston Daily Globe*, Summer 1888). Indeed serial detective stories became a standard feature of Pulitzer's *New York Evening World* with *His Secret* in 1887, *A Beautiful Victim* in 1888, *An International Mystery* in 1889, and *Done to Death* in 1890.

And S.S. McClure had been syndicating detective stories for some years before he made the rounds of the nation's papers with Malcolm Bell's serial *The Strange Footprint* in 1889.

For some papers like *The Boston Daily Globe* detective serials became a regular feature in the early 1880s. *The Globe* started the decade with a run of novels about detective Donald Dyke:

> *Donald Dyke; or, The Record of a Mysterious Case* (Summer 1882);
> *Donald Dyke; or, Who was the Guilty Man* (Fall 1882);
> *The Hoyt-Bronson Mystery; or, Donald Dyke's Most Difficult Case* (Fall 1882);
> *The Beacon Street Puzzle or, Unravelling a Tangled Skein,* by Ernest A.
>   Young (Summer 1883); and
> *A Wife's Strategy, and Her Search for Donald Dyke, The Detective Genius*
>   *Shown by a Woman* (Winter 1883)

Announcing these serials, *The Globe* ran ads like this one:

ON SATURDAY,
August the 20th,
The author of "Donald Dyke; or, Who was the Guilty Man," one of the BEST DETECTIVE STORIES EVER PUBLISHED IN THE UNITED STATES, will begin, in THE BOSTON DAILY GLOBE, a NEW DETECTIVE STORY, which in many respects, is superior to that VERY POPULAR WORK. It is entitled
THE
HOYT-BRONSON
MYSTERY;
Or
DONALD DYKE'S MOST DIFFICULT CASE.
Donald Dyke is familiar to our readers. His cunning, skill and bravery, which are able to overcome the greatest difficulties, are here put to their severest test.
Though baffled again and again, though several times narrowly escaping destruction himself, though opposed to men who are almost his equals in ability, HE IS AT LAST VICTORIOUS, PROTECTING THE INNOCENT AND PUNISHING THE GUILTY.
A novel feature in a detective story is introduced. A New York detective, one of the most accomplished in the profession, is employed to defeat the ends of justice, but HE PROVED NO MATCH FOR DONALD DYKE, WHO OUTWITS HIM.
The story is finely written, and is perfectly pure in sentiment and tone, having been undertaken mainly to illustrate detective skill and perseverance [August 19, 1882].

By mid-decade, along with short stories detective stories, serials became a regular occurrence in U.S. papers. And not only *The Globe* but other papers regularly ran ads alerting readers to their forthcoming detective serials: thus this ad about *The Diamond Button*:

> "A GREAT DETECTIVE STORY soon to appear in these Columns. If you want to be INTERESTED— absorbed — engulfed in interest — read the first chapters of this story. No Danger that You Will Not Follow It to the End [*Salt Lake Herald*, November 2, 1889].

The fashion for serial detective stories was furthered by the appearance in papers of serial versions of novels by well-known writers. First, there were versions of Julian Hawthorne's Inspector Byrnes novels. In the late 1880s Nathaniel Hawthorne's son, Julian, already a well-known literary figure, joined with Inspector Thomas F. Byrnes, head of the detective division of the New York City police department, inventor of the mug shot as well as the third degree, to produce a series of novels supposedly "from the diary of Inspector Byrnes." So sure were editors that readers would be galvanized by the Hawthorne/Byrnes books that papers like the *Isola* [KA] *Register* offered "A pamphlet containing the first three chapters mailed on receipt of a two cent stamp" on July 8, 1887 to readers who had missed the first chapters of *The Great Bank Robbery*. Hawthorne's *Another's Crime* was so popular that it was serialized in papers from coast to coast (from the *Boston Daily Globe* and the *Lowell* [MA] *Sun* to the *Galveston* [TX] *Daily News* and the *Salt Lake City Herald*) over a period of three years — from 1888 to 1891. After Hawthorne there was celebrity journalist Nellie Bly, whose *Mystery of Central Park* ran in the [New York] *Evening News* in the summer of 1889. There was also the overnight sensation Australian Fergus Hume. His first novel, *The Mystery of a Hansom Cab,* became so popular in Britain that speculators bought the rights to it and formed the Hansom Cab publishing company, and in 1888 in the U.S. the novel ran as a serial in papers across the nation, including the *Hamilton* [OH] *Daily Democrat*, and the *Cambridge* [IN] *City Tribune.*

The Mystery of a Hansom Cab and Hawthorne's Inspector Byrnes books, like other detective story serials of the 1880s, boil down to being sensation novels. In Hume's book, in addition to the complex mystery the author concocts, he adds elements that would not be out of place in one of Braddon's novels — a secret for which the hero is willing to die rather than reveal, bigamy, two competing police detectives, scenes of life among idle rich, a helpless woman heroine, missing documents, and an accused innocent. In the case of Hawthorne, with real crimes as a framework (bank robbery, extortion [*Section 558*], murder and espionage [*A Tragic Mystery*], and forgery [*An American Penman*]), the Inspector Byrnes books center on the passions and suffering of women — Mrs. Nelson in *The Great Bank Robbery*, Kitty Clive in *Section 558*, Mme. Desmond in *A Tragic Mystery*. Indeed *The Great Bank Robbery* is more about Mrs. Nelson's unbridled passions than about Inspector Byrnes tracking down the mugs who robbed the Manhattan Savings Bank. Nonetheless both writers begin to show bits of new elements in their renditions of the traditional sensation-detective novel. Unlike the detective heroes of short newspaper fiction or the swashbucklers of dime novels, Hawthorne draws a larger-than-life bureaucrat-hero:

> And there, at his desk, sits the Inspector, examining, weighing, deciding, investigating, advising, reproving, encouraging; cheerful or grave, as the case may be, even-tempered, firm, suave, stern, penetrating, impenetrable; the depository of all secrets, the revealer of none; the man who is never hurried, yet never behindhand; never idle, yet never weary; always patient, and always prompt. No position under the municipal government requires more tact than his, more energy, more courage, more experience. He must be pliant, yet immovable; subtle, yet straightforward; keen, yet blunt. He must know all the frailties of human nature, and yet be not too cynical to comprehend its goodness; he must be an advocate, and at the same time a judge. In short, he must be a chief of New York detectives; and, whatever else his office may be, it is certainly no sinecure [*Another's Crime*].

Perhaps more importantly, Fergus Hume in his novel posits a new kind of reader — one familiar with detective stories: thus these passages from *The Mystery of the Hansom Cab*:

> "But do you know anything of the detective business?" some one would ask.
> "Oh, dear yes," with an airy wave of his hand; "I've read Gaboriau, you know; awfully jolly life, 'tectives."

and

> "Murdered in a cab," he said, lighting a fresh cigarette, and blowing a cloud of smoke. "A romance in real life, which beats Miss Braddon hollow."

and

> In one of Du Boisgobey's stories, entitled "An Omnibus Mystery," a murder closely resembling this tragedy takes place in an omnibus, but we question if even that author would have been daring enough to write about a crime being committed in a hansom cab.

and

> "Puts one in mind of 'The Leavenworth Case,' and all that sort of thing," said Felix, whose reading was of the lightest description. "Awfully exciting, like putting a Chinese puzzle together. Gad, I wouldn't mind being a detective myself."

Prize Stories

That new kind of reader figures, as well, in another tactic of the newspaper wars of the 1880s and 1890s. By the 1880s inviting readers to submit stories in hopes of winning prizes became a usual way publishers used to attract readers. There was, for instance, *The Salt Lake Herald's* story contest in 1882:

> The object was to encourage and stimulate literary taste, and excite in those possessing latent ability a desire to bring their talents into activity. The results of our efforts were greater than we had anticipated. For the New Year's story prize of $50 there were ten competitors [December 31, 1882].

Story contests for some papers became a regular feature — thus at the end of the 1880s Pulitzer's *New York Evening World* ran a series of contests asking readers to submit stories about a variety of subjects — there was a sea story contest, a hunting story contest, and a fishing story contest:

> The EVENING WORLD HAS OPENED A Fish Story Contest as a novel, timely and interesting feature. The usual prize, a gold double eagle, will be given for the best fish story submitted [June 28, 1889].

But with detective stories a different kind of contest appeared in papers in the 1880s — one in which readers were asked to predict the conclusion of a detective story before the last installment was published in the paper. There was, for instance, the *Written in Red* contest in the *Boston Daily Globe*:

> "Written in Red," begins in THE GLOBE Today.
> It is the most unique of all detective stories.
> Only the authors know, as yet, the true solution of the mystery of Paul North.
> But the person who comes the nearest to finding out the true solution can have $200 by calling at THE GLOBE counting-room. If two or more persons submit equally good solutions, the money will be divided between them.
> The solutions are limited to 100 words, and must be sent in after all the story has been printed except the last chapter. The last chapter will be delayed a week or two to give all a chance.
> It is the most realistic detective story even written. Read every word of it, and then send in the result of your judgment of the plot. Remember that answers are limited to 100 words [August 3, 1888].

Two years later *The Globe* based its detective story contest on Scott Campbell's *Saved By Death*:

> At the end of the next to the last chapter the strange fate of Austin Craige will still remain unexplained. The solution of the fascinating mystery will be given in the very last chapter and not before. That solution and that chapter will not be published nor leave the author's hands until one week at least after the publication of the preceding chapter. But the readers of this story will have ample

opportunity to study all the situations and motives that enter into the mystery, which will be related fairly and candidly by the author, and an acute reasoner will thus be able to detect the true and logical secret of Austin Craige's strange fate. Watch the motives and scenes that fill this wonderfully ingenious story.

All are urged to follow the story attentively, day by day, and when the next to the last chapter has been printed, everybody should send THE GLOBE his or her judgment on the subject in letters of not more than 100 words each. No theories will be considered if received, before the last chapter has been given, and no person may send in more than one theory.

When a week or so has passed after that publication, all the letters will be carefully examined by competent persons and compared with the solution given by the author in the concluding chapter. Then the result will be announced in THE GLOBE, and whoever has come nearest the author's own explanation of the fate of Austin Craige will receive a reward of $200, while the two whose theories are next best will receive $50 each [*Boston Daily Globe*, December 27, 1890].

This kind of appeal to readers of detective stories assumes a new kind of reader — a person interested in close reading and problem solving as opposed to one interested in emotional involvement with others' real or imagined dangers. The prize stories of the 1880s also serve as precursors of the reader-writer contests run by a number of papers at the turn of the century and, more importantly, the reader-writer relationship explicit in golden-age detective fiction.

Read All About It

Newspapers played a unique role in the development of the detective story during the nineteenth century. In fact, they had a lot to do with its growth and prosperity. And that happened in a number of ways. At the beginning, American newspapers began the chain of events that would lead stories about detectives to move from the magazine in which they first appeared to the published "notebooks" that became numerous and popular in the early 1860s. Thus they were the first to notice and reprint the detective stories run by *Chambers' Edinburgh Journal* between 1849 and 1852. This led to their appearance in magazines and that specifically led to the publication of the first notebook, *The Recollections of a Policeman*, in 1852. In the 1850s and early 1860s notebooks and magazines became the focus of detective fiction, and while most American newspapers lacked the means to pay for original fiction, they helped to make the new genre popular by frequent reprints of detective stories snipped from magazines and notebooks — whether published in New York, London, or Paris. By the 1870s, on one hand detectives had become recurring, but usually incidental, characters in sensation novels, and on the other hand they had become the lead characters in harum-scarum hunt-and-chase stories in the lower tier of family story papers and dime novels. And a good bit of public criticism came to be leveled at the latter not only by Anthony Comstock who included the publishers of detective stories in his anti-vice campaigns but also in occasional newspaper pieces decrying the kind of literature to which youths were exposed. While all of that was going on, newspapers became the refuge of the detective story in the United States, printing them in increasing numbers in the 1870s and 1880s. These stories accustomed readers to a detective who was neither the cockney interloper who cleaned up messes at the big house nor the superhero who struggled to best gigantic villains and their minions. Main-line magazines shied away from publishing detective stories because of the bad reputation being attached to them. But not newspapers. Since writers had little space to develop their heroes in newspaper fiction, the role of their detectives became focused on solving people's problems, finding things that others could not, and on using that knowledge to make justice happen. It was also important to create a character and design a plot that avoided controversy. In this connection, it is surely worth noting that insofar as detective fiction in (and out of) newspapers was concerned, the Civil War did not happen — it simply is not mentioned. Organized crime is a rarity. And detective fiction throughout the period completely ignores all of the early warnings in the press about the abuses of private detectives and the mounting evidence of epic corruption in big-city police departments that would come to a head in the 1890s. Science and technology, however, were not controversial topics and that fact caused editors and writers to make it a familiar factor in shading character and making plots work. Finally, in the late 1880s and 1890s newspapers began to recognize and exploit the kind of relationship between the reader and the narrative implicit in Poe's stories — the relationship that called upon the reader to ask intelligent and even imaginative questions in an attempt to predict the plot's outcome. And that reader-writer contest would reside at the basis of the golden age of the detective story in Britain and the United States.

One, of course, should not overlook the fact that it was the thriving market for detective stories and serial novels in newspapers in the 1880s that sent syndication entrepreneur S.S. McClure on a talent scouting trip to England where he discovered "A Scandal in Bohemia" and bought the rights to it and other stories by a largely unknown author. These he introduced to Americans in their newspapers, which is where most Americans in the 1890s found Arthur Conan Doyle and his Sherlock Holmes.

Selected Bibliography

Ainsworth, William Harrison. *Jack Sheppard*. London: R. Bentley, 1839.
_____. *Rookwood*. Philadelphia: Carey, Lea, and Blanchard, 1834.
Alden, Henry Mills. "An Alibi." *Harper's New Monthly Magazine* September 1856: 513–522.
Alden, W.L. "Crime Detected — An Anecdote of the Paris Police." *Harper's New Monthly Magazine* May 1852: 768–769.
_____. "A Fourfold Alibi." *The Galaxy* June 1873: 823–828.
Alger, Horatio. *Ragged Dick or, Street Life in New York with the Bootblacks*. Boston: Loring, 1868.
"The American Library." *Blackwood's Edinburgh Magazine* November 1847: 574–592.
"Another Glimpse at My Hotel." *Putnam's Magazine* August 1857: 162–174.
Bentham, Jeremy. *A Treatise on Judicial Evidence*. London: Cradock and Joy, 1825.
Blackstone, William. *Commentaries on the Laws of England*. Oxford: Clarendon Press, 1765–1769.
Braddon, Mary Elizabeth. *Aurora Floyd*. London: Webster, 1863.
_____. *Henry Dunbar*. London: John Maxwell, 1864.
_____. *Lady Audley's Secret*. London: Tinsley, 1862.
_____. *The Trail of the Serpent*. London: Simpkins, Marshall, Hamilton, Kent, 1892.
Bragg, Henry. *Tekel; or Cora Glenco*. Philadelphia: Lippincott, 1870.
Buffum, Edward Gould. "A Case of Mistaken Identity." *The Galaxy* February 1868: 188–197.
Bulwer-Lytton, Edward. *Eugene Aram*. New York: Harper's, 1832.
_____. *Night and Morning*. New York: Harper's, 1841.
_____. *Paul Clifford*. New York: Harper's, 1830.
Burton, William E. "The Cork Leg." *The Gentleman's Magazine* March 1838: 172–180.
"The Case for the Prisoner." *All the Year Round* October 10, 1863: 164–168.
Caulfield, James. *Persons, from the Revolution in 1688 to the End of the Reign of George II*. London: H. Young, 1819.
Collins, Wilkie. *After Dark*. London: Smith, Elder, 1856.
_____. *Armadale*. London: Smith, Elder, 1866.
_____. "The Diary of Anne Rodway." *Household Words* July 19, 1856: 1–7.
_____. "A Lawyer's Story." *Harper's New Monthly Magazine* February 1855: 385–391.

_____. "A Marriage Tragedy." *Harper's New Monthly Magazine* February 1858: 334–357.

_____. *The Moonstone*. London: Collier, 1868.

_____. *No Name*. London: Samson, Low, 1862.

_____. "The Poisoned Meal." *Household Words* September 18, 1858: 313–318.

_____. "Who is the Thief?" *The Atlantic Monthly* April 1858: 706–722.

_____. *The Woman in White*. London: Samson, Low, Son, 1860.

Colquhoun, Patrick. *A Treatise on the Functions and Duties of a Constable...* London: Bulmer, 1803.

_____. *A Treatise on the police of the metropolis: explaining the various...* London: H. Fry, 1796.

"Confessions of an Attorney. Jane Eccles." *Chambers' Edinburgh Journal* February 22, 1851: 118–122.

"Confessions of an Attorney. Life Policy." *Chambers' Edinburgh Journal* October 19, 1850: 241–244.

"The Costly Kiss: A New York Detective Experience." *Harper's New Monthly Magazine* April 1859: 620–626.

Davis, C. "The Pigot Murder." *Harper's New Monthly Magazine* December 1864: 40–48.

De Fonblanque, Albany. *A Tangled Skein*. London: Tinsley, 1862.

Dickens, Charles. *Barnaby Rudge*. London: Chapman Hall, 1849.

_____. *Bleak House*. London: Bradbury Evans, 1853.

_____. "A Detective Police Party." *Household Words* August 10, 1850: 457–460.

_____. "A Detective Police Party." *Household Words* July 27, 1850: 409–414.

_____. *Doctor Marigold's prescriptions, the extra Christmas number of All the year round*. London: Chapman and Hall, 1865.

_____. *Great Expectations*. New York: Gregory, 1861.

_____. "Hunted Down." *New York Ledger* August 20 and 27 and September 3, 1859.

_____. *Martin Chuzzlewit*. London: Chapman Hall, 1850.

_____. "The Metropolitan Protectives." *Household Words* April 26, 1851: 97–105.

_____. "The Modern Science of Thief Taking." *Household Words* July 13, 1850: 368–372.

_____. *The Mystery of Edwin Drood*. London: Collins, 1870.

_____. "On Duty with Inspector Field." *Household Words* June 14, 1851.

_____. "The Spy Police." *Household Words* September 21, 1850: 611–614.

_____. "Three Detective Anecdotes." *Household Words* September 14, 1850: 577–580.

Dimitry, Charles. *The House in Balfour-street*. New York: G.S. Wilcox, 1868.

"The Drama." *The Monthly Review* December 1839: 457–472.

Dunlap, John. *A Treatise on the Law of Evidence*. Albany, NY: Gould, Banks, and Gould, 1816.

Edwards, Ann. *Archie Lovell*. London: Tinsley, 1866.

"The Enigma Novel." *The Spectator* December 28, 1861: 1428.

"Experiences of a Barrister. The Accommodation Bill." *Chambers' Edinburgh Journal* January 26, 1850: 53–56.

"Experiences of a Barrister. Circumstantial Evidence." *Chambers' Edinburgh Journal* October 20, 1849: 242–247.

"Experiences of a Barrister. The Contested Marriage." *Chambers' Edinburgh Journal* March 31, 1849: 193–197.

"Experiences of a Barrister. Esther Mason." *Chambers' Edinburgh Journal* June 30, 1849: 403–407.

"Experiences of a Barrister. The March Assizes." *Chambers' Edinburgh Journal* January 13, 1849: 24–28.

"Experiences of a Barrister. The Marriage Settlement." *Chambers' Edinburgh Journal* September 8, 1849: 147–151.

"Experiences of a Barrister. Mother and Son." *Chambers' Edinburgh Journal* May 26, 1849: 324–327.

"Experiences of a Barrister. The Northern Circuit." *Chambers' Edinburgh Journal* February 17, 1849: 107–111.

"Experiences of a Barrister. The Refugee." *Chambers' Edinburgh Journal* June 1, 1850: 340–345.

"Experiences of a Barrister. The Second Marriage." *Chambers' Edinburgh Journal* September 22, 1849: 178–181.

"Experiences of a Barrister. Writ of Habeas Corpus." *Chambers' Edinburgh Journal* June 9, 1849: 354–358.

"Fashionable Forger." *Harper's New Monthly Magazine* January 1852: 231–235.

Fay, Gaston. "How Lamirande Was Caught." *The Galaxy* March 1868: 355–365.

Felix, Charles. *The Notting Hill Mystery.* London: Saunders, Otley, and Co., 1865.

"A Few Brief Remarks on Her Majesty's Recent Providential Escape." *The Monthly Magazine* July 1840: 105–106.

Fielding, Henry. *An enquiry into the causes of the late increase of robbers...* London: A. Millar, 1751.

Fielding, John. *A plan for preventing robberies within twenty miles of London...* London: A. Millar, 1818.

Fleming, Mae Agnes. *A Wonderful Woman.* New York: G.W. Carleton, 1873.

Forrester, Andrew. *The Female Detective.* London: Ward Lock, 1864.

_____. *The Revelations of a Private Detective.* London: Ward Lock, 1868.

_____. *Secret Service: or, Recollections of a City Detective.* London: Ward Lock, 1864.

Gaskell, Elizabeth. "Disappearances." *Household Words* June 7, 1851: 246–250.

Gaspey, Thomas. *The History of George Godfrey.* London: Colburn, 1828.

"The Gentleman Beggar: An Attorney's Story." *Harper's New Monthly Magazine* October 1850: 588–592.

Godwin, William. *An Enquiry Concerning Political Justice.* London: Robinson, 1793.

_____. *Fleetwood.* London: R. Bentley, 1832.

_____. *Things as they are: or, The adventures of Caleb Williams.* London: Crosby, 1794.

Green, Anna Katherine. *The Leavenworth Case, A Lawyer's Story.* New York: Putnam, 1878.

Grose, Francis. *A Classical Dictionary of the Vulgar Tongue.* London: Printed for the editor, 1823.

Hatton, Joseph. *The Tallants of Barton.* London: Tinsley, 1867.

Henty, George A. *All But Lost.* London: Tinsley, 1869.

"History and Anecdotes of Bank Note Forgeries." *Harper's New Monthly Magazine* November 1850: 745–749.

Hitchin, Charles. *A true discovery of the conduct of receivers and thief-takers in and about the city of London: to the multiplication and encouragement of thieves, housebreakers, and other loose and disorderly persons : design'd as preparatory to a larger treatise wherein shall be propos'd methods to extirpate...* London: Printed for the author, 1718.

Holcroft, Thomas. *Memoirs of Bryan Perdue.* London: Longman, Hurst, Rees, and Orme, 1805.

Jackson, William. *The new & complete Newgate calendar; or, Villany displayed in all its branches. Containing accounts of the most notorious malefactors from the year 1700 to the present time.* London: Hogg, 1795.

James, G.P.R. "Mysterious Occurrence at Lambeth." *Harper's New Monthly Magazine* August 1855: 357–367.

James, T.P. *The Mystery of Edwin Drood. Complete. (Part Second of the Mystery of Edwin Drood.) By the spirit-pen of Charles Dickens, through a medium.* Brattleboro, VT: T.P. James, 1873.

Jeaffreson, John Cordy. *Novels and Novelists.* London: Hurst and Blackett, 1858.

Johannsen, Albert. *The House of Beadle & Adams and its Dime and Nickel Novels: The Story of a Vanished Literature.* Norman: University of Oklahoma Press, 1950.

Kelly, Gary. *The English Jacobin Novel.* Oxford: Clarendon Press, 1976.

Knapp, Andrew, and William Edward Baldwin. *The Newgate calendar: Comprising interesting memoirs...* London: Robins, 1825.

Leaves from the Diary of a Law Clerk. Brown: London, 1857.

Lee, A.M. *The Daily Newspaper in America.* New York: Macmillan, 1937.

"The Left-Handed Glove; or Circumstantial Evidence." *Stories for the Home Circle.* New York: Putnam, 1857.

Lippard, George. *The Quaker City: or, The Monks of Monk-Hall.* Philadelphia: By the author, 1847.

Logan, W. H., and James Maidment. *Pedlar's Pack of Ballads and Songs.* Edinburgh: Paterson, 1869.

Lynch, Lawrence. *Dangerous Ground or the Rival Detectives.* Chicago: Henry A. Sumner & Co., 1885.

_____. *The Diamond Coterie.* Chicago: Donnelley, 1884.

_____. *Madeline Payne, the Detective's Daughter.* Chicago: Alex. T. Loyd & Co., 1884.

_____. *Out of the Labyrinth.* Chicago: Alex T. Loyd & Co., 1885.

_____. *Shadowed By Three.* Chicago: Donnelley, Gassette & Loyd, 1879.

Mabbott, Thomas O., ed. *Edgar Allan Poe: Tales and Sketches.* Cambridge, MA: Harvard, 1978.

Martel, Charles, ed. *The Detective's Note-Book.* London: Ward Lock, 1860.

_____. *Diary of an ex-detective.* London: Ward Lock, 1860.

Matthews, Brander. "The Documents in the Case." *Scribner's Magazine* September 1879: 755–765.

McLeavy, James. *Curiosities of Crime in Edinburgh During the Last Thirty Years.* Edinburgh: W. Kay, 1861.

McWaters, George. *Detectives of Europe and America, or a Life in the Secret Service.* Hartford: J.B. Burr, 1878.

_____. *Knots Untied: or, Ways and By-Ways of the Hidden Life of American Detectives.* Hartford: J.B. Burr and Hyde, 1871.

M'Govan, James. *Brought to Bay, or Experiences of a City Detective.* Edinburgh: Edinburgh Pub. Co., 1878.

_____. *Hunted Down, or Recollections of a City Detective*. Edinburgh: Edinburgh Pub. Co., 1878.

_____. *Traced and Tracked, or Memoirs of a City Detective*. Edinburgh: J. Menzies & Co., 1884.

"Memoirs of Vidocq." *Foreign Quarterly Review* January 1829: 522–559.

"Memoirs of Vidocq." *The Westminster Review* July 1829: 162–180.

Miles, Henry Downes. *Dick Turpin*. London: W. Clark, 1845.

"Miss Whitelake's Diamonds." *Appleton's Journal of Literature* January 24, 1874: 99–104.

"Mistakes in Personal Identity." *Harper's New Monthly Magazine* December 1850: 69–72.

"Modern Novel and Romance." *The Dublin University Magazine* April 1863: 436–442.

Monk. *Going and Son*. New York: Published for the author by The American News Co., 1869.

"Mrs. Latour." *Southern Literary Messenger* April 1842: 485–508.

Newell, R.H. *The cloven foot being an adaptation of the English novel "The mystery of Edwin Drood," (by Charles Dickens), to American scenes, characters, customs, and nomenclature*. New York: Carleton, 1870.

Noel, Mary. *Villains Galore: The Heyday of the Popular Story Weekly*. New York: Macmillan, 1854.

"Our Female Sensation Novelists." *The Living Age* August 1863: 352–369.

Payn, James. *The Lost Sir Massingberd*. London: Samson, Low, Son and Marston, 1864.

Perkins, F.B. "The Boldero Murder." *Harper's New Monthly Magazine* May 1862: 818–823.

Poe, Edgar Allan. "The Balloon Hoax." *New York Sun, Extra* April 13, 1844: www.eapoe.org/works/tales/ballhx.

_____. "Barnaby Rudge. By Boz. Author of "Nicholas Nickleby, Oliver Twist." *Saturday Evening Post* May 1, 1841: www.eapoe.org/works/criticsm.

_____. "Enigmatical and Conundrum-ical." *Alexander's Weekly Messenger* December 18, 1839.

_____. "A Few Words on Secret Writing." *Graham's Magazine* July 1841: 33–38.

_____. "The Gold Bug." *The Dollar Newspaper* June 21 and June 28, 1843: www.eapoe.org/works/tales/goldbga1.

_____. "The Influence of Morals." *Southern Literary Messenger* July 1838: 415–424.

_____. Letter to Frederick W. Thomas, May 25, 1842: www.eapoe.org/works/letters.

_____. Letter to George Roberts, June 4, 1842: www.eapoe.org/works/letters.

_____. Letter to James Russell Lowell, July 2, 1844: www.eapoe.org/works/letters.

_____. Letter to Phillip Pendelton Cook. August 9, 1846: www.eapoe.org/works/letters.

_____. "Maelzel's Chess Player." *Southern Literary Messenger* April 1836: 318–326.

_____. "Murders in the Rue Morgue." *Graham's American Monthly Magazine* April 1841: 166–179.

_____. "The Mystery of Marie Roget." *Snowden's Ladies' Companion* November, December 1842, and February 1843.

_____. "The Purloined Letter." *The Gift, a Christmas and New Year's Present for 1845*. Philadelphia: Carey and Hart, 1844.

_____. "Raising the Wind; or, Diddling Considered as One of the Exact Sciences."

Saturday Courier (Philadelphia), October 14, 1843: www.eapoe.org/works/tales/diddlnga.

_____. "Review of New Books." *Graham's Magazine* November 1841: 248–249.

_____. "Thou Art the Man." *Godey's Lady's Book* November 1844: www.eapoe.org/works/tales/thartb.

_____. "The Trial of James Wood." *Alexander's Weekly Messenger* April 1, 1840: www.eapoe.org/works/misc/awm.

_____. "The Unparalleled Adventure of One Hans Pfaall." *Southern Literary Messenger* June 1835: www.eapoe.org/works/tales/unphll.

Pothier, William. *A Treatise on the Law of Obligations, or Contracts...* London: Strahan, 1806.

Potter, Humphrey Tristram. *A New Dictionary of all the Cant and Flash Languages: both ancient...* London: Macintosh, 1796.

"Recent Novels." *The Monthly Review* June 1830: 259–286.

"Recollections of a Police-Officer. Flint Jackson." *Chambers' Edinburgh Journal* November 15, 1851: 306–311.

"Recollections of a Police-Officer. "The Gambler's Revenge." *Chambers' Edinburgh Journal* July 28, 1849: 55–59.

"Recollections of a Police-Officer. Guilty or Not Guilty." *Chambers' Edinburgh Journal* August 25, 1849: 115–120.

"Recollections of a Police-Officer. Legal Metamorphoses." *Chambers' Edinburgh Journal* September 28, 1850: 195–199.

"Recollections of a Police-Officer. Mary Kingsford." *Chambers' Edinburgh Journal* May 3, 1851: 274–279.

"Recollections of a Police-Officer. The Monomaniac." *Chambers' Edinburgh Journal* April 24, 1852: 259–263.

"Recollections of a Police-Officer. The Pursuit." *Chambers' Edinburgh Journal* July 13, 1850: 23–26.

"Recollections of a Police-Officer. The Revenge." *Chambers' Edinburgh Journal* November 9, 1850: 294–298.

"Recollections of a Police-Officer. The Twins." *Chambers' Edinburgh Journal* June 22, 1850: 387–390.

"Recollections of a Police-Officer. The Widow." *Chambers' Edinburgh Journal* May 18, 1850: 313–318.

"Recollections of a Police-Officer. X.Y.Z." *Chambers' Edinburgh Journal* November 17, 1849: 308–312.

Register, Seeley. *The Dead Letter*. New York: Beadle, 1867.

"Reminiscence of a Bow Street Officer." *Harper's New Monthly Magazine* September 1852: 483–494.

"Reminiscences of an Attorney. Every Man His Own Lawyer." *Chambers' Edinburgh Journal* March 22, 1851: 178–181.

"The Reprieve; Or, the Wild Justice of Revenge." *Harper's New Monthly Magazine* August 1854: 371–381.

Reynolds, George W.M. *The Mysteries of London*. London: Vickers, 1845.

Richardson, Frances T. "Zizi, the Little Detective." *The Galaxy* July 1877: 61–70.

Richmond. *Scenes in the life of a Bow Street runner, drawn up from his private memoranda*. New York: Dover, 1976.

Riddle, A.G. *Alice Brand, A Romance of the Capital.* New York: D. Appleton and Company, 1875.

Russell, William. *Diary of a Detective Police Officer.* New York: Dick & Fitzgerald, 1864.

_____. *Experiences of a French Detective Officer.* London: C.H. Clarke, 1861.

_____. *Experiences of a Real Detective.* London: Ward, Lock and Tyler, 1865.

_____. *Leaves from the Journal of a Custom-House Officer.* London: Clarke, 1868.

_____. *Recollections of a Sheriff's Officer.* London: Aldine Chambers, 1868.

_____. *A Skeleton in Every House.* London: Darton and Hodge, 1863.

_____. *Strange Stories of a Detective.* New York: Dick & Fitzgerald, 1863.

_____. *Strange Stories of a Detective; or Curiosities of Crime.* New York: Dick and Fitzgerald, 1863.

_____. *Undiscovered Crimes.* London: Ward Lock, 1862.

"A Safe Investment." *Appleton's Journal of Literature* June 1870: 625–626.

Saunders, John. *One Against the World.* London: Tinsley, 1865.

The Scoundrel's dictionary, or An explanation of the cant words used by the thieves, house-breakers, street-robbers and pick-pockets about town. To which is prefixed, some curious dissertations on the art of wheedling; and a collection of their flash songs, with a proper glossary. The whole printed from a copy taken on one of their gang, in the late scuffle between the watchmen and a party of them on clerkenwell-green... London: Brownwell, 1754.

"Sensation Novels." *Blackwood's Magazine* May 1862: 564–584.

"Sensation Novels." *The Living Age* June 6, 1863: 435–453.

"Sensation Novels." *Quarterly Review* April 1863: 481–513.

Sharpe, Gustavus. *Confessions of an Attorney to Which are Added Several Papers on English Law and Lawyers by Charles Dickens.* New York: Cornish and Lamport, 1852.

Smith, Matthew Hale. *Sunshine and Shadow in New York.* Hartford: J.B. Burr, 1868.

Smythies, Harriet Maria Gordon. *Guilty or Not Guilty.* London: Hurst and Blackett, 1864.

Southworth, Emma Dorothy Eliza Nevitte. *Allworth Abbey.* Philadelphia: T.B. Peterson, 1865.

_____. *A Noble Lord and the lost heir of Linlithgow.* Rahway, N.J., Mershon Co., 187?.

Spofford, Harriet Prescott. "In a Cellar." *The Atlantic Monthly* February 1859: 151–172.

_____. "In the Maguerriwock." *Harper's New Monthly Magazine* August 1868: 348–355.

_____. "Mr. Furbush." *Harper's New Monthly Magazine* April 1865: 623–626.

Taylor, Alfred S. *Manual of Medical Jurisprudence.* London: John Churchill, 1844.

"The Tower of London...by W.H. Ainsworth." *Burton's Gentleman's Magazine and American Monthly Review* April 1840: 202.

Turner, Bessie. *A Woman in the Case.* New York: G.W. Carleton, 1875.

Twain, Mark. *Puddin' Head Wilson.* New York: Webster, 1894.

Vidocq, Eugene François. *Mémoires de Vidocq: chef de la police de sûreté, jusqu'en 1827, aujourd'hui.* Paris: Tenon, 1828.

_____. *Memoirs of Vidocq: principal agent of the French police until 1827.* Philadelphia: Carey and Hart, 1834.

_____. "Unpublished passages in the Life of Vidocq the French Minister of Police: The Bill of Exchange." *The Gentleman's Magazine* December 1838: 389–390.

_____. "Unpublished passages in the Life of Vidocq the French Minister of Police: The Conscript's Revenge." *The Gentleman's Magazine* May 1839: 282–286.

_____. "Unpublished passages in the Life of Vidocq the French Minister of Police: Doctor D'Arsac." *The Gentleman's Magazine* October 1838: 246–248.

_____. "Unpublished passages in the Life of Vidocq the French Minister of Police: The Gambler's Death." *The Gentleman's Magazine* February 1839: 88–89.

_____. "Unpublished passages in the Life of Vidocq the French Minister of Police: Jean Monette." *The Gentleman's Magazine* April 1839: 230–232.

_____. "Unpublished passages in the Life of Vidocq the French Minister of Police: Marie Laurent." *The Gentleman's Magazine* September 1838: 174–176.

_____. "Unpublished passages in the Life of Vidocq the French Minister of Police: Pierre Louvois." *The Gentleman's Magazine* March 1839: 146–148.

_____. "Unpublished passages in the Life of Vidocq the French Minister of Police: "The Seducer." *The Gentleman's Magazine* November 1838: 318–320.

_____. "Unpublished passages in the Life of Vidocq the French Minister of Police: The Strange Discovery." *The Gentleman's Magazine* January 1839: 39–41.

Walworth, Mansfield Tracy. *Beverly: or, The White Mask.* New York: G.W. Carleton, 1872.

Warner, Warren. *The Experiences of a Barrister.* New York: Cornish and Lamport, 1852.

Warren, Samuel. *Experiences of a Barrister and Confessions of an Attorney.* Boston: Wentworth, 1857.

Waters. *Autobiography of an English Detective.* London: Maxwell, 1863.

_____. *The Heir-at-Law and other Tales.* London: Lea, 1860.

Waters, Thomas. *The Recollections of a Policeman.* New York: Cornish and Lamport, 1852.

Watson, J.W. "The Pond House Murder." *Harper's New Monthly Magazine* 1864: 460–469.

Whitehead, Charles. *The Autobiography of Jack Ketch.* Philadelphia: Carey, Lea, and Blanchard, 1835.

Williams, John. *Leaves from the Note-Book of a New York Detective.* New York: Dick and Fitzgerald, 1865.

Wood, Ellen. *The Castle's Heir.* Philadelphia: Peterson, 1863.

_____. *The Channings.* London: Bentley, 1862.

_____. *East Lynne.* London: Richard Bentley, 1861.

Selected Digital Collections of Magazine and Newspaper Archives

Chronicling America: chroniclingamerica.loc.gov
Google Books: books.google.com
Google News Archive Search: news.google.com/archivesearch
Making of America: digital.library.cornell.edu/m/moa

Newspaperarchive.com: www.newspaperarchive.com
Proquest: www.proquest.com
The Westminster Detective Library:
www2.mcdaniel.edu/WestminsterDetectiveLibrary/Home.html

A Final Caveat

Plagiarism was epidemic in nineteenth-century magazine and newspaper publication and with current limitations of available material it is often difficult or impossible to determine the original date or even the original title of any story given the multiplicity of authorized and unauthorized versions. Thus, for example, Tinsley's Magazine *ran the story "Making up for It" in its December 1867 number. On December 21, 1867 the story crossed the Atlantic and appeared, without attribution, in* Harper's Weekly, *and on January 5, 1868 the* New York Times *ran "Making Up for It" but credited the original in* Tinsley's. *Therefore, in chapters six and seven the titles and dates of stories that appeared in magazines and newspapers may not reflect the original titles and/or original dates.*

Index